CHRONICLES

OF

COLONIAL MARYLAND

WITH ILLUSTRATIONS

BY

JAMES WALTER THOMAS

Member of the Maryland Historical Society

CLEARFIELD

Originally published
Cumberland, Maryland, 1900

Reprinted for
Clearfield Company, Inc. by
Genealogical Publishing Co., Inc.
Baltimore, Maryland
1995, 1999

International Standard Book Number: 0-8063-4544-6

Made in the United States of America

Preface.

THIS work may be classified as an historical review of Maryland, anterior to the American Revolution, though its Author bestows upon it the more modest title—Chronicles of Colonial Maryland. His chief object has been to explore and develop historic fields which have hitherto either been wholly neglected, or have received but scant notice at the hands of historians. This does not apply to the first chapter, the object of which was to re-locate a cherished landmark, "once known, but forgotten",—the historic island of Saint Clement's—and thus rescue from oblivion, the spot consecrated as the first landing place of the Maryland colonists; as well, also, to identify the exact point of landing at the place of its permanent settlement. The Author, while conscious of the laborious research and painstaking care bestowed upon it, fully realizes that a work, so largely one of original research, is inevitably not without imperfections. In submitting it, therefor, to the public, he does so with the assuring hope that the learned and generous will appreciate the difficulties attending the undertaking, and will accord consideration and justice to the motive which animated this humble tribute to his native State.

J. W. T.

Cumberland, Maryland,
    March 27th, 1900.

Contents.

CHAPTER I.

PLACE OF LANDING OF THE MARYLAND COLONISTS.

Place of first landing named Saint Clement's—Impressions of the Colonists on seeing the Country—First Mass celebrated in Maryland—Identity of Saint Clement's Island rescued—Place of Permanent Settlement selected—Place of Landing identified—View of—Name bestowed on first Maryland Town—Natives—Origin of certain Indian Names, . 9–20

CHAPTER II.

THE FIRST CAPITAL OF MARYLAND.

Location—Beauties of Situation—Baltimore's Instructions concerning it—Character of Improvements—Fort Saint Mary's—Location of principal Streets, Lots, and Houses—State House—Jail—"Old Mulberry"—Copley Vault—Taverns—First Water Mill—Roman Catholic Church—Protestant Church—Baltimore's Home—"The Castle", ... 21–54

CHAPTER III.

THE FIRST CAPITAL OF MARYLAND—Continued.

First General Assembly—Organization of—Early struggles for political freedom—Character of Legislation—Ingle's Rebellion—Religious freedom—Death of Governor Leonard Calvert—Life and character of—His Descendants—Battle of the Severn—Puritan reign—Fendall's Rebellion—Effort to have Capital removed—Maryland Coin—Protestant Revolution—Royal Government—Removal of Capital—Downfall of Saint Mary's—Calvert Monument—An historic spot, ... 55–80

CHAPTER IV.

LAND TENURE OF COLONIAL MARYLAND.

Maryland a Palatine—Rights and powers of a Court Palatine—Character of Tenure—How Land could be obtained—To whom, and in what quantity granted—Nature of the grants—Statutes of Mortmain—Remnants of Feudal Tenure—Fealty—Escheats—Fines—Relief—Quit-rents—The latter a large source of revenue to Proprietary—Difficulties in their payment—Confiscation of Proprietary rights—Contest among Heirs of last Proprietary—Curious data from Land Office. 81-102

CHAPTER V.

LAND TENURE OF COLONIAL MARYLAND.

Methods of transferring Land—Livery of Seisen—Indentures—Deeds of conveyance—Acknowledgments—Descent of Land—Manors—Primogeniture—Entailment—Influence in shaping Institutions, and habits of people—Its tendency aristocratic, ... 103-114

CHAPTER VI.

JUDICIAL SYSTEM OF COLONIAL MARYLAND.

Gradual development of the system—Justices of the Peace—County Court—Manorial Courts—Prerogative Court—Chancery Court—Admiralty Court—Assize Courts, ... 115-142

CHAPTER VII.

JUDICIAL SYSTEM OF COLONIAL MARYLAND.

Provincial Court—Origin of—Justices of—Jurisdiction of—Chief Judicial Tribunal—Court of Appeals—Appeal to King and Council—Early Reports—Characteristics of Provincial Judiciary, ... 143-162

CHAPTER VIII.

CHARACTERISTICS OF MARYLAND ESTABLISHMENT.

Protestant Episcopal Church in Early Maryland—Became established Church—Nature of Establishment—Parishes—English ecclesiastical law not in force—Induction, its uses and abuses—Church tax—Contest over—Abolished—Glebes—Church Wardens—Clerks—Registrars,
163-202

CHAPTER IX.

SOME OF MARYLAND'S EARLY CHURCHES.

Division of Province into Parishes—Number in each County—William and Mary Parish—King and Queen—All Faith—Saint Andrew's—Prince George's—Marriage Records of Latter—Newtown Church—Saint Inigoe's—Saint Joseph's—Sacred Heart—Saint Aloysius—Saint John's,
203-238

CHAPTER X.

THE GREAT SEAL OF MARYLAND AND HER FLAG.

Great Seal unique—Heraldic in design—Description of—Those in use before the Revolution—Those after—Lesser Seals at arms—Impressions of on Money—Present Great Seal—Origin of Flag—Design of—Early uses of—Beauty of—Great Seal of United States—Origin of The Stars and Stripes. 239-250

CHAPTER XI.

SAINT MARY'S COUNTY.

Oldest County organization—Theatre of Maryland's early struggles Beauties of—Resources of—Boundary of—Early civil divisions—County seat—Other early towns—Ports of entry—Roads—First mail route—Historic value of Will Records—Traditions—Early School System—Charlotte Hall—Revolution—Civil Officers, ... 251-286

CHAPTER XII.

SAINT MARY'S COUNTY.

Historic places—Character of improvements—Governor Calvert's Manors—Cross Manor—Mattapany—Susquehanna—Sotterly—Fenwick's Manor—De-la Brooke—Trent Hall—The Plains—Calvert side of Patuxent—Deep Falls—Bashford—Notley Hall—Brambly—Bushwood—Saint Clement's Manor—Tudor Hall—Portobello, ... 287-319

APPENDIX.

Letter, 1799, giving account of opening of "Copley Vault", at Saint Mary's City—Topographical Map of Maryland's First Capital, showing location of principal lots and house, ... 321-325

Illustrations.

	Page
Chancellor's Point,	18
Saint Mary's Bluff, site of First State House,	32
Maryland's First State House,	34
Foundation Lines of First State House,	54
Great Seal of Maryland under the Proprietary Government,	240
Reverse of the Great Seal used by Cecelius, Lord Baltimore,	242
Lesser Seal at Arms,	243
Plate for Stamping Seal on Money,	244
Present Great Seal of Maryland,	248
The Maryland Flag,	250
Map of Leonard-Town,	262
Map of Saint Mary's City,	Appendix

Colonial Maryland.

CHAPTER I.

Place of Landing of the Maryland Colonists.

ON the 5th of March, 1634, the *Ark* and the *Dove*, bearing the representatives of the two great principles—"political freedom and religious peace", for which Maryland became renowned—after a long and eventful voyage from the old to the new world, entered the Potomac River.[1]

Charmed with the genial climate, picturesque landscape and majestic waters that greeted them, Governor Leonard Calvert and his companions began naming the places as they passed, calling the southern point, at the mouth of the river, Saint Gregory[2] (now Smith's Point) and the northern point (now Point Lookout) Saint Michaels.[3]

---

1 "Relatio Itineris in Marylandiam."—The report of Father Andrew White, one of the Maryland Colonists, to his superiors at Rome, April, 1634; discovered by Rev. Wm McSherry in the archives of the "Domus Professa," and published by the Maryland Historical Society; "Relation of Maryland," dated Saint Mary's, May, 1634, published in London, 1634, and republished as "Shea's Early Southern Tracts", No. 1; "Relation of Maryland", published in London, in 1635, and republished, with map of the country, by Joseph Sabin, of New York.

2 Ibid.

3 The pleasing impressions which the Maryland colonists formed of their new country and surroundings, may be gathered from the following extracts from Father White's report of the voyage and landing: "The country is not without such things as contribute to prosperity and

A

Sailing up the river amid the consternation of the Indians, and by the "light of their council fires, which blazed through the land," they anchored at an island which they named Saint Clement's.[1] This island, as described at the time, was thickly wooded with cedars, sassafras and nut trees, and abounded in herbs and flowers, but had such a sloping shore that a landing could only be effected by wading.[2] It is twenty-six miles from the mouth of the Potomac, lies directly above Saint Clement's Bay, and half a mile from the Maryland shore.

Leaving the *Ark* and the greater part of the colonists there, Governor Calvert spent some days exploring the country and treating with the Indians, ascending the river as high as Piscataway, nearly opposite Mount Vernon. During his absence "a court of guard" was kept at Saint Clement's, while others of the colonists were occupied in putting together a pleasure." "The soil seems remarkably fertile, is dark and not hard, to the depth of a foot, and overlays a rich, red clay." "Fine groves of trees appear, not chocked with briars or bushes and undergrowth, but growing at intervals, as if planted by the hand of man." There are "strawberries, vines, sassafras, acorns, and walnuts"; also, "deer, beavers, and squirrels", and "an infinite number of birds of various colors, such as eagles, crows, swans geese, turkeys, partridges, and ducks". "Numerous springs furnish a supply of water". "Never have I beheld a larger or more beautiful river (than the lower Potomac.) The Thames seems a mere rivulet in comparison with it; it is not disfigured with swamps, but has firm land on each side". The Saint George's (Saint Mary's) River "has two harbors, capable of containing three hundred ships of the largest size". "The natives are very tall, and well proportioned; their skin is naturally rather dark, and they make it uglier by staining it, generally with red paint, mixed with oil to keep off the mosquitoes". "The soles of their feet are as hard as horn, and they tread on thorns and briars without being hurt". "The race are of a frank and cheerful disposition, and understand any matter when it is stated to them; they have a keen sense of taste and smell, and in sight, too, they surpass the Europeans. They live for the most part, on a kind of paste, which they call *Pone* and *Omini*, both of which are made of Indian corn,

---

1 Ibid. 2 Ibid.

barge, the parts for which they had brought with them, and in getting out material for a palisado.[1] On his return, preparations were made for religious ceremony, and on the 25th of March (the day of the Annunciation of the Virgin Mary), 1634, among the trees and flowers, they celebrated, at Saint Clement's, the first mass in Maryland. They then erected a great cross, "hewn out of a tree," as a "trophy to Christ," and as an emblem of Maryland's christian faith.[2] After this, with solemn ceremonies, they took formal possession of the country for "our Saviour and for our Soveraigne Lord the King of England."[3]

It should here be noted that it is singularly unfortunate that historians have fallen into the grave error of asserting that the Island of Saint Clement's, thus consecrated as the landing place of the pilgrims of Maryland, has long since yielded to the ravages of the insidious and relentless surf, and has almost disappeared—an error, resulting apparently, from a misapprehension of the location of the island, and the

---

and sometimes they add fish, or what they have procured by hunting or fowling. They are especially careful to refrain from wine or warm drinks, and are not easily persuaded to taste them". "They run to us of their own accord, with a cheerful expression on their faces, and offer us what they have taken in hunting or fishing", sometimes bringing "oysters, boiled or roasted". "They cherish generous feelings towards us, and make a return for whatever kindness you may have shown them". "They live in houses built in an oblong, oval shape. Light is admitted into these through the roof, by a window a foot and a half long, this also serves to carry off the smoke, for they kindle the fire in the middle of the floor, and sleep around it. Their Kings, however, and chief men, have private apartments of ther own, and beds, made by driving four posts in the ground and arranging poles above them horizontally". "One of these cabins has fallen to me". "It has been fitted up" as a temporary place of worship, "and you may call this the first chapel of Maryland".

1 Relation of Maryland, 1634.   2 Relatio Itineris.
3 Relation of Maryland, 1634.

assumption that it was the same as Heron Island, nearby, but more inland and immediately at the mouth of Saint Clement's Bay, and which, well authenticated tradition says, for more than a century and a half has been practically washed away. The pioneer Maryland historian, Bozman,[1] left the matter in doubt. Later, Dalrymple, in his valuable annotation of "The Relatio Itineris in Marylandiam", and who appears to have made it the subject of personal investigation, concluded that it was Heron Island on which the landing was made and to which the name of Saint Clement's was affixed. As recorded by him, "the name has disappeared and almost the whole of the island has been washed away by the river. * * * All that is left of it is a sand bank of about ten acres".[2] Still later authors, among them Scharf, Bryant, and even the careful and painstaking Brown have united in the confounding of Heron Island with Saint Clement's, and thus recording it as a lamentable, but nevertheless an historical fact, that the spot on which the colonists of Maryland first set foot upon her soil, and proclaimed the right of sovereignty over her domain, —than which none should be more sacred to the memory of her people—no longer exists either in fact or in name.[3]

They are not one and the same. A chronicle of the landing says, "they sayled up the river till they came to Heron Island (so-called from the large number of birds there of that name) which is about 14 leagues, and there came to anchor under an island near unto it which they called Saint Clement's."[4] A map of that time,[5] and also one of later date,[6]

---

[1] Bozman's History of Maryland, p. 27.
[2] Relatio Itineris, Dalrymple's note, p. 104.
[3] Scharf, History of Maryland, 1, p. 74; Brown, History of Maryland, p. 23; Bryant, History of United States, 1, p. 492.
[4] Relation of Maryland, 1634.
[5] Map in Relation of Maryland, 1635.   [6] Maps, 1670, Shea 1, p. 45.

as well as the early land grants of the land nearest these islands,[1] not only confirm this as to the separate identity of the two, but show that their relative position at that day was the same that the remnant of Heron Island bears to-day to the undiminished proportions of Saint Clement's. In name only has it changed. The first grant of Saint Clement's Island was to Dr. Thomas Gerrard in 1639, when it was included in the grant of Saint Clement's Manor. From him, through intermarriage of his daughter Elizabeth, with Colonel Nehemiah Blackiston, it passed to the Blackistons, and from long possession in them, it came to be called Blackiston's Island, the name it bears to-day. It is true, Father White and the Relation of 1634, the authorities perhaps, by which Maryland historians have been misled, say the landing was made on the first one of the group called Heron Islands which the colonists reached, but they clearly meant the first one of the three islands which lie in the Potomac, between Saint Clement's Bay and the Wicomico River, and known as Saint Clement's, (Blackiston's) Saint Katherine's, and Saint Margeret's.

The Relation of 1634, indeed, practically establishes the identity of these islands as being the same as those above mentioned. It says, "the first of those islands we called Saint Clement's; the second, Saint Katherine's, and the third Saint Cecelia's," now Saint Margaret's. It is, happily, a fact that Saint Katherine's Island has always retained the name first bestowed upon it. At the time they were named, it was the second in the trio, and lay above Saint Clement's—to-day its position is second, and it lies next above Blackiston's Island. It would therefore, have been a physical impossibility to have named the islands in the order in which they stand, and to

---

[1] Patents to Wm. Britton for Little Britton, and Thomas Gerrard for Saint Clement's Manor, 1639 in Land Office, Annapolis.

have placed Saint Katherine's second in the line, without the island now known as Blackiston's being the first in that course, and the one lying next below it. Again, in 1678, a new patent was issued for Saint Clement's Manor, and the three islands, in the language of the patent, "lying in the Potomac River, at the mouth of the Wiccocomoco River, called by the names of Saint Clement's Island, Saint Katherine's Island, and Saint Margaret's Island" were included in the grant,[1] which three islands are there to-day, and known as Blackistone's, Saint Katherine's, and Saint Margaret's.

It should be noted that Heron Island—now scarcely discernible—which lies more inland, and somewhat out of the direct course in sailing up the river, was most likely very diminutive and practically valueless even at that date, as no patent appears ever to have been issued for it. It was also, apparently, deemed too insignificant for a new name when bestowing names upon the three lying further out in the river, and it to-day retains its first name—Heron—the one by which the entire group was originally known.

The records also of the devises and alienations of the island covering a period of more than a century, refer to it alternately as Blackiston's or Saint Clement's Island, which, with a direct chain of title from the Lord Proprietary to the present time, incontestably establishes the fact, that the beautiful Blackiston's Island of to-day, gracefully slumbering upon the bosom of the lower Potomac, is the historic Saint Clement's Island of the past.[2]

---

[1] Liber 20, p. 5, Land Office.

[2] Patents to Thomas Gerrard, 1639 Liber 1, p. 48, and Justinian Gerrard, 1678, Liber 20, p. 5, Land Office; judgment in suit, Nehemiah Blackiston vs. Justinian Gerrard, 1686, Provincial Court Records, Liber D. S. A., p. 532; will, Elizabeth (Blackiston) Guibert, Liber 14, p. 224, Annapolis; wills, John Blackiston, Liber 1, p. 352, and Nehemiah

THE LANDING

It is also worthy of note that Saint Clement's has passed into history as possessing, at the time of the landing, an area of four hundred acres, the result, perhaps, of an error in the copy of Father White's report at Rome, the authority for the statement.[1] By the return of the Surveyor General, in 1639, five years only after the narrative was written, it contained eighty acres,[2] which is about its size to-day. Father White most probably said it contained four score, and not four hundred acres.

Before the colonists left England, Lord Baltimore sent to Governor Leonard Calvert a set of instructions for the government of the colony upon their arrival in Maryland, in which he urges him in selecting the place of settlement, that his chief care be "to make choice of a place first, that is probable to be healthfull and fruitfull; next, that it be easily fortified, and thirdly, that it be convenient for trade both with the English and savages".[3]

Following these instructions, and deeming it imprudent to locate high up the river, where retreat would be difficult in the event of attack, Governor Calvert, already impressed with the superior advantages of that section of the province bordering on the lower Potomac for the Maryland settlement, concluded to visit next the Indian village of Yaocomico. This he

---

Blackiston, Liber 3, p. 435, both of Saint Mary's County; deeds, John Blackiston to R. H. Miles, Liber F, vol. 1, p. 8, and R. H. Miles to J. M. Goldsmith, Liber F, vol. 1, p. 328, Land Office; deeds, G. W. Morgan, sheriff, to B. G. Harris, B. G. Harris to J. L. McWilliams, R. C. Combs, attorney, to F. A. Denison, F. A. Denison to Mary E. Swan, Saint Mary's County.

1 Relatio Itineris, p. 32.   2 Old Maryland Manors, p. 29.

3 The original draft of this paper, in Baltimore's own handwriting, and the oldest original document, except the Charter, belonging to Maryland's early history, has only very recently been discovered, and is now in the Maryland Historical Society. It has also been published by Brown, "Makers of America", p. 45.

was also induced to do by Captain Henry Fleet, an Indian trader, whose familiarity with the country gave his opinion importance and weight, and who represented that section of it in glowing terms and as being well adapted in every way to their purpose.

Leaving both ships at Saint Clement's Island, and accompanied by Captain Henry Fleet and a small body of men, he sailed in his barge down the river about sixteen miles to a bold, deep tributary flowing into the Potomac from the north, and which they named Saint George's (now Saint Mary's) River. Ascending this river, and naming its two "great harbors," the one Saint George (now Saint George's River), and the other, more inland, Saint Mary (still Saint Mary's), and between Church Point and Chancellor's Point, he anchored at Yaocomico, situated on the eastern bank of the river, and about five miles from its mouth.

He sought interview with King Yaocomico, and informed him of the object of his coming, to which, says the Relation, "he made but little answer, as is their manner to any new or sudden question, but entertained him and his company that night in his house, and gave him his own bed to lye on—which is a mat laid on boards—and the next day went to show him the country."[1]

The Governor was convinced of the superior fitness of the the place, and that his entry there could be safely made, and to avoid "every appearance of injustice, and to afford no opportunity for hostility on the part of the Indians, he waived all question of right or superior power in the premises, and agreed to buy their town and territory. The Yaocomicos having previously resolved to move higher up the country, to avoid the Susquehanocks, a more powerful tribe, and their

---

[1] Relation of Maryland, 1634.

THE LANDING

enemy, this was accomplished without difficulty, and for cloth, axes, hatchets, rakes, hoes, and knives, they agreed that the colonists should occupy a part of their town and land, reserving a part for themselves until their corn could be gathered, when the whole should be surrendered. It was further mutually agreed, that the two nations should live peaceably together, and that if any injury was done on either side, the offending party should make reparation.[1]

Much historical encomium has been lavished upon William Penn, for his famous treaty with the Shackamaxon Indians for the land upon which the city of Philadelphia stands, but neither the annals of Pennsylvania, or of any other American colony, present a more conspicuous example of humanity and justice towards the Aboriginees, than is portrayed in the spirit which animated Maryland on that occasion, and, indeed, throughout, in that regard, and it should, with equal justice, adorn the pages of her history.[2]

The ships dropping anchor in Saint Mary's harbor, the colonists landed on the "right hand side", or southern arm

---

[1] Relatio Itineris; Relation of Maryland, 1634.

[2] Speaking of the religion of the Indians found in and around Saint Mary's, the Relation of 1634 says: "First, they acknowledge one God of Heaven, which they call our God; and cry a thousand shames upon those christians that so lightly offend so good a God. But they give no external honour unto Him, but use all their might to please an Okee (or frantic spirit), for fear of harm from him. They adore, also, Wheat and Fire, as two gods, very beneficial unto man's natures In the Machicomoco, or Temple of Patuxent, there was seane by our traders this ceremony. Upon a day appointed all the Townes mett, and a great fire being made; about it stood the younger sort, and behinde them againe the elder. Then taking a little deer suet, they cast it into the fire, crying, Tabo, Tabo, and lifting their hands to heaven. After this, was brought before them a great Bagg, filled with a longe Tobacco pipe and Poake, which is the word they use for our Tobacco. This was carried about the fire, the youth following, and singing Tabo, Tabo, in very good tune of voice, and comely gesture of body. The round ended, one comes reverently to the Bagge, and opening it, takes out the Pipe, and

of the harbor (Chancellor's Point), and, walking about a mile around the river bank, came to the place selected for their permanent settlement, and laid out the plan for the first town in Maryland.

Father White's report (the most valuable record of the times, and the only one that attempts to detail this feature of the landing) says : " The left side of the river was the abode of King Yaocomico. We landed on the right hand side," and about a mile from the town.[1] This clearly means *Saint Mary's harbor*, and *not* the *river* (or Saint Inigoe's harbor, as has been suggested), and identifies with certainty, Chancellor's Point as the place of landing. The town of Yaocomico and the place of landing could not have been on opposite sides of the river, for the colonists walked from one place to the other, which could only have been accomplished, if on opposite sides, by going around the head of the river—a journey not of one mile only, but of at least twenty. The two, however, could have been on opposite sides of the harbor—a deep indentation made by the two long headlands, now known as Church Point and Chancellor's Point.

The Indian town, it is conceded, occupied the northern or Church Point arm, which placed it on the *left side* in sailing up, thus making the southern, or Chancellor's Point arm, the *right hand side* in entering the harbor ; the southern extremity (Chancellor's Point) of this arm, being also about a mile distant from the town they laid out—Saint Mary's.

The event of landing and unloading the ships was made with as much formality as circumstances would permit, and

---

divides the Poake, from one to one. As every one tooke his draught, hee breath'd his smoke upon the limbs of his own body, as it were to sanctifie them by this ceremony, to the honour and service of their God, whomsoever they meant."

[1] Relatio Itineris.

CHANCELLOR'S POINT.

was done under military escort, parade under colors and arms, and firing of musketry and cannon.[1]

Then and there, Governor Calvert, on the 27th of March, 1634, with appropriate ceremonies, proclaimed formal possession of Maryland, and named its first town Saint Mary's. Then and there, says a distinguished historian,[2] "landed the Pilgrims of Maryland, and then and there were laid the foundations of the old city of Saint Mary's and of our present State."

"The landing of the Pilgrims of New England, has been the burden of many a story, and the theme of many an oration. The very rock upon which their feet were first planted, is consecrated in the estimation of their descendants, and its relics are enshrined as objects of holy regard. They were freemen in search of freedom ; they found it, and transmitted it to their posterity. It becomes us, therefore, to tread lightly upon their ashes. Yet, while we would avoid all invidious contrasts, and forget the stern spirit of the Puritan, which so often mistook religious intolerance for holy zeal ; we can turn with exultation to the Pilgrims of Maryland, as the founders of religious liberty in the new world. They erected the first altar to it on this continent ; and the fires first kindled on it ascended to Heaven amid the blessings of the savage."

May the memory of the spirit and character of Maryland's Pilgrim fathers be sacredly cherished and zealously guarded forever by their descendants.[3]

---

1 Bozman, II, p. 30.   2 McMahon, p. 198.

3 The following definitions of Indian terms used in this chapter are taken from Maryland Historical Society Pub. No. 7. Potomac (Botomeg) a "river full of swarms of small fry—where fishes spawn in shoals." (Kerchival, History, Valley of Virginia, 145 and 149, says : the Potomac above its confluence with the Shenandoah, was called Cohongoronta.) Piscatowa, (Biskatowe) "one who has his hair plaited up sideways and

backwards." Anacosta, (Nanakoita) "one who prepares himself for defence, to resist attack." Yaocomico, (A(i)ago-mo-ago) "he that is floating on water, tossed to and fro." Susquehanocks, (Saskweonag) "those who live in a place where the surf is heard beating (grating) on the shore." Patuxent. (Portuxeud) "the place where grows portu (tobacco)."

CHAPTER II.

The First Capital of Maryland.

SAINT MARY'S CITY,[1] the first Capital of Maryland, was situated on the east side of the Saint George's (now Saint Mary's) River, a tributary of the Potomac, about five miles from its mouth, and sixteen miles from Point Lookout, the southern extremity of the western shore of Maryland.

A gentle slope from the eastern hills, then a spacious plateau of singular beauty, elevated about forty feet above the water, and terminating in a bold bluff between two broad expanses of the river, formed the site of the City.

A crescent shaped indentation, made by this bluff[2] and a headland about a mile lower down the river,[3] gave the City a capacious harbor.

The river skirted two sides of the town, afforded depth and security of navigation, and adding beauty and grandeur to its other attractions, made the situation of Saint Mary's one of surpassing loveliness.

---

[1] Much of the material in this chapter was incorporated in an address entitled The First Capital of Maryland, and delivered by the Author on the occasion of the two hundredth anniversary of the removal of the Capital of Maryland, from St. Mary's to Annapolis, and which, together with other addresses on that occasion, was published by the State of Maryland in memorial volume entitled "Removal of the State Capital."

[2] Church Point.   [3] Chancellor's Point,

A river possessing more enchanting scenery than the Saint Mary's may not easily be found, and at no place along its banks is this displayed to greater advantage than at the site of old Saint Mary's. Looking from thence, either towards the north, where its clear and glittering waters are first seen winding down the blue vista of the distant hills, with its sloping banks, and intercepted by its long, narrow capes and jutting cliffs; or towards the south, where its waters, growing bolder and deeper, with its high, grassy banks, upland slopes, abrupt declivities, white, winding beach, pebbly shore, and (as seen from the direction of its mouth) its interlocking promonitories, giving it the appearance of a series of lakes, rather than a stream of regular width, it presents a picture of rare and exquisite beauty.

Saint Mary's City occupied the site of the Indian village of "Yaocomico," at which place the Maryland colony was induced to settle by the glowing description of Captain Henry Fleet, son of a member of the Virginia Company, whose familiarity with the country gave his opinion importance and weight. and, who described it as a location, desirable alike for its commanding commercial advantages and its safety of defense, as well as for its temporary improvements and its natural beauty and attractiveness; or, in his own language, "a spot, indeed, so charming in its situation that Europe itself can scarcely show one to surpass it"; and, having first purchased the Indian title thereto (the details of which are given in the preceding chapter), Governor Calvert, on the 27th of March, 1634, assumed formal possession, and named the first town of Maryland—Saint Mary's.[1]

Under the instructions of Baltimore, containing the details and rules for the government of the colonists, they were di-

---

[1] Relatio Itineris, p. 35.

rected, after having selected a suitable place for their permanent settlement, 'to seate a towne", in which they were "to cause streets to be marked out", and to require the buildings to be erected "in line" with such streets, and "neere adjoining one to another"; all the houses to be built in as "decent and uniform a manner" as circumstances permitted, the land in the rear of the houses "to be assigned for gardens and such uses". The first choice of lots was to be for a "fitt place and a competent quantity of ground for a Fort", and "within", or "neere unto" this lot, a site was to be chosen for "a convenient house, and a church or chappel adjacent", for the "seate of his Lordship, or his Governor or other Commissioners", the two latter buildings to be completed only so far "as is necessary for present use", and not "in every part as fine as afterwards they may be". He also directed that a plat of the town, its situation and surroundings, be made by the Surveyor General, and sent to him by the first opportunity.[1]

The next official notice with reference to laying out of the town of Saint Mary's, is the following order, from Baltimore to Governor Calvert, dated Warden Castle, England, August 29th, 1636:

"I would have you pass in freehold to every of the first adventurers that shall claim or desire it, and to their heirs, ten acres of land within the plats assigned or to be assigned for the town and fields of Saint Mary's, for every person that any of said adventurers transported or brought into Maryland, according to their conditions first published; and five acres of land to every other adventurer for every other person which he hath or shall transport thither since the time of the first plantation, until the 13th day of August, which shall be in

---

[1] Instructions, Nov. 13, 1633. In Maryland Historical Society.

the year of our Lord 1638, and for so doing, this shall be your warrant ".[1]

In 1684, another grant of land was made to Saint Mary's, to be divided into lots of one acre each, and of sufficient quantity to make, with those already there, one hundred lots within the limits of the town.[2]

Undisturbed for several year, either by domestic factions or external dissensions, Saint Mary's, for a colonial town, grew with considerable rapidity. Brick and other builders' supplies were imported, which, with the home products available for the purpose, afforded, from an early period, abundant building material.

While Virginia, as late as 1638, was making its laws in an ale house,[3] and, indeed, in 1716, Jamestown, its first capital, contained only "a church, Court House and four other buildings",[4] Saint Mary's, in a comparatively short time after its settlement, had, besides the home of Lord Baltimore, a church, a pretentious State House, a jail and other public offices, and about thirty houses.[5] Soon thereafter, it had sixty houses (which number it never much exceeded),[6] protected by two forts, Saint Mary's and Saint Inigoes, each well mounted with the ordnance of that day.

As the place for holding the General Assemblies, the seat of the Provincial Court, and the port where all ships trading

---

1 Kilty, p. 33.   2 Archives (Ass. Pro. 1684) p. 119.
3 Streeter Papers, p. 15.   4 Lodge, p. 51.
5 Archives Ass. Pro. 1641 and 1676; Scharf, 1, p. 294.
     Baltimore, in his report in 1677, to the committee of Trade and Plantation in England, stated that the houses at St. Mary's "excepting my own home and the buildings wherein the Public offices are kept," did not exceed thirty, built at considerable distance from each other, and the most of them after the manner of the smaller farm houses of England.
6 McMahon, p. 250.

with the Province had first to resort, Saint Mary's soon became a place of importance, and, in 1668, it was by letters patent, incorporated and erected into a city, with privileges and immunities above and beyond any other place in the Province. Its officers consisted of a Mayor, Recorder, six Aldermen and, ten Councilmen, and among its special prerogatives were those of a "Weekly Market" and an "Annual Fair".[1]

In 1671, Saint Mary's received a new accession to its prerogatives, that of sending two representatives to the General Assembly,[2] the first being Mr. John Morecroft and the Honorable Thomas Notley.[3]

It is to be regretted that no chart of the City of the Calverts was made before it had disappeared—except in name and in memory—from the banks of the Saint Mary's; but from original surveys and grants, ancient transfers, and re-surveys, together with the many natural boundaries and landmarks still visible, the map shown in the appendix was platted. By this data, obtained through laborious and exhaustive research, and applied with painstaking care, the outlines of the City, and the location of its public, as well as its more prominent private lots and buildings, have thus been happily preserved.

The plain upon which the City of Saint Mary's stood, was about a mile square, the limit prescribed by its charter, with a water front made extensive by the many and acute meanderings of the river. This plain was broken by two creeks making into it from the river—Saint John's and Key's (the latter now a small ravine)—and upon the peninsular

---

1 This, the first municipal charter granted in Maryland, may be found in Liber F. F. p. 645, etc., in Land Office, Annapolis. The Town Ordinances adopted for Saint Mary's City may be seen in Archives, Council Proceedings, 1685, p. 418-422.

2 McMahon, p. 251.   3 Archives (Ass. Pro. 1671) p. 311.

plateau which they formed, and bounded on the northeast and southwest respectively, and which contained about one hundred acres, were erected the public buildings of the Province, and it became the more thickly settled part of the town. On this plateau the houses, which "passed through the various stages of architectural transition", from the log cabin to the substantial frame and brick building, were scattered irregularly, the lots being unsymetrically arranged, of irregular size, and large, none of them being less than a quarter of an acre, and many of them large enough for extensive grounds, and gardens sufficiently capacious to supply the needs of the household.

It may be proper to preface a more detailed account of the improvements at Saint Mary's, with the general statement that they consisted of its fort, or palisado, which, though a rude structure compared with those of more modern date, was solidly built and well enough mounted to protect the inhabitants against the warfare of that day; its massive and dignified State House, with its thick walls, tile roof, and paved floors; its stout jail, with its iron-barred windows; its market house, warehouses, and several ordinaries; its unique brick chapel, the victim of the Roman Catholic persecution of later times; its quaint Protestant church; its pretentious and fortress-like executive mansion; which, with its offices, private houses, and shops—of varied architectural design—numbering, it is said, about sixty, and scattered over the elevated, but level plain, studded, we are told, with primeval forest trees, constituted the picturesque little metropolis of early Maryland.

In 1664, an Act was passed under which all houses thereafter erected, had to be not less than twenty feet square, and two-and-a-half stories high, with brick chimneys.[1]

---

[1] Archives (Ass. Pro. 1664) p. 539.

Of the streets which traversed the town, but two have been definitely located, which, with the broad river beach, seem to have formed the principal thoroughfares of the City— the one running northwest and southeast from the State House to Saint Inigoe's Creek, and known as "Middle Street"; the other, northeast and southwest from "Saint Mary's Hills" to the southwestern extremity of the town, and known as "Mattapany Street".[1]

The first improvement of a public character made at Saint Mary's (excepting the temporary buildings designed for storing the common supplies of provisions for the colonists), was "Saint Mary's Fort". It was erected in 1634, and was located on a small bluff, at the mouth of "Key's Creek", or branch, on the north side of the creek, and immediately between Governor Leonard Calvert's lot and the chapel land.[2] This location indicates that it was intended as a place of rendezvous and protection against Indian invasions, rather than as a fortification of the town against naval attacks, it being guarded from incursions of so formidable a character by "Fort Saint Inigoe's", situated a short distance below. The colonists, at the time the fort was built, were in the midst of erecting their houses, but becoming alarmed by the war-like attitude of the Indians (excited by the intrigues of Clayborne), they ceased building, and at once set to work to erect a fort for their better security, which, it is recorded, they completed in about six weeks.[3]

---

[1] See grant to Mary Throughton, Liber I. p. 67; Robert Carvile, et al., Liber 20, p. 269; Elizabeth Baker to Charles Carroll, Council Book, H. D. No. 2, p. 150.

[2] It has been stated that it stood on the bluff on the south side of Key's Creek. This is an error. See patent to Leonard Calvert, Liber 1; p. 117; and deed from Thomas Copley to C. Fenwick, Liber I. p. 121; see also Archives (Ass. Pro. 1638) p. 78.

[3] Relation, 1634.

Governor Leonard Calvert described it as "a pallizado of one hundred and twentie yards square, with fower flankes", mounted with one piece of ordnance and six murderers, placed in parts most convenient—"a fortification sufficient, we think, to defend against any such weake enemies as we have reason to expect here",[1] but the Relation, 1634, says, they had "four murderers and seven pieces more to mount forthwith".

The manner of its construction, the records have left in obscurity. Traditionary history, however, says, it consisted of a large, log block-house and magazine, protected by stockades and ramparts of earth. Intrenchments, still visible, indicate that this may be correct as to the earthen parapets, and, since the colonists were engaged, while at Saint Clement's, in "cleaving pales for a palisado", it is not improbable that the stockade was also a feature of it. That the building within was of considerable size, is sustained by the fact, that in it most of the public business of the Province was transacted, prior to 1638, and that the first three sessions of the General Assembly were held there, one of which contained ninety members.

In 1638, an Act was passed for the building of a "town house" at Saint Mary's. Of the style and location of this building (if erected), nothing is known, and it is merely referred to as illustrating the method deemed most available at that time, of getting whatever buildings of a public nature, which the colony needed. The Act provided, that "every housekeeper should be contributory to said building, either in stuff, workmanship, labor, or tobacco, in such manner and after such rates proportionally to each man's personal estate".[2]

---

1 Maryland Historical Society Fund Pub. No. 35, p. 21.
2 Archives (Ass. Pro. 1638) p. 78; Bozman, p. 33.

THE FIRST CAPITAL

Adjoining the Fort, on the south and east, was "Saint Mary's Chapel yard", while on the north and west was the land of Governor Leonard Calvert.[1] The latter, when first laid out, was a large lot, known as "Governor's Field", and embraced a considerable part of the little plateau before mentioned.[2]

After the death of Governor Calvert, Margaret Brent, his excutrix, assumed to make sale of this property to Governor William Stone, who occupied it as his residence while Governor of the Province; but, in 1659, William Calvert, son and heir of Governor Leonard Calvert, and in England at the time of his father's death, through proceedings in the Provincial Court, recovered possession of the house of his father at Saint Mary's.[3] Subsequently the lower, or northern, part of this lot came into the possession of Hugh Lee, and at a later date it was purchased by the Province of Maryland.

Of the architecture of the Calvert House, but little is known. In the inventory of his estate, however, it is described as a "large frame building", and the site it occupied is still pointed out. This places it about one hundred yards from the Fort, about two hundred and fifty yards from the river, and about the same distance from Middle Street, on which it fronted.[4]

---

1 Liber I, p. 119-121.

2 The patent for this land was dated August 13, 1641. It was bounded on the west by the River, on the north by the Bay, on the east by Mill (Saint Johns) Creek to a distance of 47 perches above the Mill, and where Saint Peter's and the Chapel land meet and on the south by a line drawn from thence to the River. Liber I, p. 121.

3 See Note, Chapter III.

4 In 1707, this property was in the possession of George Parker, in right of his children, by his wife, then deceased, the daughter of Gabriel Parratt. Rent Rolls, Saint Mary's.

Lower down the plateau, on the same side of Middle Street, and nearly adjoining the Calvert lot on the northwest, was the Lee Residence before mentioned, and which embraced the whole of the lower end of the plateau. In 1662, this property was purchased by the Province, for a "Government House", at a cost of twelve thousand pounds of casked tobacco,[1] and was used as such until 1676, when new public buildings were erected. This was the first real estate ever owned by the Province of Maryland, and that part of the lot known as "Saint Mary's Bluff", became the site of its first State House and other public buildings. The house (in accordance with the custom of the times) was used also as an "ordinary".[2] The lessee was Lieutenant William Smith, and one of the conditions of the lease was, that he plant on that part of the lot set apart for him, three acres, "forty apple or pear trees".[3] It was known as "Smith's Town House".[4] Of this building, prominently as it was connected with the history of the times, nothing remains except the depression which marks the spot where once it stood—about three hundred yards from the river—and a few scattered, moss-covered bricks, the more durable fragments of its historic ruins.

That part of the "Country's lot" which lay between Smith's Town House and Middle Street, was the residence of Mark Cordea. On the lot he also appears to have had a shoe shop. This property subsequently became the residence of Colonel William Digges, Secretary of the Province. Adjoining it on the northwest, and fronting on Middle Street, was the residence of John Baker, and subsequently of Attorney General Charles Carroll. The lot contained one and a quarter acres, and in the house, when owned by John Baker, several

---

1 Archives (Ass. Pro. 1662) p. 455.   2 Ibid, 1666, p. 29.
3 Kilty, p. 220.   4 Ibid.

sessions of the Council were held. Near this lot, on the northwest, and fronting on the same street, was the "Van Sweringen Tavern", owned by Garrett Van Sweringen. Northwest of this lot, fronting on the same side of this street, were the Law Chambers, owned by Robert Carvile, Christopher Rousby, and Robert Ridgely. The lot contained one acre, and was granted in 1679; it was called "Triple Contract". Between this and the State House lot, on the same side of the street, were the lots of Nicholas Painter and Captain John Quigley; the latter, lying nearest the State House, being one of the taverns of the town. Each of them contained one acre.

Bordering on the river, and running up to the three last mentioned lots, was the lot on which stood the Secretary's Office, Council Chamber, and "Saint Mary's Room". This was one building; it was erected in 1664, and at a later period was referred to as the "Old Court House". In the Council Chamber the first General Assembly under the royal government in Maryland was prorogued in May, 1692, after which it repaired to the State House. Bordering on the river, also, and lying between the Secretary's Office and Smith's Town House, was the home of Daniel S. Jenifer, Clerk of the Provincial Court. The lot contained four acres, and, as directed by the order for the grant, was not to be "layed out soe neare the Ordinary House or Secretary's Office as to prejudice eyther the Office or the Ordinary's orchard or garden.[1]

---

[1] As the authorities for the above have to be largely used conjunctively, they are given in the following order: Archives, Pro. Cl. 1686, p. 531; Ibid, 1684, p. 301; Council Book No. 2 p. 150; Archives, Pro. Cl. 1678, pp. 178, 201, 203, 204, 205, 207; Ibid, 1692, p. 420; Liber No. 20, pp. 260, 269; Archives, Pro. Ass. 1678, p. 32; Ibid, 1664, p. 539; Ibid, 1666, p. 34; Ibid, 1676, p. 482; Archives, Pro. Cl. 1678, p. 174; Archives, Pro. Ass. 1692, p. 349; Ibid, 1666, p. 123; Resurvey of "Governor's Field", in 1754, now in possession of the author.

At the end of Middle Street was the State House lot, called "Saint Mary's Bluff", containing about three acres, and which embraced the entire end of the plateau forming the northwestern extremity of the town. The bluff, by an abrupt descent of about twenty feet, terminates in a broad, sandy flat, and thence into a long point, on which stood, it is said, the town wharf and warehouses, the latter occupying the flat immediately below the bluff, and between it and the wharf.

About ninety feet from the summit of the bluff stood the State House. It was a strikingly beautiful situation, and commanded an extensive view of the town, the river, and the surrounding country; and to those approaching the City, either by land or water, it formed a prominent and picturesque feature of the landscape.

The Act under which the State House was erected, was passed in 1674, and the building was completed in October, 1676. The contractor was Captain John Quigley, and the contract price for it, and a jail, was 330,000 ℔s. of tobacco, of which Saint Mary's City contributed 100,000 ℔s. The State House was forty-five feet long and fifty feet deep. An enclosed two-story "porch" in front, "12 by 16 feet in the clear" and a corresponding wing in the rear for the stairway, "16 by 16 feet in the clear", gave it a cruciform shape. The main building was two-and-a-half stories high; the porch and stairway wing being two stories only. It was all built of dark, red vitrified brick, with walls twenty-eight inches thick to the "water table", which was three feet high and "shelving", and twenty-four and nineteen inches thick in the first and second stories, respectively, with steep roof, covered with tile, from the centre of which shot up an iron spire,[1] with ball,

---

[1] Captain Randolph Jones, author of "The Buccaneers", and who died a few years since at an advanced age, informed the author that he

SAINT MARY'S BLUFF, SITE OF FIRST STATE HOUSE.

supporting near its top a vane, on which was inscribed, "1676", the date of its erection. The lower floor of the main building, contained at first, no divisions, and is referred to as "Saint Mary's Hall". The floor of this hall was paved with brick; its ceiling was twelve feet high, and entrance to it from the porch, was obtained through a door ten feet high and five feet wide. The second story contained three rooms, and, in 1682, the lower floor was divided by a brick partition, into two halls for the accommodation of the Upper and Lower Houses of Assembly.

The first and second stories were lighted by eight windows, with "double lights and transoms", those below being "eight feet high and four feet wide", and those above, "five feet high and two-and-a-half feet wide". The openings in the porch consisted of a central arch "six feet wide and eleven feet high" (extending from the "keystone" to the floor), and two smaller arches on the "sides above the bentles", the second story having one window immediately over the central arch. The opposite wing contained an oak "half pace" stairway, that extended to the "attic", and which had a window upon each "half pace of the stairs".

By a singular coincidence, the State House was erected without chimneys, owing to a controversy over the proposition to allow it, in conformity with the custom of the times, to be used as an Ordinary, or eating-house, the opposing and predominant faction, in order to make this impracticable, caused

---

distinctly remembered this old spire, and its dismal creak and twang. It was about twelve feet high, and the hollow iron ball, which was near the centre of the spire, was about two feet in diameter. After the State House was pulled down, this ancient structure lay for some time unprotected in the Church yard, at Saint Mary's. It ultimately disappeared, most likely by the hands of the "iron speculator", and has, probably, long since been "scattered by the thousand winds of trade". O! ye sons of the times, where slept your vigils?

them to be omitted altogether. In 1678, however, three outside chimneys were put up : one at each gable end, and one at the rear of the stairway wing, and which, with a partition in the stairway wing, cost 20,000 ℔s. of tobacco. In 1682, outside wooden shutters, and suitable furniture (tables and formes) for the building, were ordered to be purchased.[1] The year previous, in order to avoid the expense of maintaining a Drummer for the convening of the Assemblies and Provincial Courts, a "public bell"[2] was ordered for the State House.[3]

In 1688, the northwest wing was ordered to be made five feet deeper, and the fireplace ten feet wide in the first story, and eight feet wide in the second, each to be provided with a white oak mantle [4]

The accompanying picture of the State House, at Saint Mary's, which the author of this work is happily able to here present, was reproduced from one in his possession, and which it is believed, is the only one extant, or indeed, which ever existed of this old memorial of colonial times, and which, at the time it was built, was not only the "architectural glory" of Maryland, but, perhaps, the finest specimen of architecture in America. The engraving was taken from a *mechanical*

---

[1] Archives (Ass. Pro, 1674), p. 404; Ibid, 1678, pp. 27 and 32; Ibid, 1682, pp. 299 and 30^.

[2] This is probably the bell at Georgetown College, and which is supposed to have belonged to the little chapel at Saint Mary's. The State House bell is the only one of the kind, which the records mention as being at Saint Mary's, and the one at Georgetown, bearing the date of the purchase of the State House bell, leads to the conclusion that it is the same one. The tone of the bell is exceedingly sweet, and the appliances for hanging and ringing it, very curious. The handsome English-walnut, elliptical-shaped table, known as the "Council table", and which stood in the Council room in the State House, is also at Georgetown College, where it was taken a few years ago, from Saint Inigoe's Manor. It is well preserved, and is an exceedingly interesting relic.

[3] Archives (Ass. Pro. 1681) p. 144.   [4] Ibid, 1688, p. 223.

MARYLAND'S FIRST STATE HOUSE.

drawing, made from actual measurements of its earth-covered foundation, but excavated for the purpose, and from the specifications set out in the Act of Assembly[1] authorizing the building to be erected, defining its dimensions, character, and style, and which was, in effect, the contract between the Province and the builder—Captain William Quigley. The iron spire was not a part of the original contract, and its size could only be approximately determined from an early written description of it, and from data obtained from persons who distinctly remembered it, both while it was on the building and after the latter was pulled down.[2] This picture has never before been presented to the public, except that, in 1894, on the occasion of the celebration of the two hundredth anniversary of the removal of the Capital from Saint Mary's to Annapolis, permission was given the Baltimore Sun to print a wood cut of it in connection with its account of those ceremonies.

On the "State House Square", about seventy feet distant, stood the historic "Old Mulberry" tree, under whose broad, spreading branches the first colonists of Maryland assembled, and under which, also, traditionary history says, the first mass at Saint Mary's was celebrated, and the treaty between Governor Calvert and the Yaocomico Indians was made. Of this venerable tree, whose mass of foliage continued for two hundred years afterward to crown the State House promontory, it is further recorded, that "on it were nailed the proclamations of Calvert and his successors, the notices of punishments and fines, the inventories of debtors whose goods were to be sold, and all notices calling for the public attention." Within comparatively recent years even,

---

[1] Archives (Ass. Pro. 1674) p. 404.
[2] The late Doctor Alexander Jones, in Leonardtown Herald, in 1840, and the late Doctor John M. Brome, and Captain Randolph Jones.

curious relic hunters were able to pick from its decaying trunk, the rude nails which there held the forgotten State papers of two centuries and more ago.[1]

This aged tree had watched over the City in its infancy; in its development and prosperity, and in its pride and glory, as the metropolis of Maryland; it had seen it stripped of its prestige and its honors, and lose its importance and its rank; it had witnessed its battle with adversity and its downfall and decline, and it had mourned the departure of nearly every symbol of its existence and memorial of its glory, which, under the winning game of time, had one by one, faded and passed away; and still it stood—stood as a "silent sentinel of time, whose watchword is death"—stood "daily distilling the dews of Heaven" upon the sacred ground around it—stood, sheltering the generations of men who were buried beneath its luxuriant shade—stood telling the story of the first Capital of Maryland, and marking the spot where once it was—stood until 1876, when, like the almost forgotten City—the companion of its prime—its time-worn and shattered trunk laid down to rest.

About fifteen feet northeast of the State House, stands what is called the "Calvert Vault", and which is said to contain the remains of Governor Leonard Calvert, Lady Jane Calvert, wife of Charles Lord Baltimore, and Cecelius Calvert, their oldest son,[2] but it is highly probable that it is the *Copley*

---

[1] Bryant, p. 504.

[2] Stanley, in Pilate and Herod, p. 16, says: "About thirty or more years ago (1823), (for I write from memory of a vestry record, and a verbal explanation or statement, made to me by a then vestryman of the Parish, the late Richard Thomas, of Saint Mary's, a worthy man) some young men, while under the influence of liquor, broke into this vault, forced open a leaden coffin, and discovered the corpse of a lady, supposed to be Lady Ann Calvert, adorned with trinkets of gold and such a dress as denoted her rank." It may be added that these young men were

THE FIRST CAPITAL 37

and *not* the Calvert vault. The tradition is certainly incorrect as to Lady Jane Baltimore, who died in England and was buried at "Saint Giles", on the 24th of January, 1701,[1] and from the fact that no allusion was made to it as the place of Governor Calvert's interment, or even to the existence of a vault, at the time the lot on which it stands was purchased for State purposes (fifteen years after his death), it is fair to assume that he, also, is not buried there. It is, however, a matter of record, that the first Royal Governor of Maryland, Lionel Copley, and Lady Copley, his wife, are both buried at Saint Mary's, and in a vault which was built by order of the State, at the State's expense, and presumably, upon the State's property.

On July 27th, 1694, it having been made known "to his Excellency, that the bodies of the late Governor Copley and his Lady, deceased, lye still at the Great House", and "confessing it was expected an order would have been received for carrying them by some man-of-war to England", it was ordered by the Council, "that they be interred in a vault, to be built for the purpose, at Saint Mary's, and that the ceremony be performed by the next Provincial Court, with all the decency and grandeur the Constitution and circumstances of affairs will admit of, and that three brass guns, being all that's to be had, be in readiness, and also the militia of adjoining parts".[2] Pursuant to this order, the interment took place October 5, 1694.[3]

---

were most probably influenced by curiosity, rather than drink, as would appear from the interesting letter in the Appendix, written only a few days after the occurrence, by one of the participants. It should also be noted, that Lady Ann Calvert was never in Maryland. She died in London, in 1649.

1 Genealogist, vol. 1.   2 Cl. Pro. H. D. 2, p. 43.   3 Ibid, p. 65.

Governor Copley left three children, two sons and one daughter.—Ibid, p. 98.

On the north side of the State House lot, and on the declivity facing Saint John's Creek, stood the jail. It was erected in 1676; was two stories high, twenty-four feet long and fifteen feet wide, in the clear, with ceilings nine feet high, and was built of brick, with tiled roof and paved floor. It had three windows, each having "three iron bars upright and two across", into which the upright bars were wrought.[1] Below the jail was "Gallows-green", the property of Richard May, Chief Clerk to the Secretary, and which, as first granted, says the record, extended beyond the "gallowes", and across the plateau as far as the "great white mulberry tree".[2] This, however, subsequently became a part of the State House lot.

On the northeast side of Middle Street, adjoining the State House lot, and extending through it to Saint John's Creek, was the lot on which stood the famous hostelry, known as "Jellie's Tavern".[3] It was built of brick; was about thirty-five by forty-five feet, and was two-and-a-half stories high. The walls and chimneys of this building were standing within the recollection of a few very old people living up to a recent period, and its site is still pointed out, near that of the present rectory of Trinity Church. It was owned and operated by Robert Jellie, and from the following proceedings taken against it, by the Council, in 1686, it may be inferred that in its latter days, its reputation for order and sobriety became somewhat tarnished:

"It is considered by this Board, that the House wherein Robert Jellie keeps Ordinary at the City of Saint Mary's, is very inconvenient and prejudicial to the public, for that at the time of Provincial Courts, the Jury, attorneys and suitors are at said House often detained and disordered, * * * and said

---

[1] Archives (Ass. Pro. 1674) p. 406.
[2] Liber 16, p. 594, Land Office.   [3] Re-survey, 1723.

THE FIRST CAPITAL

House being also near the State House, wherein the Public Offices of the Province are kept, the Clerks of said offices are often found to frequent said House, by which means there is great occasion to suspect that the public affairs of the Province are much impeded by reason of said Ordinary. * * * This Board does, therefore, represent the same as a Public grievance to the Mayor and Aldermen of said City, in order to have the same suppressed ".[1]

In the ravine, below this tavern, was located the "Town Spring".

Adjoining the tavern lot on the east, fronting on Middle Street, and extending through to Saint John's Creek, was the residence of Philip Lynes, Mayor of Saint Mary's City at the time of the removal of the Capital to Annapolis,[2] and adjoining it on the east, was the traditional site of the Protestant Episcopal Church. It is alleged that Trinity Church, on Trinity (Smith's) Creek, six miles below, erected in 1642,[3] and probably the first Protestant church built by the Maryland colonists, was moved to Saint Mary's,[4] and located, according to tradition, in the "Creek lot", close by the old graveyard,

---

1 Archives (Cl. Pro.) pp. 494, 498.

Among the tavern keepers at Saint Mary's, from time to time, may be mentioned, William Smith, Robert Ridgely, John Baker, Garrett Van Sweringen, and John Quigley, the two latter being partners. Ordinaries were regularly licensed, and were subject to stringent laws, both as to accommodations and rates. At Saint Mary's, each innkeeper was required to have at least twelve feather beds, and to provide stable room for at least twenty horses, and was limited to the following charges: Lodging in bed with sheets, 12 pence ; diet, 1 shilling per meal ; brandy, malaga, and sherry, 10 shillings per gallon ; canary, 12 shillings; French, Renish, Dutch, and English wines, 6 shillings ; Mum, 3 shillings ; plain cider, 25 and boiled cider, 30 ℔s. tob. per quart. Archives (Ass. Pro. 1666-1676) pp. 295, 407, 554, and Ibid, 1682, p. 429 ; Archives (Cl. Pro. 1672) p. 118, and Ibid, 1692, p. 420.

2 Re-survey, 1723 ; Scharf, 1, p. 347.

3 Allen, Who Were the Early Settlers of Maryland.

4 Butler, p. 23.

now crowned with cedar and holly trees. It being most probably a wooden structure, and the State House at an early date having been dedicated to Protestant worship, the history of this little church appears to have passed away with its usefulness. That there was, however, a Protestant church at Saint Mary's at an early period, is clearly established,[1] and of its architecture, it is also known that it had an "arched ceiling", after the design of which the State House ceiling was subsequently modeled.[2]

Adjoining the church lot on the east, stood the residences of John Llewelyn and Philip Evens. Of these houses little is known; the records, as well as tradition, being silent, both as to their character and size, except that the former furnishes a scant notice of the home of Clerk of the Council, John Llewelyn,[3] from which it may be inferred that it was a house of comfortable proportions.

A little further east, and near the point where Mill Creek falls into Saint John's, stood the town water mill, erected in 1635. The mill site and lot contained nine acres. It was built by Thomas Cornwaleys, who having completed it, proceeded, as he said, to "build a house to put my own head in". In 1723, it had ceased to be operated, and the "old dam", remains of which are still visible, was all that was then left of its ruin.[4]

It is worthy of note, that this was not only the first water mill set up in Maryland, but was one of the earliest in America, and was one of the few in the country which was

---

1 See statement of Governor Seymoure, in trial of Father Brooke, Scharf, 1, p. 369.

2 See Extracts from William & Mary Parish Records, in Whittingham Library, by Allen.

3 Archives (Cl. Pro. 1684) p. 308; Re-survey, 1723.

4 Relation, 1635; McSherry, p. 57; Re-survey, 1723.

erected as a private enterprise, rather than by public contribution.[1]

In 1639, the Assembly authorized another mill to be built at Saint Mary's, the cost not to exceed 20,000 ℔s of tobacco, to be raised by general taxation.[2] As the assessment, however, for this mill appears not to have been made, it is highly probable that it was never erected.

The records also speak of a "wind mill" at Saint Mary's, the property of Major General Edward Gibbons, and purchased by Lord Baltimore, in 1656, for £100 sterling, and which, he directed, should be specially cared for and improved.[3]

Between the mill lot and Middle Street was the traditional site of "Market Square". Under the charter, a "market" was to be held weekly; the town officers also being authorized to hold an "Annual Fair", to which the ancient Court of "Piepoudrea"[4] was to be an incident.

On the south and east side of the Fort was the "Chapel land". It extended from Key's Creek, across the plateau to to the fresh of Saint John's (above tide-water, called Mill) Creek. The Chapel itself, stood near the intersection of "Middle" and "Mattapany" Streets, fronting northeast, and

---

[1] Improvements of this character were of slow growth at that time. The first water mill in Massachusetts was built in 1633, five years after the colony had been settled. The same year a saw mill was erected near London, but it was deemed a machine which would deprive the laboring people of employment and it was demolished.—Bozman.

[2] Bozman, p. 156. [3] Archives (Pro. Cl.) p. 326.

[4] The lowest—and at the same time the most expeditious Court of Justice known to the law of England, is the Court of Piepoudrea, *curia pedis pulveri zati*, so called from the dusty feet of the suitors, or according to Sir Edward Coke, because justice is there done as speedily as dust can fall from the foot. It was held at markets so that attendants on the markets might have their causes heard and determined expeditiously, and thus lose no time by the delays of the law. Blackstone, vol. III, p. 31.

on the former street. It was a brick building, and, judging from its foundation lines (visible until a recent period), it was about eighteen by thirty feet. Over the altar, was a carved representation of clouds,[1] and of the flames of Pentecost.[2] The exact date of its erection has not been ascertained, but it was prior to 1638,[3] and it was undoubtedly (barring the little wigwam fitted up by Father White, and called by him the " first Chapel in Maryland ") the first church built by the Maryland colonists.

It has been suggested, in proof of the harmony and concord existing between the Protestants and Roman Catholics in Maryland at that time, that this Chapel was built by their joint contributions, and used in common between them, where " each at his appropriate hour might offer up his sacrifice to the Most High "[4]—a theory which seems to be sustained by the records of the times.

That " *the Chapel* " was the early place of worship for the Protestants in and around Saint Mary's City, is clearly established by the records in the proceedings against William Lewis, showing the complainants on their way to "the Chapel, July 1st, 1638, to procure the signatures of the Protestants there assembled, to their petition asking for protection and redress " ;[5] and also by the case against Doctor Thomas Gerrard, for "taking away the key of the Chapel", and removing the books there used in Protestant worship.[6] It is equally clear, that this Chapel was also the

---

[1] Bryant, p. 498.

[2] Fragments of this altar piece may still be seen at Georgetown College; the altar stone, chalice, and paten are at Woodstock College.

[3] See proceedings against Lewis. [4] Day Star, p. 34.

[5] Archives (Pro. Ct. 1638) p. 35.

[6] Archives (Ass. Pro. 1642) p. 119.

Roman Catholic place of worship during the same period. Apart from the fact that the church and lot belonged to the Jesuit Priest in charge at Saint Mary's[1], the Roman Catholic graveyard there was "ye ordinary burying place in Saint Mary's Chapel Yard".[2]

If, however, the Protestants acquired any rights to the use and occupation of this Chapel by reason of having contributed to the cost of its construction or otherwise, they were relinquished at an early date, and it became exclusively a Roman Catholic Church.

In April, 1641, the Chapel lot and buildings were purchased by Governor Calvert, for the Proprietary, for £200 sterling.[3] Why this purchase was made, is one of the many mysteries and obscurities in Maryland's early history, which the records fail to elucidate.

In 1683, the Proprietary, having disposed of a part of the Chapel land, ordered that such quantity as was deemed necessary for the "Chapel and burying place at the City of Saint Mary's", be supplied from some other of his Lordship's land lying contiguous thereto.[4]

---

1 The Chapel lot was first surveyed for Mr. Ferdinand Poulton, a Jesuit Priest, officially known as Father Brock, and who was accidentally shot while crossing the Saint Mary's River. The patent, however, was obtained by Mr. Thomas Copley, a Jesuit Priest, known officially as Father Philip Fisher. It contained twenty-five acres, and was bounded as follows; "on the east by Saint Peter's; south by Gile's Brent's land; west by Key's Branch, and north by a line drawn from Key's Branch, at the 'Vayle', to the brook where Saint Peter's ends, being about forty-five perches above the Mill".—Liber 1, pp. 32 and 117; Shea, pp. 38 and 55.

2 Will of John Loyd, 1658; Day Star, p. 34.

3 Archives (Pro. Cl.) pp. 136 and 143; Ibid, (Pro. Ct.) pp. 217, 243, 263, and 266.

4 Kilty, p. 123.

By the Act of 1704, to "prevent the growth of Popery in Maryland", the celebration of mass in this Chapel, in common with other Roman Catholic churches in the Province, was prohibited. In September of that year, two priests, Robert Brooke and William Hunter, were arraigned before Governor Seymour, on the charge of holding service in Saint Mary's Chapel, contrary to law. It being, says the record, their "first offence", they were "dismissed with a mere reprimand", but one, it should be said, which was singularly conspicuous for its arrogant tone and intolerant spirit. By advice of the Council, the Governor at the same time issued an order, directing the sheriff of the county to lock up the "Papish Chapel at the City of Saint Mary's" and "keep the key thereof", "and that no person presume to make use thereof under any pretence whatever".[1] Thus, under this order, issued September 19th, 1704, this, the first church erected by the Pilgrims of Maryland, was forever closed to public worship.

While the American Revolution swept away the legislation of the times against the Roman Catholics the title to this property, had, in the meantime, become vested in others, and the "Chapel land at Saint Mary's", where stood the first Church of Rome, in Maryland, was forever lost to the object and purpose of its dedication. The Chapel building and furniture, however, were taken to Saint Inigoe's, and the manor house, erected in 1705, under the auspices of Father Ashby, was built of the bricks taken from the old Chapel at Saint Mary's.[2]

---

[1] Scharf, 1, p. 369; Shea, p. 354.
[2] Bishop Fenweck's Maryland; Shea, p. 370.

THE FIRST CAPITAL 45

It is stated that further inland, in the little ravine above "Governor's Spring", "the first burial ground of the colony was made, and where the Jesuit fathers placed the block cross at the head of every christian grave".[1] Be this as it may, certain it is, that the "Chapel yard" was "ye ordinary burying place" for Roman Catholics, as early as 1658[2]—an entirely different location.

On the east side of Mattapany Street, and near the head of "Governor's Run", stood what was probably the most pretentious residence at Saint Mary's. It was called the "Governor's Castle". The lot on which it stood was granted in 1638, to Thomas Cornwaleys, and was called "Saint Peter". The situation, while not as picturesque perhaps, as some others, was nevertheless, an attractive one. The house fronted the west, and commanded a pleasing view of both the land and water. The records speak of this house as early as 1639,[3] and in 1640, its substantial character and superior style of architecture were deemed worthy of special note.[4]

In 1664, it was owned by Philip Calvert, and later by Lord Baltimore,[5] by whom it was probably embellished, if not enlarged. Even within the present century, the walls, chimneys, and tiled cellar floor of this early colonial mansion, were still partly standing, and the site, covered with fragments of brick and tile, is still clearly discernible.

It was built of dark red brick, ornamented with black, was square in general shape (about forty feet each way), was two stories high, with arched brick porch in front, and two large chimneys, which were near the centre of the build-

---

1 'Bryant, p. 505.   2 Will, John Loyd, 1658; Day Star, 34.
3 Liber 1, p. 67.   4 Bryant, p. 505.
5 Rent Rolls.

ing. A cellar, which extended under the whole structure, was paved with square tile. A massive and high brick wall enclosed the building and court,[1] which, while adding doubtless to its imposing appearance, must have given to it much the aspect of a fortification.

An eminent Maryland author,[2] in 1838, from details furnished by living witnesses of a time when this building and its surroundings, while not, perhaps, in their pristine glory, were still standing, wrote the following description of them: "A massive building, of dark brick, two stories in height, and penetrated by narrow windows looking forth, beyond the fort, upon the river, constituted the chief member or main body of the mansion. This was capped by a wooden balustraded parapet, terminating, at each extremity, in a scroll, and in the middle, sustaining an entablature that rose to a summit on which was mounted a weathercock. From this central structure, right and left, a series of arcades and corridors served to bring into line a range of subordinate buildings. * * * In the rear of the buildings, a circular sweep of wall and pailing reached as far as a group of stables and sheds. Vanward, the same kind of enclosures, more ornate in their fashion, shut in a grassy court. * * * Ancient trees shaded the whole mass of dwelling-house, court and stables, and gave to the place both a lordly and comfortable aspect. It was a pleasant groupe of roof and bower, of spire and tree to look upon from * * * the fair villiage—city, studding the level plain with its scattered dwellings."

This building may have been occupied by Charles, Lord Baltimore during the latter years of his residence in Maryland, but it does not appear to have been the "executive

---

[1] Bryant, p. 505.   [2] Kennedy, Rob of the Bowl.

mansion" of the Province, until the establishment of the Royal Goverment in Maryland, when it was used as such by Sir Lionel Copley, the first Royal Governor,[1] and his successors, and when it was probably given the name, by which it was afterwards known, "Governor's Castle".

About twenty yards below the house was a spring, which is still known as "Governor's Spring", and noted for its abundant flow of pure, clear water.

On the opposite side of the ravine from the "Governor's Castle", was the Throughton house, said to have been one of the finest private residences at Saint Mary's. The lot was granted in 1639,[2] and was improved by a capacious brick building, one-and-a-half stories high, with steep roof and dormer windows. This house was occupied by the Mackalls, and later by the Bromes, until the early part of the present century, when it was destroyed by fire. The chimneys and gables of the building now there are said to be constructed of material saved from the ruin of its predecessor.

Adjoining Mrs. Mary Throughton's lot, on the east, was "Courtney's Fancy", the residence of Thomas Courtney, while still further inland were "Saint Mary's Hills", and "Paris and Galloway", owned respectively, by Major Nicholas Sewall, and Attorney General Robert Carvile.[3]

On the opposite, or northerly, side of Matapany Street, and about two hundred and fifty yards from its intersection with Mill Creek, was "Saint Barberry", the home of Attorney General Robert Carvile, and subsequently of his daughter, Mrs. Cecelius Butler.[4]

Adjoining "Saint Barberry" on the north, was the residence of John Lewger, the first Secretary of the Province. It

---

1 Archives (Pro. Cl. 1692) p. 382.   2 Liber 1, p. 67.
3 Rent Rolls.   4 Resurvey, 1723.

was called "Saint John", and stood on the bluff formed by the union of Saint John's Creek with Saint Mary's Bay—a commanding and singularly beautiful situation. The warrant for "Saint John" was issued in 1637, and the patent in 1639. As early as the 11th of February, 1638, the records speak of "our Secretary's house at Saint John", and on the 25th of the same month, the General Assembly adjourned at Fort Saint Mary's to meet at the "mansion house" there,[1] which from that time, continued to be the place at which most of the public business of the Province was transacted, until the "Government House", heretofore mentioned, was purchased.

When Mr. Lewger returned to England, "Saint John" was sold to Richard Bennett. In 1650, John Lewger, Jr., who remained in Maryland, and who, in 1648, when but twenty years of age, was Clerk of the Assembly, secured the historic home of his father, at Saint Mary's.[2] It was subsequently sold to Lord Baltimore, who ordered a large area of adjacent land, lying within and beyond the limits of Saint Mary's, to be added to it, the whole to be erected into a manor, and to be granted to his son, Charles Calvert,[3] then Governor of the Province. "Saint John" was the home of Charles, Lord Baltimore, for about twenty years, and for a period quite as long, nearly all of the meetings of the Council of State were held there".[4] In 1684, when he visited England, destined never to return to Maryland, the "mansion house, orchard, and garden" were put in charge of William Smith, of Saint Mary's.[5]

---

1 Archives (Ass. Pro. 1638) pp. 28 and 32.
2 Archives (Pro. Ct. 1650) pp. 66 and 70; Neil's Maryland, p. 72.
3 Kilty, p. 95.   4 Archives (Pro. Cl. 1662-1684).
5 Kilty, p. 220.

THE FIRST CAPITAL

Of this building, no traces are left to indicate its style or character, except the still visible outlines of its cellar, and the broken brick and tile which are commingled with the soil around it. But repeated instances are furnished in which Baltimore, during the sessions of the Assembly and Courts, entertained there, for weeks at a time, a large number of persons,[1] from which it may be inferred, that it was, at least, a building of no inconsiderable propartions.

The residence of Speaker of the House, Kenelm Cheseldine, was called "East Saint Mary's". The house stood on the north side of Chancellor's Creek, on a site now crowned with trees and remnants of its ruin, and a little southeast of the present dwelling on the property, which still bears its original name. This building, which was standing less than fifty years ago, was about thirty by thirty-five feet, was built of brick, and was one-and-a-half stories high, with steep roof and sharp dormer windows. "East Saint Mary's", was in 1639,[2] patented to Nathaniel Pope.[3] It was subsequently owned by Lord Baltimore, and later by Kenelm Cheseldine, for several years Speaker of the Lower House of Assembly. During the greater part of the time it was owned by Baltimore, it was, by order of the Council, constituted the place of general rendezvous for the militia, and was the "Port of Entry" for Saint Mary's City.[4] "East Saint Mary's" is also historic as the place at which the sessions of 1669 and 1671, of the General Assembly were held.[5]

---

1 As an illustration see Archives (Ass. Pro. 1674) p. 432.
2 Liber 1, p. 54.
3 His daughter, Ann, married Colonel John Washington, the great-grandfather of General Washington.—William & Mary Quarterly, 1893.
4 Archives (2 Pro. Cl.) pp. 23, 31, and 93.
5 Archives (2 Ass. Pro.) pp. 156 and 239.

"The residence of Deputy Governor Giles Brent,[1] stood on the cliff on the south side of "Key's Branch". The lot was patented to him in 1639, and fronted eighty perches on the river. It was beautifully situated and was called the "White House".[2]

Adjoining this lot on the south, was "Brent's Forge"[3] while still further south was the residence of Mistress Margaret and Mary Brent. The latter lot was patented in 1639,[4] and was called "Sisters' Freehold".[5]

---

[1] Giles Brent came to Maryland in 1639; was appointed Treasurer, and during the visit of Governor Calvert to England, in 1643, was commissioned Deputy Governor of the Province. He was the son of Richard Brent, of Gloucester, England. He had a brother, Fulk Brent, and sisters Margaret, Mary, Catherine, Elizabeth, Eleanor, Jane, and Ann. Of these, Mary and Margaret, and his brother Fulk, came to Maryland with him. It was this Mistress Margaret who was such a prominent figure in early Maryland history. She was the executrix of Governor Leonard Calvert, and represented Lord Baltimore in various important matters of State, in all of which she displayed marked talent, courage, and ability. She enjoys the distinction of having been the first woman in America (and, perhaps, in the world, if we except the ingenious Portia, of dramatic fame), who exercised the rights of an attorney at law. The records furnish repeated instances in which she appeared before the Courts in that capacity. She was also a strong—and perhaps, the earliest—advocate of woman's suffrage, having demanded, not only a seat in the General Assembly of Maryland, but a vote therein, both in her individual capacity, and as the representative of the estate of Governor Leonard Calvert. Two votes to one woman, however, was more than even the gallantry of the sons of early Maryland could accord. Could the wife of Governor Leonard Calvert—whose identity is still shrouded in obscurity—have been one of the sisters of this notable woman? If so, it would account for the high offices bestowed by him upon Colonel Giles Brent, and the close bond of intimacy and apparent relationship which existed between them.

[2] Kilty, p. 71; Rent Rolls.   [3] Kilty, p. 71.
[4] Liber 1, p. 32.   [5] Deed, E. Clocker, to J. Milburn, 1756.

THE FIRST CAPITAL

Adjacent to this property on the south, was the residence of Governor Thomas Green.[1] It was patented in 1639, and was called, at first, "Green's Rest",[2] and later, "Saint Ann".

All of these houses stood near the river, and were located in what is now known as the "Rectory Field". The site of each, as well as the graded slope from the houses to the river, can still clearly be seen.

The house of Governor Green—a two-story frame building, with brick gables, was occupied as late as 1820,[3] and its brick chimneys were standing within the recollection of many persons still living.

In the same general locality, but further inland, and bordering on Saint Andrew's Creek and Saint Inigoe's Creek, were, "Town Land", the residence of Robert Clark, Surveyor General;[4] "Lewis' Neck", the residence of Lieutenant William Lewis, subsequently of Daniel Clocker;[5] "Van Sweringen Point", the residence of Garrett Van Sweringen, subsequently of Clerk of Council, Robert Ridgely;[6] "Saint Peter's Key", the residence of John Harris, subsequently of William

---

1 It is said by Browning that Thomas Green married Elizabeth a sister of Governor Leonard Calvert. He had sons named Leonard, Francis, Thomas, and Robert.—Davis, p. 182.

2 Liber 1, p. 42; Rent Rolls; Archives (2 Pro. Ct.) p. 337.

3 By the father of the late Doctor John Mackall Brome. To Doctor Brome, a most estimable man, and his venerable mother, both now deceased, whose residence at Saint Mary's had, together, covered nearly a century of time, and, consequently, had seen much of the old City before it crumbled to ruin, the author is indebted for much valuable information and data, which could otherwise only have been secured, if at all, at the expense of enormous research and labor.

4 Kilty.   5 Ibid; Will of Benjamin Clocker.

6 Patent, Land Office; Resurvey, 1710.

Goldsmith ;[1] and "Cross Neck", the residence of Elizabeth Baker, who devised it, in 1701, to William and Mary (P. E.) Parish.[2]

About midway between Robert Clark's and the intersection of Middle and Mattapany Streets, and near the latter street, was one of the principal taverns of the City, in the latter part of its history. It was owned by Garrett Van Sweringen, in 1671, but was shortly afterward destroyed by fire. It was rebuilt, however, and in 1698 was known as "The Coffee House". He also owned, in 1698, the house at Saint Mary's called "The Council Room".[3]

South of Saint Andrew's Creek, and on the promontory which formed the southern arm of Saint Mary's Harbor, was the house of Chancellor Philip Calvert. It was known as "the Chancellor's Point"[4]—the name it still retains. It was a singularly commanding and beautiful situation, but nothing remains, save the name and a few fragments of its ruin, to mark the spot where once stood the historic home of Maryland's first Chancellor.

Adjoining "Chancellor's Point" on the east, and bordering on Saint Inigoe's Creek, were "Clocker's Fancy" and "Justice's Freehold", the residences respectively, of Daniel Clocker and William Deakins.[5]

Still further down the peninsula, was the Walstenholme residence. This place is familiarly known as the home of the "Collector", a position with which it was associated as late as the American Revolution—Daniel Walstenholme, its owner,

---

1 Patent, Land Office ; Rent Rolls.
2 Archives (Pro. Cl. 1692) pp. 395 and 420 ; Resurvey, 1750 ; will of Elizabeth Baker.
3 Archives (Pro. Cl. 1692) p. 420; will, Liber P. C. III.
4 Patent.   5 Deed, Elizabeth Clocker to John Milburn, 1756.

THE FIRST CAPITAL 53

and son of his predecessor in that office—being, until 1776, Collector of the Potomac District.[1] The house, a capacious frame building, with brick gables (and until recent years, double-roofed and triangularly-capped dormer windows), and finished with handsomely carved woodwork ornamenting both ceilings and side walls, is still in good preservation. It stands to-day, the only monument of its time, and furnishes a handsome and interesting specimen of the style of architecture and interior embellishment of that day. It occupies the summit of the high, bold bluff at the juncture of Saint Inigoe's Creek with the river, and commands an extensive and picturesque view of both land and water, embracing in its sweep, Saint George's Island, the broad Potomac, and the dim, mountain-like lines of the distant Virginia shore. It is now the mansion house of the beautiful estate called "Rose Craft".[2]

---

[1] This house, it is said by persons in position to know, retains its original style of architecture, except, that about thirty years ago its precipitous roof and triangularly-capped dormer windows were removed, and the present roof substituted. It is also worthy of note that this house is frequently referred to as the home of "Anthony Warden, Collector". No such person ever lived at Saint Mary's, or ever was the Proprietory Collector in Maryland. The name was first introduced in Maryland literature, by Kennedy, in his interesting legend of Saint Inigoe's, ' Rob, of the Bowl ", which, while an historical novel of great value, introduces its characters through fictitious names.

[2] Journal and Correspondence, Council of Safely, July, 1776; deed, John Mackall to A. Livers Lee, 1810.

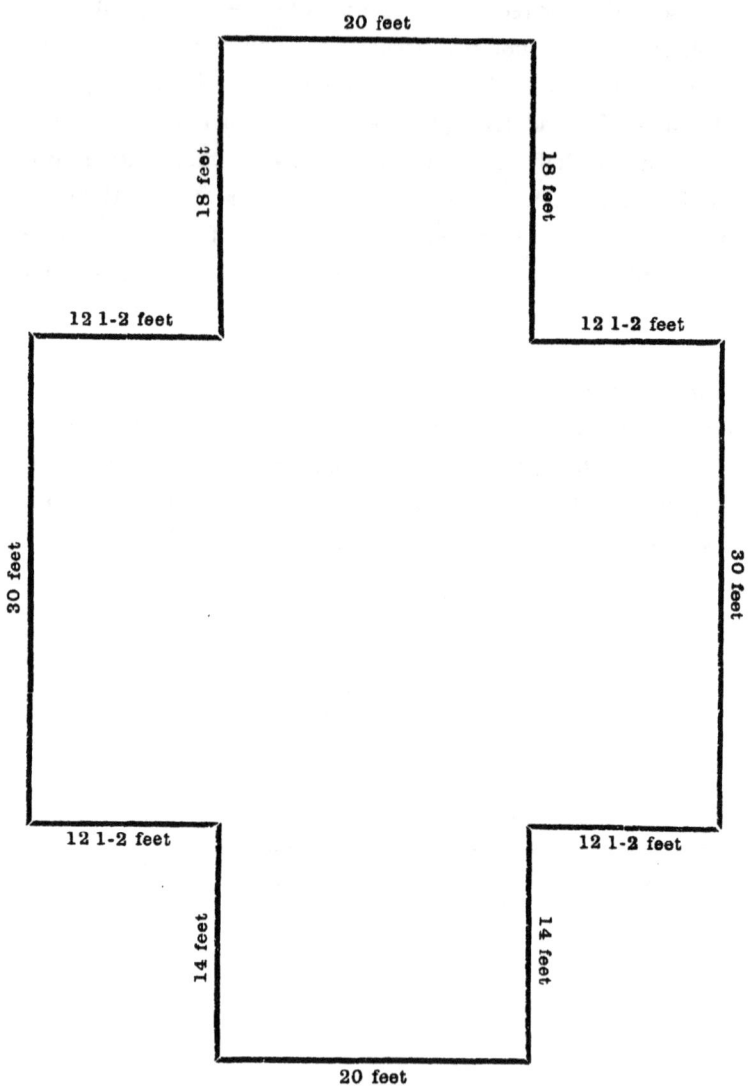

FOUNDATION LINES
OF MARYLAND'S FIRST STATE HOUSE

CHAPTER III.

The First Capital of Maryland.

THE first General Assembly held in Maryland, met at Saint Mary's, on the 26th of February, 1635. The Acts of this session, Baltimore refused to approve, because, as he claimed, the right to originate laws resided, under the charter, exclusively in himself; the power of the Assembly being limited to assent and dissent to such as he propounded. The freemen of Maryland, convinced that they possessed equal and co-ordinate rights, in matters of legislation, with the Proprietary, with the courage of their conviction, vindicated their position, by rejecting, at the next session of the Assembly, the whole body of bills drafted and submitted by him for their adoption, and enacted in their stead, a code which eminated from themselves, though substantially the same as the one that he had propounded. After this, the right of the Assembly to initiate legislation was not contested, and the right of the Proprietary was, in practice, limited to his veto. This right he always retained the privilege of exercising personally, and, while the Governor of the Province was invested with the power of assenting to or rejecting laws passed by the Assembly, his assent only gave them efficacy until the Proprietary's *dissent* was declared.[1]

---

[1] McMahon, p. 145; Brown, pp. 35 and 44; Johnson's Foundation of Maryland.

The freemen, successful in their opposition to what they deemed an encroachment upon their charter rights, thus planted in Maryland, at the session of 1637, that germ of liberty which underlies the right of free self government.

The Legislature consisted at first of one branch, and until 1639, was composed of the Council and all the freemen in the Province, either in person or by proxy, convened by proclamation and summons, with the Governor as its President. In 1639, burgesses were elected from every hundred, who with the Governor and Council, composed the House of Assembly. With this change from a primary to a representative Assembly, two curious anomalies still existed—the one conceding to the Governor the right to summons additional members at will ; the other, the right of every freeman who failed to vote for the burgess elected, to claim representation in person.

In 1650, the organization of an Upper and a Lower House of Assembly was established ; the Governor, Council, and those summoned by special writ, constituting the Upper House, and the burgesses elected, the Lower House. The number of delegates to be elected was within the Governor's discretion, and was regulated by the proclamation for the election, usually from two to four from each hundred (subsequently, each county), until 1681, when the number was uniformly fixed, and reduced to two, which continued until 1692, when it was, for the first time, regulated by Act of Assembly, and when the number was increased to four from every county—a basis of representation which continued until the Revolution.[1]

It should here be said that the legislation enacted at the little Capital of Saint Mary's, during the sixty-one years in which it was the seat of Government, forms, to a great

---

[1] McMahon, p. 147; Brown, p. 43; Doyle, p. 291; Scharf, 2, p. 282.

extent, the foundation and outlines of the present legal, civil, and social structures of Maryland, and of some of its most cherished institutions.

It was then and there, that the great struggle for popular sovereignty, between the bold and courageous yeomanry of Maryland and the Lord Proprietary was inaugurated, and which resulted in setting upon a firm foundation, that principle, which formed the basis of Maryland's early system of free self-government, and which, "in process of time, and course of events", developed into a reality, the sublime doctrine of constitutional liberty.

It was also, by the legislation then and there enacted, that the famous "Toleration Act", giving legal sanction to liberty of conscience, which shed such brilliant renown upon the legislative annals of Maryland, won for it the name of the "Land of the Sanctuary", and which extended to all who believed in Jesus Christ, whatever their form of worship, "shelter, protection, and repose", became engrafted by law upon its government.

Though religious toleration had existed, in practice, in Maryland, from its earliest settlement, it had never been made the subject of legislative enactment, and to the General Assembly, of 1649, does this, "the proudest memorial" of Maryland's colonial history, belong. "Higher than all titles and badges of honor, and more exalted than royal nobility", is the imperishable distinction which the passage of this broad and liberal Act won for Maryland, and for the members of that never-to-be-forgotten session, and sacred, *forever, be the hallowed spot which gave it birth!* [1]

---
[1] In a recent publication, "Religion Under the Barons of Baltimore", the author indulges in lengthy and ingenious arguments in an endeavor to show that religious toleration had no existence in Maryland, under the Barons of Baltimore, and that the claims made by Maryland and

But, besides being the historic battle field of Maryland's early struggle for political freedom, and the scene of its first legislative confirmation of religious peace, Saint Mary's presents in its history, as the capital and metropolis of the Province, all "the glowing incidents and martial virtues" which characterized and gave inspiration to that eventful and heroic period—the period in Maryland history which has truly been styled, "the golden age of its colonial existence"; the period in which the foundation of its government was being broadly and deeply laid; the period of its great political turmoils and religious agitations; the period in which were the defiant spirit and persistent rebellion of Clayborne; the artful sedition

---

some historians, that it had, is "unhistorical and apochryphal", and based upon, what at best, is only a "legendary tale". For more than two centuries and a half, Maryland has enjoyed her unique position in the matter of early religious toleration. It is the keystone of the great archway in her history, as it was the keynote of her earliest code, and is too firmly set to be easily shaken. Whether for religious, prudential, or commercial reasons, the fact remains—and it is one than which none other in Maryland history is more incontestably established—that religious toleration, and in a broad sense for that day, had practical existence in Maryland, from the date of its settlement, and that it continued throughout the successive administrations of Cecilius and Charles Lord Baltimore, except when the government was in the hands of Cromwell's Commissioners and the Puritan element, from 1652 to 1657; and except, also, when it was under the jurisdiction of the English Crown, from 1692 to 1715. Injustice to none, and christian toleration and charity to all who believed in Jesus Christ, was a cardinal rule established by Cecilius, continued by Charles, Lord Baltimore, and which those in authority under them rigorously enforced. This is abundantly proven by the instructions sent out with the colonists in 1634, which provided that all Protestants should be treated "with as much mildness and favor as justice will permit", and that all Roman Catholics abstain from public "discourse concerning matters of religion", as well as that their religious duties be "done as privately as may be"; by the proceedings against Lieutenant William Lewis, a Roman Catholic, who, in 1638, on the complaint that he would not allow the Protestant servants under him to read a certain book of sermons, and that he had spoken disrespectfully of the ministers of their church, was arraigned, convicted, and fined 500 lbs. of

THE FIRST CAPITAL

and destructive warfare of Ingle; the reflex action upon Maryland of England's parliamentary disturbances, resulting in the usurpation of the Proprietary rights; the turbulence and ascendancy of the Puritan, whose reign was so conspicuous for its political proscription of those who hospitably received and generously treated them when outcast and homeless, and of sectarian persecution of those who did not worship at the altar of their shrine; the repeated efforts of the Proprietary to reduce them to subjection, beginning with the memorable battle upon the Severn, and ending only with the turn of affairs in England which took from them their moral support; the rise and fall of the intriguing and ambitious Fendall, the

---

tobacco, and placed under bond for his future good behavior in that respect; by the proclamation, issued before 1638, for the suppression of all "disputes tending to the opening of a faction in religion"; by the case against Doctor Thomas Gerrard, also a Roman Catholic, who, in 1642, on complaint of the Protestants against him for interfering with their worship, was, upon conviction, fined 500 ℔s. of tobacco, to be given for the support of the first Protestant minister that should arrive in the Province; by the oath to be administered to the newly-appointed Protestant Governor, Stone, in 1648, which provided that he would "not directly or indirectly trouble, molest, or discountenance any person, whatsoever, in the Province, professing to believe in Jesus Christ, and in particular, no Roman Catholic, for or in respect to his religion, or in his free exercise thereof within the said Province"; by the "Toleration Act", of 1649, giving to the code, already existing in practice, legislative confirmation, which if not drafted by the Proprietary, certainly received his approval and sanction; by the "Protestant Declaration", of 1650, signed by Governor William Stone—whose churchmanship and veracity are not in doubt—and by a large number of the leading Protestants of the Province, in which it was distinctly stated, "that according to an Act of Assembly here, and several other strict injunctions and declarations by his sayd Lordship for that purpose made and provided. we doe heere enjoy all fitting and convenient freedom and liberty in the exercise of our religion under his Lordship's government and interest, and that none of us are in any wayes troubled or molested, for or by reason thereof, within his Lordship's sayd Province"; and by the case against the Rev. Francis Fitzherbert, who, while acquitted upon the charge of threatening excommunication of a member of his church unless he compelled his

Cromwell of Maryland; the introduction of the printing press, that emblem of liberty which was not found in any other American colony; the embroiling designs and the insurrection of the apostate, Coade; the Protestant revolutional, in 1689; the fall of the Proprietary government; the administration of affairs by the representatives of the Crown, and the establishment of the Church of England, by law, in the Province—all pass in review, and stand in "characteristic light and shade"[1] upon its historic panorama.

Protestant wife and children to attend the Roman Catholic Church, was promptly arraigned and tried. Other concrete examples could be cited to show that religious liberty in early Maryland was not a fancy, but a condition—not a theory, but a fact. The above, however, are surely sufficient to give the liberality of her religious spirit its proper place— that of a fundamental principal underlying the Baltimore polity and the Maryland government—and to demonstrate that it was zealously guarded and practically maintained. But while Maryland is entitled to the credit, and enjoys the honor of having first unfurled and firmly planted on her ramparts, the banner of religious liberty in the New World, her "Toleration Act", of 1649, was not the first legislative enactment on that subject. In 1645, a Toleration Act was introduced in the Assembly at Plymouth Rock, but it did not pass. In 1647, however, Roger Williams and his small band of followers, who were independents and non-conformists in the broadest sense, and who, unable to adapt themselves to the rigidly organized government of Massachusetts, and determined to live only "with those of a like way of thinking", had settled the Providence Plantation of Rhode Island. There, after much internal strife and dissension--inevitable among extremists—and several ineffectual efforts to establish a government, they at length succeeded in forming a structure, which, while of short duration, was yet long enough to have engrafted in its code, the enactment that, "all men may walk as their consciences persuade them, every one in the name of his God; and let the saints of the Most High walk in this colony without molestation".—For this Note, see "Baltimore's Instructions", 1633, in Maryland Historical Society and "Makers of America", p. 46; Archives (Pro. Ct. 1638) p. 35; Ibid, p. 38; Ibid (Ass. Pro. 1642) p. 119; Ibid (Cl. Pro. 1648) p. 209; Ibid (Ass. Pro. 1649) p. 244; Bozman, II, p. 72; Day Star, pp. 35-66; Moore's "Lives of the Governors of New Plymouth and Massachusetts Bay"; Pro. 1st. Gen. Ass. of Providence, 1647, p. 50.

1 The Buccaneers.

THE FIRST CAPITAL

The year 1644 is conspicuous in the annals of Saint Mary's, as the beginning of a series of dissensions in Maryland, in which the Provincial Capital was the theatre of action, and which, with slight interruptions, continued to disturb the peace of the Province for about sixteen years. In November of that year, Richard Ingle, who had shortly before been arrested at Saint Mary's, for "treason", and had escaped, filled with revenge and burning for retaliation, entered the Saint Mary's River in command of the armed ship *Reformation*. Finding much disturbance and divided sympathy in the colony, over the contest then pending in England, between the King and Parliament, he met with but little difficulty in exciting the disaffected to rebellion. This accomplished, he invaded and seized the City, mutilated the records, pillaged public and private property,[1] and drove Governor Calvert to Virginia. Calvert, however, after much delay, gathered there all available forces, and, pledging his own and Baltimore's estates to pay them, crossed the Potomac, and after a short and bloodless contest, regained the Provincial Capital.[2]

But he did not long enjoy the fruits of his victory. On 9th of June, 1647, and at the early age of forty,[3] he died at Saint Mary's, where his remains, it is said, still repose under its revered and holy soil.

---

[1] The case of Captain Thomas Cornwaleys, illustrates the rapacity of Ingle's rule at Saint Mary's, and the extent to which private property was pillaged. After Ingle's return to England, Cornwaleys sued him there to recover £3000 damages, and alleged in his declaration, that he had a comfortable dwelling-house, furnished with plate, brass, pewter, bedding, and linen hangings; his plantation, also, being well stocked with horses, cattle, swine, sheep and goats; and that Ingle took possession of his mansion, burned his fences, killed his swine, carried off his horses and cattle, wrenched off the locks of his doors, and otherwise greatly damaged his property.—Scharf, vol. 1, p. 149.

[2] Bozman, p. 290; Brown, p. 60; Scharf, 1, p. 149.

[3] Neil, p. 60.

Of the life and character of Leonard Calvert, historians have said but little. While there is no desire to detract from the unfading lustre which they have accorded to the Proprietaries of Maryland, truth and justice alike, demand that of the pioneer Governor of the Province, and the founder of Saint Mary's, it should here be said, that he, who left his native land to lead the pilgrim colonists to Maryland; he who faced the perils and dangers, and stood the heat and fire of storm and battle, which so often darkened its early colonial days; he who first proclaimed and laid in practice those fundamental principles which underlie the priceless boon of liberty of conscience; he, who, with untiring energy, fidelity, and zeal, devoted the best years of his life to the development and glory of Maryland, and to the prosperity and happiness of its citizens; he, whose undaunted courage, wise and liberal statesmanship, and mild and gentle government, are so closely associated with the foundation, early growth, and permanent establishment of Maryland, should stand upon the pages of history no less distinguished and renowned, as long as valiant service to early Maryland has an admirer, or civil and religious liberty a friend.

From the fact that the records of the Province, prior to his death, make no mention of wife or children, and that his brief, nuncupative will did not refer to them, Governor Calvert has passed into history as having died a bachelor, but recent investigation proves this to be an error, and that he was not only married, but left children.[1]

---

[1] In Pro. Court Records, 1658-62, p. 459, etc., may be found the proceedings in the suit of the Lord Proprietary, guardian of William Calvert (then in England), son and heir at law of Governor Leonard Calvert, vs. Thomas Stone, son, and Valinda Stone, widow of Governor William Stone, for the recovery of Governor Calvert's house and lot, at Saint Mary's, and which Stone, in 1650. had purchased of Margaret Brent, executrix of Governor Calvert, under the supposition that she had the

THE FIRST CAPITAL

In 1652, the Commissioners of the English Parliament, arrived at Saint Mary's, deposed Governor William Stone, who had been appointed Governor of the Province in 1648, and named a Board of Councilors, for the government of Maryland, of whom Robert Brooke, of De La Brooke, was President, and, as such, acting Governor of the Province. On the dissolution of Parliament, however, Stone, in 1654, proclaimed Cromwell "Lord Protector", and reorganized the Proprietary government. This excited the violent opposition

---

power to convey it.—Archives (Pro. Ct. 1650) pp. 106 and 172. The verdict was for the "plaintiff for the land and costes"—thus establishing the fact of both marriage and issue. William Calvert came to Maryland about 1662, where he held many positions of distinction, among them Judge of the Testamentary Court, member of the Council, with rank directly after the Chancellor and Secretary of the Province. He was drowned in 1682.—Archives (Pro. Cl. 1682) p. 366. His widow, Madam Elizabeth Calvert, was living in 1692.—Ibid, 1692, p. 492. She was the daugter of Governor William Stone, and Valinda, his wife, the sister of Thomas Sprigg, of Northampton, Prince George's County. William Calvert left sons Charles, George, and Richard, and daughter, Elizabeth who married, in 1681, James Neale, Jr., and left daughter, Mary, born in 1683, and who married first Charles Egerton (ancestory of the Egertons of "Piney Neck"), and second, Garrett Van Sweringen.—See case Daniel Dulauey vs. Charles Calvert, et al., in High Court of Chancery of Maryland, August, 1720; wills, Charles Egerton, 1698, and James Egerton, 1765, Saint Mary's County. Governor Leonard Calvert also left a daughter Ann, who came to Maryland in 1663. In September of that year, Governor Charles Calvert wrote Lord Baltimore as follows: "Att the same time, my cousin William's Sister arrived here and is now at my house and has the care of my household affairs. As yett noe good match does present, but I hope in a short time she may find one to her own content and yr. Lspp's desire".—Calvert Papers, vol. 1, p. 224. She married, about 1664, Baker Brooke, of De La Brooke, member of the Council and Surveyor General of the Province. Through this marriage she was the ancestress of Monica Brooke, the mother of Chief Justice Roger Brooke Taney and Catharene Boarman, the wife of Major William Thomas. Ann (Calvert) Brooke married, second, Henry Brent, Deputy Surveyor General of the Province, and third, Colonel Richard Marsham. See will, Baker Brooke, P. C. No. 1, p. 114, Saint Mary's County; Kilty, p. 62; Test. Pro. Liber 13, Annapolis.

of the Puritan element in Maryland, who, with all available forces, invaded Saint Mary's, and finding Governor Stone without the means of effectual resistance, removed the records to Mr. Richard Preston's, near Saint Leonard's, on the Patuxent River, appointed from their own party, officials for the government of the Province, and passed laws ignoring Lord Baltimore's territorial rights, disfranchising Roman Catholics, and repealing the Toleration Act. of 1649, enacting in place of the latter, an Act concerning religion in obedience to the inspiration of their own phylosophy.[1]

Governor Stone succeeded in capturing the records and restored them to the Provincial Capital, as well, also, the magazine and arms designed for the defense of Saint Leonard's, but in his effort, through the memorable battle at Providence—the first land engagement in Maryland—to reduce the insurgents to subjection, he was overwhelmingly defeated,[2] and they continued to hold the reins of government until 1657, when, through an agreement, induced by the turn of affairs in England against Puritans, it was formerly surrendered and re-instated at Saint Mary's.[3]

---

1 Bozman, II, p. 505; McMahon, p. 206.

2 This battle took place on the 15th of March, 1654. Stone's "battle cry" was "Hey, for Saint Mary's", while that of the Puritans was, "God is our strength". Stone has been criticised for starting into this engagement with such a small body of men—about 130 only—but it should be remembered that the military organization of the Province had been much neglected, and at that time was very poor, and that he was, in consequence, limited to such men as he could muster in and around Saint Mary's. After this, the militia was put upon a much better footing. The Province was divided into military districts, commanders appointed for each, arms and ammunition looked after, and the whole fighting population was mustered in and trained. Under such conditions, the black and gold ensign of Maryland would probably not have fallen.

3 Bozman, II, p. 505; McMahon, p. 206.

THE FIRST CAPITAL

The year 1659, is noted in connection with Saint Mary's for the attempted rebellion of Governor Josias Fendall, in which he made the unsuccessful effort to "play the part in Maryland which Cromwell had just performed in England", by conspiring with the Assembly to overthrow the Proprietary government and establish a republic, with himself as its head.[1]

While not within the scope of this work to enter into the details of this tragedy, it may be proper to state, that the scheme by which Fendall expected to accomplish this, was to surrender his commission from Baltimore, have the Legislature declare its independence of the Proprietary, and, as the direct representatives of the people, elect him Governor of the Province. On the 12th of March, 1659, the Lower House declared its independence of *all power*, and denied the right of the Upper House (composed only of representatives of the Proprietary) to sit longer as a branch of the Legislature. To this Fendall, of course, assented, and, on the 14th of March, dissolved the Upper House, surrendered his commission from the Proprietary, and was elected by the Legislature thus constituted, Governor of the Republic of Maryland.[2] After a fruitless effort, however, to enlist public interest in this nefarious scheme, Fendall abandoned his government thus established, and when his arrest was ordered, voluntarily submitted himself to the mercy of the Baltimore government, which, in the meantime, had been reorganized, with Philip Calvert as Governor. He was tried and convicted, but after a short imprisonment was discharged from all the penalties imposed by the Court, except those of being disfranchised

---

[1] McMahon, p. 212; McSherry, p. 81.

[2] For an interesting discussion as to the causes of this rebellion, see the able treatise of Doctor Sparks on "The Maryland Revolution of 1689", page 30-36.

and prohibited from holding public office—humanity which he lived long enough to repay by an effort, many year afterwards, to excite another rebellion in the Province.[1]

Early in 1662, the Honorable Charles Calvert arrived at Saint Mary's, and entered upon the duties of Governor of the Province. He subsequently established a temporary residence at Mattapany, but about the time he became, by the death of his father, Baron of Baltimore and Proprietary of the Province, he resumed his residence at Saint Mary's. As an expression of their pleasure at his return to the Provincial Capital to live, the General Assembly presented him with an appropriation of 30,000 ℔s. of tobacco.[2]

Charles, Lord Baltimore, was, perhaps, more closely identified with the development of Saint Mary's, than any other man connected with its history. It was during his administration that it was incorporated into a city, and the privilege of sending two representatives to the General Assembly was granted; it was also, during his proprietorship that the State House and other public buildings were erected, and to sustain its privileges and importance, and give it permanency as the seat of government, he gave the City a written assurance that it should continue to be the Capital of the Province as long as he remained its Proprietary.[3] This promise he faithfully observed, and though efforts were made, and inducements offered from time to time, to get the seat of government removed, he firmly resisted them all. One of these propositions came from the inhabitants of Anne Arundel, accompanied by the generous offer to build at the Ridge, in that County, at their own expense, a Governor's house, as

---

1 McMahon, pp. 213 and 214.
2 Archives (Ass. Pro. 1674) p. 454.
1 Petition of Mayor and Council to Governor Nicholson, in Scharf 1, p. 345.

THE FIRST CAPITAL

well, also, as a State House, jail, and necessary offices, the latter buildings to be paid for only when completed.[1]

In 1661, an Act was passed for the establishment of a Mint in Maryland (at Saint Mary's) for the coining of money corresponding in purity, and equal in value to English coins of similar denominations.[2] Whether or not the Mint was actually operated, the records do not show. A writer, in 1708, says it was established, but not much used.[3] It may be of interest to note here the curious method for getting money introduced among the people, as adopted by the Act of 1662, under which every householder in the Province was required to buy at least ten shillings for every taxable person in the family, paying for it in tobacco, at two pence per pound.

As early as 1689, a printing press, probably the first in Maryland,[4]—and, indeed, in America—had been established at Saint Mary's. There is, apparently, no data from which the exact time it commenced operations can be ascertained, but it was certainly as early as the above date, when the "Declaration of the Protestant Associators", probably the first pamphlet ever printed in Maryland, was issued from it.[5]

---

[1] Archives (Ass. Pro. 1674) p. 78

[2] Specimens of the coins struck for Maryland, of about this date, are exceedingly rare, but a few of them are preserved in the Maryland Historical Society. They consisted of shillings, sixpence, and groats, their weight being respectively, 66, 34, and 25 grains of silver. A part of the legend on these coins was, *Crescite et Multiplicamini*, and their advent into Maryland marks, also, as far as the records show, the introduction of that motto into the Province, and which was ultimately destined to become, for a short time, the motto of the State.—See Crosby, ", Early Coins of America", p. 123.

[3] British Empire in America, p. 344.

[4] Chalmers, p. 384; Neil, p. 174.

[5] Scharf, vol. 1, p. 190, says: A printing press was set up in Maryland by the Jesuit Missionaries, on which was printed Father White's catechism for use of the Indians, and that it was destroyed or carried off

The press belonged to Richard Nuthead, and was the only one in Maryland, of which the records speak, until 1696, when William Bladen took a press to Annapolis and became the public printer of the Province.[1]

Shortly after the accession of William and Mary to the English throne, the "religious fever which had just shaken England to its centre", was used by certain leaders in Maryland, under color of religious zeal, as the instrument for precipitating a crisis in the affairs of the Province. In April, 1689, an "Association in arms for the defense of the Protestant religion and for asserting the rights of King William and Queen Mary to the Province of Maryland", was formed, and this act was followed by open revolution.

On the 16th of the following July, information was received by the Council, at Saint Mary's, that companies of militia were being formed in different parts of the Province. An envoy was at once dispatched from Saint Mary's to ascertain their movements, but he was arrested and held as a spy. Learning, however, of their intended march upon, and near approach to the Provincial Capital, Colonel William Digges, of Saint Mary's, prepared for defense. He mustered in one hundred men, and took position in the State House, which was to be the point of attack. While these preparations were being made at Saint Mary's, Colonel Henry Darnell and Major Nicholas Sewall went up the Patuxent and raised a force of one hundred and sixty men, but they did not arrive in time to assist in the defense of the Capital.

---

in 1655; but I can find no authority for the statement. Same author, vol. I, p. 362, says: Another printing press was set up in 1660. This seems to be based upon an inference drawn from the Act of that year, providing for the publication of the laws of that session. Reference to the Act, however, shows that publication by proclamation only was meant, and not by printing.

1 Scharf, I, p. 362.

THE FIRST CAPITAL 69

When the revolutionists reached Saint Mary's, they numbered seven hundred men, under command of Captain John Coade, Colonel Henry Jowles, Major John Campbell, Mr. Nehemiah Blackiston, and Mr. Ninian Beall. Colonel Digges, finding his men unwilling to fight against such superior numbers, after a short skirmish, evacuated the State House and surrendered.[1]

The Council were driven to the Garrison at Mattapany,[2] which being also captured, articles of formal surrender were signed on the 1st day of August, 1689, by which the "Associators" were placed in absolute possession and control of the Province.[3]

A full history of the motives and causes underlying and prompting this revolution, which swept away the Proprietary government, and, as events showed, marked the downfall of Saint Mary's, would involve too much detail, but it may be proper to note the fact that the records indicate the uprising to have been the result, not so much of the fear of violence to the Protestant religion, as it was of the alarm of physical danger, produced by the report that the Roman Catholics were conspiring with the Indians to massacre the Protestants, kindled and fanned by a few captious spirits, who were emulous of power, at whatever cost, and fired with ambition and expectation of royal favor from a Protestant King.[4]

With the power in their own hands, Coade and his associates, issued the famous "Declaration of the Protestant Associators",[5] selected a Council for the government of the Province, of which Nehemiah Blackiston, of "Longworth

---

[1] Archives (Cl. Pro. 1689) pp. 147-163 ; Scharf I, pp. 310, 313, 315.
[2] Mattapany—see Chapter on Saint Mary's County.
[3] McMahon, p. 237.   [4] Day Star, p. 87 ; Brown, p. 150.
[5] Archives (Cl. Pro. 1689) p. 101.

Point", was President,[1] and sent an address to William and Mary, in which they detailed the results of the revolution, assigned the "defense of the Protestant religion" as the reason for it, and asked that the Province be placed under the protection of the English Government.[2]

The revolution received the Royal sanction and Maryland was placed under a Royal government. Sir Lionel Copley, the first Governor appointed by the Crown, arrived at Saint Mary's, in 1691. His associates were Sir Thomas Lawrence, Chancellor and Secretary, and Captain John Courtes, Mr. Thomas Brooke, and eight others as Councilors.[3]

The first Assembly under the Royal Government, convened at Saint Mary's, May 10th, 1692, with Nehemiah Blackiston, President of the Upper, and Kenelm Cheseldine, Speaker of the Lower House.[4]

The most conspicuous of the Acts of this session, was the one overthrowing religious freedom—so long the pride of Maryland—and constituting by law, the Church of England, as the established church of the Province.[5]

Governor Copley's residence at Saint Mary's, however, was of short duration. His wife died there on the 5th of March, 1692 O. S.,[6] and he died on the 27th of September, 1693.[7]

---

1 Ibid, p. 206. 2 Ibid, p. 108.
3 Ibid, 1691, p. 271. 4 Archives (Ass. Pro. 1692).
5 For the particulars of this Act, see Chapter on Some of the Early Churches of Maryland.
6 Archives (Cl. Pro. 1692) p. 479.
7 Liber H. D. No. 2, Cl. Pro. pp. 65 add 98.

The cases of Governor and Lady Copley furnish strong examples of efficiency in the art of embalming at that early period. Governor Copley died about six months after his wife—as computed by the English system then in vogue, the legal year beginning the 25th of March—and yet for, ten months after his death, the bodies of both of

THE FIRST CAPITAL

In July, 1694, Francis Nicholson, Esq., became Governor of Maryland, and one of his first official acts was to sound the death knell of Saint Mary's. He summoned an Assembly to convene in September, not at Saint Mary's, but at Anne-Arundel-Town—now Annapolis. This act "foreshadowed the doom" of Saint Mary's, and at that session of the Assembly, the removal of the Capital was decided upon.[1]

The consternation which Saint Mary's felt at this sudden, and, to it, disastrous movement can well be understood. It solemnly protested, pathetically appealed, and graciously offered. Through its Mayor, Aldermen, Recorder, and Council, it sent a protest to the Governor and Council,[2] in which the point was made, that the "power of appointing a place for the Supreme Court of Judicature and Seat of Government" of Maryland was the special prerogative of the Crown, and that it could not be done by Act of Assembly, and urged that they "reject said bill" until their Majesties' pleasure could be ascertained.[3] This they supplemented with

---

them lay in the "Great House", at Saint Mary's, awaiting orders to ship them to England. It was not until July, 1694, that the Council ordered a vault to be built for their interment—a ceremony which did not take place until the following October. It is further worthy of note that as late as 1790, when the only vault known to be at Saint Mary's, and hence, presumably the Copley Vault, was broken into, the remains of the woman there interred, were found to be in a state of perfect preservation, until exposed to the air, when they crumbled into dust. For further particulars of the berial of Governor Copley and Lady Copley, see pages 36 and 37. See also "Pilate and Herod", page 16, note.

[1] Scharf, I, p. 347.   [2] Ibid.

[3] Those who signed the protest and the petition were, Philip Lynes, Mayor; Kenelm Cheseldine, Recorder; Henry Dutton, John Lewellyn, Jo. Watson, Thomas Beall, Philip Clark, Edward Greenhalgh, Aldermen; Thomas Waughop, William Aisquith, Thomas Price, Richard Benton, Robert Mason, W. Taylard, Samuel Watkins, Common Councilmen; Wm. Diggs, J. Bouye, Clerks; G. Van Sweringen, Josh Brodbert, Ro. Carville, Chas. Caud, Robt. King, George Layfield, John Coode,

a lengthy petition, in which, after dwelling upon the ancient rights and privileges of Saint Mary's, sustained by long enjoyment, and confirmed in the most solemn manner by the late Proprietary, and upon the advantages of a site well-watered, with a commodious harbor, and a healthful and pleasant situation, they proposed to obviate all objections as to want of accommodations and the difficulty of access, by keeping a coach or caravan, to run daily during the sessions of the Legislature and Provincial Court, between the City and the Patuxent, and weekly at other times, and at least six horses with suitable furniture, for riding post, etc.[1]

The appeal, however, was of no avail. Governor Nicholson had removed the Capital of Virginia from its ancient seat,[2] and had come to Maryland resolved upon the same course towards Saint Mary's. He went through the form of submitting the addresses to the Assembly, from whence they were returned to him—whose wishes were probably well understood—with a reply, conspicuous only for its vindictive spirit, bitter acrimony, and extreme coarseness; in which they ridiculed the idea of being bound by Proprietary promises, denied the advantages of Saint Mary's, mocked at its calamities, and laughed at its proposals.[3]

Henry Wriothesley, W. Bladen, James Cullen, Thomas Hebb, James B. Baker, Stephen Blatchford, Daniel Bell, Jonathan Clarke, Edward Kelsey, Abraham Rhodes, Joseph Edto, Roger Tolle, Henry H. T. Taylor, James Reckets, John Wincoll, Edward Fisher, John F. Noble, Thomas Hutchins, Richard Sowler, Thomas [his X mark] Guyther, Robert Denry, Claudius Dutitre, Samuel Wheeler, Constables; John I. M. Mackye, Peter Dent, Wm. Guyther, John [his X mark] Janner, John [his X mark] Little, Thomas H. Hickson, William Nuthead, Richard Griffin, Isaac Paine, Peter Watts, Robert Carse, John Evans, Wm. Lowry, —— Anderson, Eben Cooke, Zacharias Van Swearingen, Leon D. Hukenett, William Harpenos, Michael Chevers, Elias Beech, Thomas Guinurn, John Freeman, and Joseph Doyne, Freemen.

1 McMahon, p. 252.   2 Brown, p. 187.
3 Scharf, I, pp. 344-346; Riley, History of Annapolis, p. 62.

On the receipt of the reply from the Assembly, the Governor and Council thus tersely recorded their views on the matter: "This Board concurs with the said answers made by the House of Burgess".[1]

In February, 1695, Governor Nicholson issued an order for the removal of the archives, records, etc., "from Saint Mary's to Anne Arundel Town, they to be conveyed in good strong bags, and to be secured with cordage and hides, and well packed, with guards to attend them night and day, to be protected from all accidents, and to be delivered to the Sheriff of Anne Arundel County". The final removal was made that winter, and on the 28th of February, 1695, the General Assembly commenced its first session in the new Capital of Maryland.[2]

The reason alleged for this change, was that Saint Mary's, being on the verge of the Province, was difficult of access to the masses of the people. This may not have been altogether without weight, but it was more probably due to the fierce political struggle and the bitter sectarian strife, which existed there at that time—between the advocates of the Proprietary and the adherents of the King—between the Church of England and the Church of Rome.

"It was", says one of Maryland's eminent historians, McMahon, "the interest of the new government, to destoy, as far as possible, the cherished recollections which were associated with the departed Proprietary power; and there was no object so intertwined with all these recollections, as this ancient city, consecrated by the landing of the colonists, endeared to the natives as the first home of their fathers, and exhibiting, at every step, the monuments of that gentle and

---

[1] Riley, p. 62.
[2] Riley, p. 62; Ridgely, History of Annapolis, p. 88.

E

liberal administration, which had called up a thriving colony out of the once trackless wilderness. The Catholics of the colony dwelt principally in that section of it; and, under the joint operation of these causes, it had been distinguished during all the troubles consequent upon the civil wars in England, by its unshaken attachment to the Proprietary. Without these considerations to prompt the removal, the recollections and the attachments, which centre the feelings of a people in in an ancient capital, would probably have contributed to preserve it as such; until, by the denseness of the population, and the increasing facilities for traveling, thereby afforded to the remote sections of the State, the objection to its location would have been in a great measure obviated; and the City of Saint Mary's would, at this day, have been the seat of our State government. The excitement of the moment made its claims to recollection, cogent reasons for its destruction, and the public convenience came in as the sanction ''.

After Saint Mary's ceased to be the Capital of the Province, it soon began to decline. The removal of the government officials, in itself, seriously diminished its population, and, in 1708, it ceased also to be the county seat of Saint Mary's County, the last symbol of its official character. The same year, it lost its long honored privilege of sending delegates to the General Assembly, and soon after, lost its rank as a city.

No longer the commercial emporium of the Province, with no manufacturing interests at that day to sustain its vitality, and completely stripped of its official importance, it was left without means of support. Its population gradually departed; its old fort sank to the level of the earth; its houses—one by one—fell to ruin, and, in a comparatively short time, nothing remained, save the old State House and a few of the more durable buildings, the latter used as homesteads for the farms into which the site of the old city became converted.

In 1695, permission was given the Justices of Saint Mary's County, to use the State House for a Court House and church. In 1708, the public buildings and land at Saint Mary's, were ordered to be sold. They were, however, not sold, and, in 1720, the General Assembly vested the old "State House and grounds in the Rector and Vestry of William and Mary Parish, and their successors, in fee simple, for the use of the Parish, forever ".[1]

The changes deemed necessary to adapt the old edifice to church purposes, were made the following year, the contractor for the work being Joshua Dayne. The attic and second story floors, and all the partitions were removed, and the building was ceiled "square with the top of the arch after the model of the old Chapel at Saint Mary's". A railing was put across the transept of that arm of the cross which originally formed the porch, and which was converted into a chancel, its large central arch being bricked up and giving place to the altar, which was of heavy oak, ornamented with carvings, and above it, a fresco picture, representing "the flight into Egypt"; while in place of the two smaller arches, windows were substituted, each eight feet high, and twenty-two inches wide. The opposite, or "stair-way", arm of the cross became the vestibule of the church, and was made to correspond, in design and appearance, to the original entrance to the building; while in the northern and southern transepts, galleries were erected. As thus changed, it would accommodate about four hundred persons.[2]

---

[1] Act, 1695, c. 13; 1708, c. 3; 1720, c. 4.
[2] Allen's MSS.; Extracts from Vestry Record.

There was so much opposition manifested, it is said, on the part of the Roman Catholics, to the old State House being used for Protestant worship, that the latter, about the year 1700, applied to a British man-of-war for assistance, and three cannon were placed there for their protection, and which remained in the church yard until 1823, when they were removed to Washington City.[1]

The old State House continued to be used as a church for more than a century; but, in 1829, this historic old building was pulled down, and its material used in the construction of Trinity Church, which stands nearby. This old monument might well have been "spared all but the ravages of time", and—had it been saved from the sacrilege of man—it might to-day be standing to "point a moral", and "adorn the history" of the founders of Maryland.[2]

In 1839, the State of Maryland purchased from William and Mary Parish, the eastern half of the State House lot, and to commemorate the spot where "civilization and christianity were first introduced into our State", erected on it the imposing and classic building, known as the "Saint Mary's Female Seminary". It also, a little over two years ago, did tardy justice to Maryland's first Governor—Leonard Calvert—by erecting to his memory a handsome granite shaft, placing it on the site of the "Old Mulberry"; and, at the same time, in order to perpetuate the foundation lines of the old State House, planted at each of its twelve corners, a massive granite marker.

---

[1] Scharf, Historical Address, June, 1891.

[2] Much of the furniture in the present church is made of the wood of the "Old Mulberry". Some of this wood has also been worked up into "relics" and sold, the proceeds having been used to keep the church in repair.

THE FIRST CAPITAL

The shaft is thirty-six feet high, and six feet square at the base. Above the inscription blocks, are two bronze medallion plates, bearing the Coat of Arms of Maryland. The monument contains the following interesting inscriptions:

To the Memory of
LEONARD CALVERT,
First Governor of Maryland,
This Monument is
Erected by
The State of Maryland.

Erected on the Site of the
OLD MULBERRY TREE,
Under which the
First Colonists of Maryland Assembled
To Establish a Government
Where the persecuted and oppressed of every creed and every clime might repose in peace and security, adore their common God, and enjoy the priceless blessings of civil and religious liberty.

LEONARD CALVERT,
Second Son of George Calvert,
First Baron of Baltimore,
and Anne, His Wife,
Led the First Colonists to Maryland,
November 22, 1633—March 3, 1634,
Founded Saint Mary's, March 27, 1634,
Died, June 9, 1647.

By His Wisdom, Justice, and Fidelity, He Fostered the Infancy of the Colony, Guided it Through Great Perils, and Dying, Left it at Peace. The Descendants and Successors of the Men He Governed, Here Record Their Grateful Recognition of His Virtues, November, MDCCCXC.

Thus did the ancient City of Saint Mary's spring into being, flourish, and pass away.[1] In the "very State to which it gave birth"; in the State whose foundations it erected; in the State, many of whose most valued institutions, and more ancient principles of organic law it established, it to-day stands almost a "solitary spot, dedicated to God, and a fit memento of perishable man".

But it is one, which, as long as civilization shall endure upon the earth, will be memorable in the history of its development. The philosopher and the statesmen, when tracing back the progress of the political systems of men, from the loftiest heights they shall ever reach, will always pause upon the banks of the Saint Mary's to contemplate one of the

---

[1] Among the papers recently purchased by the Maryland Historical Society, from Mr. John Roland Phillips, is a letter from Governor Leonard Calvert to his London partner, Sir Richard Lechford, dated, Point Comfort, May 30th, 1634, and which is of special value as showing the dimensions of Fort Saint Mary's—a fact hitherto unknown. As described by him, it was "one hundred and twentie yards square, with fower flankes", and was mounted with "one piece of ordnance" and six "murderers". Another paper in the above mentioned collection of much general historic interest, is "A brief relation of the voyage unto Maryland", supposed to have been written by Father White, and which was sent as a supplement to the above letter. Both of the documents describe the location of Saint Mary's as being half a mile from the river. The fact that the first Provincial Capital was immediately on the river, the State House lot, indeed, being bounded on two sides by it, leaves no room for doubt, that what was meant was, that the site of the town was that far distant from the place of landing, just as the Relation must have referred to the place of landing, rather than the place of settlement and to Saint Mary's Harbor, rather than the river, when it stated that the village of Yaocomico was on one side of the river, and the Maryland settlement on the other—a physical impossibility, since the site of Yaocomico and Saint Mary's were one and the same. The distance from the place of landing to the site of the town, as given in these two documents, is just half of that which it was stated to be in the Relatio Itineris. They were, probably, all rough estimates only, as was the estimate of the acreage of Saint Clement's Island, as stated in Relatio Itineris, for the correction of which see page 15, see also page 18.

greatest epochs in their history. It was there that, under the auspices of the founders of the State of Maryland, the injured freemen of England found a refuge from the depredations of Royal power; it was there that the inherent rights of man found opportunity for growth to strength and vigor, away from the depressing tyranny of Kings; it was there that the ancient privileges of the people, that came down with the succeeding generations of our fathers, from the morning twilight of Anglo-Saxon history, struggling through the centuries with varying fortunes, at last found a home and a country as all-pervading as the atmosphere around them; it was there that these principles and rights first entered into the practical operations of government; it was there that was established the first State in America where the people were governed by laws made by themselves; it was there that was organized the first civil government in the history of the Christian world, which was administered under that glorious principle of American liberty—the independence of Church and State in their relations to each other; it was there, too, that freedom of conscience, in all of its breadth and fullness, was first proclaimed to men as their inherent and inviolable right, in tones which, sounding above the tempest of bigotry and persecution, were to continue forever, from age to age, to gladden the world with the assurance of practical Christian charity, and ultimately find expression in the political systems of every civilized people.[1]

Such was the halo surrounding Maryland's early colonial metropolis, and yet, the present generation asks when and where it was; such the renown of Maryland's first capital, embodying in its history, the germ of so much of that which gave grandeur and glory, as well as inspiration and pride, to

---

[1] Honorable Richard T. Merrick, Historical Address, 1884.

the later annals of the State, and yet, history has recorded its birth without a smile, and written its epitaph without a tear.

In desolation and ruin, as it is, and though its hearthstone is buried beneath the moss of so many years, it should be revered as a hallowed spot; sacred to the "proudest memories" of Maryland; endeared in the pride and in the affection of its sons and its daughters; the glory of every American patriot; for it was the spot where first arose the radiant morning sun of our religious freedom; the spot where first broke and brightened into effulgent daylight, the early dawn of our civil liberty.

CHAPTER IV.

The Land Tenure of Colonial Maryland.

BY the Maryland Charter, the Baron of Baltimore was made the "true and absolute Lord and Proprietary" of Maryland, and invested with all the "rights, prerogatives and immunities" that had ever been enjoyed by the Bishop of the County Palatine of Durham—than which, no higher grant was ever made to an English subject.

Of the Counties Palatine (so called, because in *a Palatio*, the owner was the supreme power, as fully as was the King in his palace), Durham, was the only one in England at that time, which was held by a subject, and hence, the one named in the Charter.[1]

---

[1] Kilty, Landholder's Assistant, p. 12.

But the *juro regatio*, which attached to the person of the King, did not attach to Lord Baltimore. He did not have the incidental prerogatives of the King, and only such of the direct ones as were expressly granted by the Charter.--2 H. & J. Maryland Reports, p. 250.

The Proprietor had even more power than any Bishop of Durham ever had. Within the Province of Maryland, the Proprietor had regal power. It was his justice that was administered in the courts, and all writs and warrants were issued in his name. These courts were appointed by him, and he determined their jurisdiction and manner of proceeding. In them he had the laws executed, and passed sentences amounting even to confiscation and death. He likewise had the royal power of pardon, and had admirality jurisdiction. The Proprietor could erect towns, boroughs, cities, and ports of entry and departure.

As the "ruler of the Province and the owner of its soil", Baltimore was also expressly authorized and empowered to dispose of the whole or any part of the premises, or of any estate or interest in its lands, for such time, and on such terms as to him might seem most expedient. The Charter also invested him with the right to introduce in Maryland, the feudal system, which had then been practically broken up

From the Proprietor all land was held. He received all escheats and fines for alienations, and had sovereign title to all mines, wastes, forests, and chases. He could erect manors with court leet and court baron. The Proprietor could raise troops and levy defensive warfare, even pursuing enemies without the limits of the Province. He could impose duties upon ships and merchandise. He could establish churches and chapels, and have them consecrated according to the ecclesiastical laws of England. He held their patronage and advowsons. Only through the Proprietor could the King do anything in the Province. All these powers belonged to the Palatine of Durham, and all except the ecclesiastical were exercised by the Proprietor of Maryland.

In the matter of legislation there is a difference. There was no provision in Durham for the assembling of the people to make laws. If the Palatine wanted any new laws, they were passed by his Council, which was composed of the chief men of the county. The Proprietor, however, had the right to call assemblies of the freemen and enact laws with their assent. But the colonists insisted on their right to propose and enact laws with the assent of the Proprietor. This right was obtained. The Proprietor retained his right to initiate some legislation but not all. Maryland laws, like those of Durham, were published in the courts. The Proprietor was not obliged to submit these laws to the Crown for approval. In addition, the Proprietor could publish ordinances not extending to life, member, or property. This has been aptly designated as a police power. Again, the Proprietor possessed an advantage over the Bishop of Durham, in that cases between the Bishop and his subjects could be appealed to the Court of Exchequer in London, whereas cases between the Proprietor and his subjects were finally settled in the Proprietor's courts, from which there was no appeal to the King. Parliament levied taxes on the Bishop of Durham, and these were collected by his officers, as taxes were collected in Maryland by the Proprietor's officers, but Parliament had no power to tax the Proprietor of Maryland, and the Charter exempted him from royal taxation.

The administrative machinery of the Proprietary Government bears some likeness to that of the Durham Palatinate. The Governor of Maryland was its administrative head. He had the highest judicial

in England, and further provided that the statute of "Quia Emptoris",[1] intended to prevent subinfeudation, and which had, in effect, abolished the manorial system in England, should be dispensed with, and conferred upon him the privilege of erecting manors in Maryland, with all the manorial rights which had been incident to such estates in England—thus making the Baron of Baltimore the sole tenant of the crown, and at the same time securing to him, as the exclusive landlord of the Province, all escheats, fines, and forfeitures.[2]

---

jurisdiction, and presided over the Court of Chancery. Thus he resembled the Chancellor of Temporalities of the Bishopric of Durham. In both governments are seen the Receiver General. In both the Sheriff was the executive officer of the Palatine, collected the revenue, and was responsible to the Palatine alone. The Seneschal of Durham bore some resemblance to the Surveyor General of Maryland, and the Bailiff to the Constable. The Bishop's Council had its counterpart in the Proprietor's Council, which, while it had less legislative, had more judicial power, and also retained great influence in legislation.

The division of the Courts into County Courts and Halmote Courts, was followed in the powers given to the Provincial, Chancery, Admiralty and Council, and to the County Courts. While allegiance to the King was reserved, the oath of fidelity was taken to the Proprietor, and all writs ran "in the year of our dominion". In the period now to be considered, it will be seen that the Proprietor had vastly more power in Maryland than the King had in England, and freely exercised his power. In no other American colony was there such despotic authority. In none was such absolute government ever established as existed in Maryland in this period.—Causes of The Maryland Revolution of 1689, pp. 27-29, Sparks.

1 The statute "Quia Emptoris", enacted in the reign of Edward I, directed that in all sales or feoffments of land, the purchaser of the land should not hold of his immediate feoffer, but of the chief lord of the fee. The aim of the statute was to strengthen the hands of the King, and to prevent the intermediate lords from subinfeudating their lands. This great land law, marking an epoch in the constitutional history of England, enacted in 1290, was virtually set aside by Charles I, after an interval of three and a-half centuries, and the privilege denied the great feudal barons of England was bestowed in all its fullness upon the young Irish peer.—Local Institutions of Maryland, p. 13, Wilhelm,

2 The Charter; Kilty, p. 28; Ground Rents in Maryland, pp. 11-13.

The Maryland grant was to be held by Baltimore *of the "Kings of England, * * in free and common socage, by fealty only for all services,"* and subject to the annual render of "two Indian arrows from those parts", to be delivered at Windsor Castle on Tuesday of Easter week in every year, and also, the fifth part of all the gold and silver found within the Province.[1]

By a species of tenure similar to that under which he held the Province, Baltimore granted land to the Maryland Colonists. The fact that his lands would be unproductive unless they were occupied, prompted him at once to adopt and publish a general land system. It proved a good one, not only as a means of producing a constantly increasing revenue to himself, but in its results upon the economic welfare of the community and the material development of the Province.[2]

To encourage persons to come and bring their dependents and servents with them, his lands were offered on the most generous terms. These, it is true, were less liberal at a later period than at first, but they were always sufficiently so to stimulate the growth of the Colony, and at the same time,

---

[1] Maryland Charter.

[2] The area of Maryland is 6,000,000 acres, exclusive of its water area, which is about 1,000,000 acres. The territory within its charter limits comprised about 10,000,000 acres of land, embracing, in addition to its present domain, the entire State of Delaware, that part of Pennsylvania lying south of the parallel of Philadelphia, extending to the most westerly ridge of the Alleghenies, a part of the Eastern Shore of Virginia, and that part of West Virginia lying between the North and South Branches of the Potomac —McMahon, pp. 18-59; Brown, pp. 134 137; Local Institutions of Maryland, pp. 8-9. While not within the scope of this treatise to deal with the methods by which Maryland was robbed of her territory, it should be noted in passing, that they furnish a disgraceful commentary upon the times, reflecting alike upon the English Crown and the beneficiaries of the spoils.

afford a source of lucrative revenue to the Proprietary. The conditions upon which land could be obtained, and the terms and character of the grant, were fully set forth in proclamations, or "Conditions of Plantation", as they were called, issued by the Proprietary from time to time.

Under the first "Conditions of Plantation", every freeman who came to Maryland to "inhabit and plant" was entitled, without cost or charge, except the annual quit rent, to one hundred acres of land for himself, a like quantity for his wife, every child over sixteen, and each servant, and fifty acres for every child under sixteen years of age, to be held by "him and his heirs and assigns forever", in free and common socage" of Baltimore as the Lord Proprietary.[1]

In 1641, the amount of land given, was reduced to fifty acres for every adult, and twenty-five acres for every child.[2]

If those transported exceeded a certain number, he was entitled for their transportation, not only what they could each separately have claimed, had they come at their own expense, but to an additional quantity, proportioned to the number, age, and sex of such persons transported, the largest premiums being paid for males between sixteen and fifty, and females between fourteen and forty, years of age—thus inducing small but vigorous settlements in the Province, which would become the industrial centres of their respective localities.[3] It also depended upon the time of immigration. At first 2000 acres were given for the transportation of five men, but, in 1636, the number was increased to ten, and, in 1641, to twenty able men and women, between the ages above

---

[1] The grants, it appears, were intended to be for an indefeasible estate of inheritance in fee simple.—Kilty, p. 32.

[2] Kilty, pp. 29-31; Relation, 1635; Archives (Cl. Pro. 1636 and 1641) pp. 47 and 99.

[3] Local Institutions of Maryland, p. 15.

mentioned.¹ A further consideration imposed by the last mentioned proclamation, was that each of said twenty persons, as a means of giving additional military defense, should come provided with the following arms and ammunition : " one musket or bastard musket ; 10 ℔s. of powder ; 40 ℔s. of lead, bullets, pistol and goose shot, each sort some ; one sword and belt, and one brandeleer and flask ".² Special grants of larger size were sometimes made from personal considerations, or on account of public or private services rendered.

In 1683, however, Baltimore, deeming these inducements no longer necessary to insure the success and prosperity of the colony, abolished them, and adopted a new "land system", under which no premiums were offered for the transportation of person, and those desiring to obtain land had to pay, in addition to the annual quit-rent, a definite amount of purchase money. This was called "caution money", because it had to be paid before the warrant could issue.³ At first, the amount charged was only 50 ℔s. of casked tobacco for every fifty acres, if along the seaboard, or 100 ℔s. if in the interior.⁴ Subsequently it was increased to 40 shillings per one hundred acres, and, in 1738, to £5 sterling, on which basis it continued until the American Revolution.⁵

Under the first proclamation the right to take up land, was without restriction as to nationality, but by the one of 1636, it was expressly limited to persons of "British and Irish descent",⁶ except that grants could be made, after 1648, to persons of "French, Dutch, and Italian descent", in the

---

1 Kilty, pp. 29-31 ; Archives (Cl. Pro. 1636 and 1641) pp. 47 and 49.
2 Ibid.
3 Kilty, p. 124.   4 Archives (Cl. Pro. 1683) p. 142.
5 Ground Rents in Maryland, p. 19.
6 But this included natives of Scotland, the union having previously taken place, and also natives of Wales, who were *British* by a still older title.

discretion of the Governor[1]—a limitation which was not removed until 1683, when, for the first time, the lands of Maryland were open to all persons "living in or trading within the Province", who choose to purchase them.[2]

This right, however, did not extend to corporations, religious or temporal, which, indeed, as early as 1641, were prohibited from acquiring or holding land in Maryland in any manner whatsoever, or enjoying any of the uses in them which were forbidden by the "Statutes of Mortmain prior to Henry VIII", without special license under the hand and seal of Lord Proprietary.[3]

---

1 Archives (Cl. Pro. 1636, 1641, 1648) pp. 48, 99, 222.

2 McMahon, p. 173.

3 In the interval between the settlement at Saint Mary's, in March. 1634, and the meeting and adjournment of this General Assembly (1637), various events had transpired which produced momentous results. The colony had been reinforced by numerous additions. The Jesuit, zealous in propagating their faith, and in proselytizing, had made many converts among the lower order of Protestants, and had been eminently successful among the Indians. Emperors and kings, with their people, had embraced the Cross, and been baptized into the Church.

As a natural consequence, great grants of valuable land were made by the aboriginal chiefs to the Fathers who had converted them to the faith. King Pathuen had given them the valuable estate of Mattapany, in Saint Mary's County, near the mouth of the Patuxent, where the Jesuits had established a mission, and besides that, Thomas Copley, whose status as a Jesuit Priest is not disclosed by the records, had demanded large grants under the conditions of Plantation * * * and under the conditions of 1636. he received the title to twenty thousand acres, and he held it to the use of the Society of Jesus. In January of 1637, when the Proprietary was preparing his Code of Laws, he commissioned John Lewger "Commissioner in causes testamentary, to prove wills, and to grant letters of administration, etc". * * *

By the Great Ordinance of 1638-9, it was enacted that the laws should be equally enforced against and concerning all persons, lay and ecclesiastical, without distinction, exemption, or privilege to any. Its twelfth section ratified the commission to Lewger, by providing "that the Secretary shalt prove wills, and grant administrations, and use and appoint all power and means necessary or conducing thereto".

In no other State did the statutes of Mortmain take root, but the early act of Baltimore in introducing them in Maryland, made a lasting impression. His order, as applicable to ecclesiastical bodies, was substantially incorporated in the Maryland Bill of Rights, and it is the law of Maryland to-day, that lands cannot be given, sold, or devised to religious

---

The jurisdiction of the temporal authority therefore, had been distinctly asserted by his Lordship's act, over all ecclesiastical persons and their property, and over all causes testamentary, and over the administration of the estates of decedents. This had been done deliberately, in carrying out a mature policy.

This assertion of jurisdiction by the temporal prince, over ecclesiastical persons and things on the one side, and the acquisition of lands from the Indians, and by Copley for the use of the Jesuits on the other, made a distinct issue in Maryland that had been contested in England, for six hundred years, and had only shortly before then been finally settled. It was the old question as to whether the Canon Law prevailed and was in force *jure divino* in a State, or whether it was only allowed so far as adopted by the Prince or State itself. Under all the circumstances, it was, perhaps, natural that such a question should arise.

In the organized State of England, it had been definitely settled, but in such a country as Maryland, then a savage wilderness, with a few hundred Christians, founding a new society upon Christian principles, which were to pervade, control, and direct it for all time, the enthusiasts who had braved the hardships of emigration, and the terrors of the unknown by land and by water, to carry the Cross to the heathen, may well have believed that the power of the Keys should prevail over the power of the Sword, and that their duty to religion and truth, required them to assert the supremacy of the ecclesiastical authority over the temporal power. At any rate, the missionary priests at once claimed that the Canon Law prevailed in Maryland *proprio vigore*, without the license, assent, or adoption of Prince or people. It existed because it was the law of the Church. This was the old claim of the extension of the *corpus juris canonici* over England. * * *

The Jesuit Fathers, in this conflict of Law, as they supposed, very naturally held on to the law which bound them, until it was shown that they were bound by the law of England in this behalf. Great issues were at stake, and the discussion of them naturally aroused feeling. Secretary Lewger had been a Protestant. He was an Englisman —an educated scholar of the University of Oxford. He knew the history of the struggle in England against the authority of the Canon Law, against the exemption of ecclesiastics, their persons and their

bodies, or for religious uses, except to the extent of two and a-half acres for church and church yard, without sanction of the General Assembly[1]

At first, the grant was obtained by filing an application with the Secretary of the Province. If the claim was duly substantiated by proof of the date of immigration, etc., a certificate to that effect was issued and addressed to the Governor, who, on application of the holder thereof, issued a

---

property, from the temporal jurisdiction, the enormous abuses that had grown out of their usurpation of the exclusive cognizance of causes testamentary and matrimonial, and the great evils, political and social, produced by the holding of great estates in Mortmain. He understood the policy of the Proprietary, which he had been selected and sent to carry out—to transplant to Maryland all the safeguards against these abuses, and the remedies for these evils, and the guarantees for liberty, which the experience of Englishmen had demonstrated to be necessary to preserve their institutions, and which their sagacity had devised, their wisdom adopted and their courage secured.

Therefore it was that Lewger, carrying out the purposes of the Proprietary, set himself against this claim of the authority of the Canon Law, and procured the Assembly to unite with Baltimore in asserting the supremacy of the temporal power of freemen and Proprietary in General Assembly.

He followed this up in the Assembly which met the following autumn on the 25th of October, 1640, by procuring to be passed the act touching marriage. The persons who can celebrate it, the parties who are permitted to marry, and the conditions upon which they shall marry are all declared and specified. The whole subject of marriage thus passed under the control of the temporal power.

He further insisted that all grants of land to the Jesuits should be vacated, whether to them from the Indians or from the Proprietary to Thomas Copley, who held the land for the use of the Society.

Baltimore pressed his policy that the Common Law of England should be the law for everybody in Maryland, lay and ecclesiastical, and no great estates should grow up in Mortmain, to be a future menace to the liberties and free institutions of the Province.

Immediately after the adjournment of the General Assembly, Lord Baltimore brought the matter before the highest authority of the Church, and " petitioned the Sacred Congregation of the Propagation of

---

[1] Maryland Bill of Rights; Maryland Constitution, Article xxxviii.

warrant to the Surveyor General, commanding him to "survey and lay out" the land therein specified. On the execution of this warrant, and on the application of the holder, a patent was issued, signed by the Governor and attested by the Secretary and Surveyor General of the Province.[1]

There being no time at first fixed for the surrender, and the certificates and warrants being assignable before the patent was issued on them, owing to the scarcity of coin, and the inconvenience of tobacco as a currency, they were frequently transferred and passed about as so much money.[2]

But, in 1643, it appearing that many persons had long since obtained certificates and warrants for land for which no patent had been issued, (thus depriving the Proprietary of his "quit rents", which did not commence until after the date of the patent), a proclamation was issued, requiring the holder to surrender them and take out grants for the same within twelve months from that date, under "pain of being

---

the Faith, in the name of the Catholics of Maryland, to grant a Prefect and secular priests authority to take charge of the Maryland mission". In August, 1641, permission was given Baltimore to remove the Jesuits, and the authority to take charge of Maryland issued to Don Rossetti, Archbishop of Tarsus.

In November, 1641, he issues Conditions of Plantation, to take effect in the following January, and they put in actual operation in Maryland all the provisions and prohibitions of all the Statutes of Mortmain, which had been enacted in England before that time. * * * The Provincial also exacted a release in full, of all lands acquired, and of all right to acquire lands from Indians, and conveyed to th Proprietary the estate of Mattapany, granted to the Society by King Pathuen; the Manor of the Immaculate Conception, and that of Saint Gregory, and all other domains held in the Province, either by Indian grant or by grant to any person for the use of the Society. * * * —Foundation of Maryland—Johnson.

In the same admirable treatise may be found the deed of Release above referred to, as well also the correspondence leading up to it.

---

1 Kilty, pp. 64, 65; Local Institutions in Maryland, p. 27.
2 Kilty, p. 77.

THE LAND TENURE

refused the grant after said time ",[1] which largely did away with their value as a circulating medium.

While it would seem that the Proprietary intended from the outset, that all land grants should be under the great seal of the Province, for many years they were issued under the hand and seal of the Governor alone, and it was not until 1644, when the duty of authenticating patents devolved upon the Chancellor of the Province, that the great seal was attached.[2] In 1680, the "Land Office", under the supervision, at first of a "Register", but later of a "Land Council", and still later of a "Judge of the Land Office", was established, and it became the place where all proceedings relating to the sale and granting of land were subsequently conducted.[3]

The Lord Proprietary, by the express terms of the Charter, held his lands of the Crown, in *"free and common socage, by fealty only for all services"*, and *his* grantees held of *him* by the same tenure.[4]

---

[1] 1st Council Book, p. 98; Kilty, p. 35.
[2] Bland, Maryland Reports, 1, p. 308. [3] Ibid.

The first "Surveyor General" of Maryland, was John Langford, and his commission, dated March 24, 1641, furnishes the only instance on record of an office held for life. The first Register of the Land Office was John Llewellin, who had been Chief Clerk to the Secretary of the Province and was hence familiar with its land affairs. The first "Land Council", appointed 1684, consisted of Major Nicholas Sewall, Colonel Henry Darnall, Colonel Edward Digges and Mr. John Darnall. The first Judge of the Land Office appointed 1715, was Mr. Philomea Lloyd, then Deputy Secretary of the Province. He was succeeded in turn by Edmond Jennings, 1732; Levin Gale, 1738; Phillip Thomas, 1743; (the last sole Judge) Benjamine Tasker and Benjamine Young, 1746; Benedict Calvert and George Steward, 1755; who continued until the Revolution.—Kilty, pp. 64, 111, 270.

[4] The estates held by the settlers were called freeholds in Acts of Assembly and elsewhere, but they were not freeholds of the present day. Being subject to the annual quit rent, they were estates in trust,

Tenure is the "stipulated condition under which real property is held" and *socage* tenure was that class of them in which the conditions were honorable in respect to quality and certain in respect to quantity and the time of exacting them, as distinguished from other species of tenures, which were base and servile as to character of conditions, and precarious and uncertain as to quantity and time.[1] At the date of the Maryland Charter, this was the most popular of all the English tenures, and the "free, certain, and pacific services" incident to it, gave it advantages, as applicable to Maryland, in encouraging immigration and promoting industry, which none other possessed.[2]

It was a remnant of feudal tenure, and to maintain its character as such, the Proprietary grants were so framed as to require the land to be held as of one of his manors, named in the patent, the grant to him being held of the Castle of Windsor.[3]

The condition and services attached to the grants, were also of a feudal nature, and while many of the feudal incidents of socage tenure in England appear never to have prevailed in

rather than allodial estates, and were feudal in form, if not in essence. The holdings being assignable and transmissable, formed an actual estate of inheritance.

Restrictions, however, could be placed by lords of manors upon their under tenants, and there is no evidence that a manor could be sub-divided into smaller manors by the tenants. It was quite common for the lords of manors to subinfeudate parts of their estate. This privilege was granted by the conditions of 1649 They were empowered to grant any portion of their manor, save the demesnes to any English subject, either in fee simple or fee tail for life, lives, or years, and under such rents not prejudicial to his lordship's royal jurisdiction.—Local Institutions of Maryland.

---

1 Kilty, p. 24, McMahon, p. 168.   2 Ibid.
3 Ground Rents in Maryland; Kilty, p. 24.

Maryland, those of fealty, rent, escheat, relief, and fines for alienation and devises were exacted.

Fealty—allegiance or fidelity to the Lord Proprietary—was an inseparable incident of every grant, and all persons holding land in the Province, were required to take either the "oath of fidelity" or "subscribe the engagement" (a substitute for the oath) before the patent was issued. And this could be demanded more than once, under penalty of being "proceeded against as rebels and traitors", and seizure and forfeiture of the lands.[1]

Escheats, as they existed in early Maryland, may be defined to be, the reversion to the Proprietary, of the land granted, upon the conviction of the tenant of crime, or upon his death without heirs—the land being taken in lieu of the feudal services, which there was no one to perform. They still exist, but upon a wholly different principle—that of property without an owner, and which reverts to the State, to be held for the benefit of all of its citizens. For many years it was deemed necessary here, as in England, to establish the fact of the escheat by the inquisition of a jury, before the lands could be again disposed of by the Proprietary, and for that purpose an "Escheator" was appointed. But in the interval between 1692 and 1715, when the government of the Province was in the hands of the Crown, although the Proprietary's right to the soil was admitted, it was found impracticable to have the "inquest of office" executed, and grants for escheated lands came to be made without it, a practice which continued after the government was restored to the Proprietery, and the one which has been followed ever since.[2]

---

[1] H. & McH. Maryland Reports, 3; Bozman. p. 403.
[2] 10th G, & J. Maryland Reports, p. 451; 1st Bland, Ibid, p. 307; 1st Gill, Ibid, p. 506.

Fines were the charges imposed upon the tenant for the privilege of selling or devising the land. Under the socage tenure, the tenant could not pass his title to another without the consent of the landlord, who, for the trouble and inconvenience of accepting a new tenant, was entitled to compensation. In Maryland this consisted of one year's rent, equal in amount to the quit-rent reserved on the land disposed of, and it had to be paid before the sale or the devise became effective or capable of passing the title.[1] This badge of feudalism was abolished in England as early as 1660, but remained in force in Maryland until 1780, except fines for devises which were suspended by order of the Proprietary, in 1742.[2]

Relief, as applicable to Maryland, bore close analogy to fines, it being the sum exacted upon the tenant dying intestate, and the land passing to the heir at law. It, too, was equal in amount to one year's rent, and had to be paid before the title could vest in the heir, after which the estate was "relieved" from the lapsed state into which, by theory of the feudal law, it had fallen.[3] This, like fines for devises, was considered by the inhabitants of the Province a great hardship, and, in 1742, it was abolished.[4]

Rent, as an acknowledgment of the tenancy, as well as for the revenue, was always reserved in the grants of Maryland lands. These rents were called "quit rents", because being a fixed sum reserved in lieu of the indefinite feudal services due the lord of the fee, the tenant was "quit" and

---

[1] Ground Rents in Maryland, p. 31.   [2] McMahon, p. 175.
[3] Ground Rents in Maryland, 23 and 24.
[4] Proclamation of Governor Bladen, October 20, 1742,

discharged from the performance of such services.¹ They were payable annually, and were perpetual in point of duration and irredeemable.² The amount depended upon the date of the grant, or rather the date of the "Condition of Plantation" under which it was issued. In the earlier grants it was only 10 ℔s. of wheat per annum for every 50 acres. This was soon increased to 15 ℔s., then to one shilling, and, in 1648, it was raised to four shillings,³ on which basis it continued until the Revolution. After 1648, manorial lands were subject to 40 shillings for every 2000 acres, for the first seven years; 40 bushels of wheat, or £6 sterling, for each of the succeeding fourteen years, after which to the twentieth part of the annual yield of the land, or £10 sterling.⁴ In a few special cases, however, grants were made, by order of the Proprietary, for a mere nominal consideration, exacting as a token of fealty only, for the whole tract granted, the annual render of a capon, a pair of pullets, an indian arrow, or a bushel of corn.⁵

Owing to the scarcity of money in the Province, quit rents were, in 1671, commuted to payments in tobacco, at the rate of two pence per pound, a duty of two shillings (half for the Proprietary personally, and half for the defense of the Province) being imposed on all exported tobacco, in consideration of an agreement on his part to receive his rents and fines in that commodity.⁶ This continued until 1717, when an

---

1 1st Bland, Maryland Reports, pp. 43, 96; Ground Rents in Maryland, p. 15.

2 See interesting and valuable criticism of Mr. Lewis Mayer ("Ground Rents in Maryland," 15 and 16) as to whether Maryland quit rents were "rent charges" or "rent service".

3 Archives (Cl. Pro. 1636, 1641, 1648) pp. 47, 99, 221.

4 Ibid, 1648, p. 223   5 Kilty.

6 Act, 1671, C. 11; McMahon, p. 178.

Act was passed giving to the Proprietary, for his exclusive use, a duty of two shillings sterling on every hogshead, and four pence sterling per hundred on every box of tobacco exported from the Province, in full discharge of his rents and fines.[1] But, this Act expired in 1733, and they again became payable either in money, or in the commodities of the country, as the patent prescribed.[2]

The "Maryland quit rents" were, from an early period, a source of trouble to the people of the Province, and a constant subject of their complaint, not because of the amount involved, but the inconvenience and difficulties attending the payment of them. This was particularly the case after the system of allowing payment in tobacco, and the subsequent provision for payment by an export duty, expired. Repeated efforts were made to get these systems renewed, or to obtain some other which would afford an easy mode of payment. In 1744, the Assembly offered to increase the former export duty on tobacco to two shillings and six pence sterling, if the Proprietary would accept it in lieu of his rents, but the proposition was declined. The following year an effort was made to purchase them, the Legislature offering to pay the Proprietary, in consideration of his rents and fines, five thousand pounds sterling annually, but this likewise failed, and they continued to be collected, according to the requisition of the patents, until the American Revolution,[3] when, the Proprietary being a British subject, his rents and other landed rights in Maryland, were seized and confiscated by the State, which, declaring quit rents to be "incompatible with absolute sovereignty", promptly abolished them, and forever "exonerated

---

1 Act, 1717, C. 7.   2 McMahon, p. 170.
3 McMahon, p, 170.

THE LAND TENURE 97

and discharged" the citizens of the State from the further payment of them. Constructively, fines were also abolished, so that by this Act, the people of Maryland were relieved of two features of their land tenure, which they had so long regarded a source of public grievance.[1]

The quit rent, though not in all respects analogous, was the origin and foundation of the present ground rent system in Maryland. It was a small rent when considered individually, but collectively it was a large source of revenue to the Proprietary, estimated, in 1770, to amount to £8,400 sterling,[2] and, at the time of the Revolution, his rents and other revenues from land were estimated at £30,000 sterling annually.[3]

In 1780, the General Assembly passed an Act which provided, "that all property within this State (debts only excepted) belonging to British subjects shall be seized, and is hereby confiscated to the use of the State", and at the same time, William Paca, Uriah Forrest, and Clement Hollyday, were appointed commissioners to preserve said lands.[4]

It was subsequently contended that this Act was ineffective, inasmuch as it provided for confiscation without formal entry and seizin. But the Supreme Court of the United States held, that under the Act no seizure was necessary, and that "the commissioners were, by operation of law, in full and actual seizure and possession of the property, though no entry or other act had been made or done", and also, that the law, itself constituting the actual confiscation and seizure,

---

1 Act, 1780, C. 18,

The abolition of the Proprietary "quit-rents" did not of course interfere with rents issuing from long leases, known as "ground rents" and owned by private individuals.

2 McMahon, p. 172. 3 Scharf, 2, p. 374.

4 Act, 1780, C. 45, 49.

embraced all land in the State held by British subjects, even though it was not discovered until after the treaty of peace, 1783, which declared that no more confiscations should be made.[1]

Henry Harford, to whom the Province was devised by Frederick, the last Lord Baltimore, estimated the loss of his lands, rents, and fines in Maryland, through the "Confiscation Act", at £447,000 sterling, and filed a claim against the British Government for that amount. He was only allowed £90,000, of which £20,000 went to Louisa, the wife of John Browning, and Caroline, the wife of Sir Robert Eden—the devise to Harford being subject to a charge of £10,000 to each of the said sisters of Frederick, Lord Baltimore.[2]

In 1783, Harford applied to the Legislature of Maryland to compensate him for the loss of his "quit rents", alleging that they were not within the "Confiscation Act", but the Assembly determined that they were "subject to all the rules and consequences of real estate", and refused either to pay for or restore them, declaring at the same time that the people of Maryland should not occupy "the degraded condition of tenants to a superior lord, a foreigner, and a British subject".[3] A similar effort was made as late as 1821, by Charles Browning, son and heir of Louisa Browning, with like result, and five years later, it was attempted to establish the right to them through the Supreme Court of the United States, upon the ground that the Proprietorship of Maryland belonged to Louisa Browning on the death of her brother, Frederick, without lawful issue.[4] This interesting question, however,

---

1 6 Cranch, United States Supreme Court Reports, p. 286.

2 Scharf, 2, p. 394.   3 Ground Rents in Maryland, p. 37.

4 Charles Lord Baltimore, died in 1751, having devised the Province of Maryland to his son Frederick and his assigns, for life; remainder to

was ignored by the Court, which decided that whatever rights Louisa Browning may have had in the premises, they had been extinguished (for the purposes of that case) by an agreement made in England between all the parties in interest, that, for certain considerations, the devise of the Province to Henry Harford should be allowed to stand.[1]

The last public use and official notice made of the old "Rent Rolls"[2] and "Debt Books", in which were kept the rents and fines due by each individual, and the land on which

---

the sons of said Frederick, lawfully begotten, successively in tail male; remainder to the daughters of said Frederick; in default of such issue, then to his oldest daughter, Louisa (wife of John Browning), in fee, subject to a charge of £20,000 sterling in favor of his daughter, Caroline (wife of Governor Robert Eden). Frederick Lord Baltimore, died in 1772, without lawful issue, having devised the Province to his illegitimate son, Henry Harford and his heirs male, lawfully begotten, and in default, to the heirs male of his illegitimate daughter, Frances Mary Harford, subject to a charge of £20,000 sterling for his two sisters, Louisa Browning and Caroline Eden. In 1761, and again in 1767, Frederick Lord Baltimore attempted to *dock* the entailment of Maryland made by his father's will. Query—Could the Province itself be entailed? If it could, was it practicable to *dock* the entailment by a common recovery suffered by the Proprietary, in person or by attorney, in one of his own courts in Maryland? By the will of Frederick, Lord Baltimore, £1500 sterling were bequeathed to Peter Prevost, and a like sum to Robert Morris, and made chargeable upon Maryland. Peter Prevost married Hester Wheland, the mother of Henry and Frances Wheland, alias Harford, and Robert Morris married Frances Harford.—2d H. & McH. Maryland Reports, p. 277; Scharf, 2, pp. 137, 139.

1 Cassell vs. Carroll, 11, Wheaton, p. 136.

2 When Cecilius, Lord Baltimore, established his "Conditions of Plantations", he furnished the basis of a pretty accurate census of the early settlers of his little American kingdom. From the first, lands were granted to those who transported persons into the colony, "to inhabit", and the names of those "transports", as they are called, are entered in the records of the Land Office of the Proprietary. At least this is true up to about 1680, a few years after the death of Cecilius, when the practice seems to have fallen into disuse, and from that time on, the record of immigrants is fragmentary and of little value. Prior to that

it accrued, was in 1777. That year, land in Maryland, for the first time, was made the subject of direct taxation. The Act under which this was done—one of the earliest passed by the first General Assembly of the Republic—provided that from "them" should be made "complete lists of the names and quantity of acres of every tract of land, and to whom the

time, however, it is safe to say that nearly every one who came as a "transport" had his name recorded, and of these an index has lately been compiled in the Land Office of the State.

It was found that of the 20,859 persons who came to Maryland prior to 1680, 15,640, or 74.98 per cent., were males, and 5,219, or 25.02 per cent., were females. Eighty-two family names were represented by more than twenty-five persons each, and aggregated 4,471 immigrants, being 22.87 per cent. of the whole number. The Smiths lead with 262 representatives, but the Joneses are a close second, with 254, and if we include the twenty five Joaneses—evidently a misspelling—they lead the Smiths by seventeen. The Williamses hold a respectable third place, with 194 names, and the Johnsons are not a bad fourth, with 133. The Davises and Taylors each number over a hundred.

There is little doubt that the different spellings of the same sounding name are to be attributed more to the clerks, who had no settled rule about it, than to the fancy of the individuals, very few of whom, probably, could spell at all.

Twenty-nine of the ships, which traded with the mother country, are recorded in the index, including the *Ark*, and among them we find the names, *Baltimore, Cecilius, Constant Friendship, Golden Wheat Sheaf, King Solomon, Maryland Merchant, True Love*, and others.

Most of the old noted families of the State, have here recorded the first of their names who came to Maryland—the Lloyds, Goldsboroughs, Tilghmans, Dents, Winders, and scores of others. There was also an Arnold Elzey in those days. Naturally, there were some odd names— "Ringing Bell" and "Thomas Birdwhistle" have a cheerful sound; "Peter Blackboard", is decidedly pedagogic; "Nicholas Broadway", smacks of arrogance; while, "Samuel Churchyard", casts a gloom over the company, which needs "Hannah Godsgrace", as an antidote. "John Godsgrass" and "James Tendergrass" are properly within easy reach of "Mary Greengoose". We run across "John Halfway", "John Halfehead"—who, by the way, sat in the first Assembly, in 1634 and 1635—and "Thomas Halfpenny". "Margaret Nutbrown" suggests the fields and forests of merry England. "Edward Rainbow" seems to have faded away in the morning of the young commonwealth, as we

same belonged", for the tax commissioners of the several counties, as a means of supplying the data and information by which the new law was to be put into operation.[1]

Thus was the fabric of Maryland's early land tenure swept away by the storm of the American Revolution. All landed rights which were granted under the Charter to Cecilius

---

find no further trace of him. "Robert Sidebottom" is a little contradictory. "Francis Silversides" was a palpable anacronism ; he should have lived in our day, and represented Nevada in the Senate of the United States. "James Wildgoose" led quite a flock into the colony, but they seem to have sought other feeding grounds. In "All Saints Buelis" and "Jehovah Jones", we catch a strong whiff of the Puritan element in Baltimore's followers. "John the Fidler " is suggestive of revelry.

While the Maryland colony was, in the main, free from hostile Indian incursions, its early history had, nevertheless, its tragic side, as we discover in the following entry : " Richard Thompson further prayeth, in consideration of transporting his wife, child, maidservant, Donsabel Gladdus, and other two men servants, that is to say John Thompson and Hubert Smith, to have confirmed to him the island to the southward of the Isle of Kent, called Poplar's Island, which he was possessed of by grant of Capt. Wm. Claybourne, and where he inhabited till in the year 1637 they were massacred by the Indians.

Negroes were brought in very early, the first entry being of "Dina" in 1637. A few others are named including Mathias Tousa, "a molatto." It would seem that lands were not always granted for negroes transported. Thomas Skinner, in 1664, transported fifteen persons, including the negroes Robert, Francis and Maria, but "rights" were refused for the negroes.

Lord Baltimore made many special grants of land to friends, and gave substantial recognition to those who had performed meritorious service. Thus, in a special warrant dated at London, May 22, 1637, his lordship recites :

" Whereas we are informed that Cyprian Thoroughgood hath done unto us and the colony good service, especially in the business of Pocomoke, we have therefore thought fit, at his request and for his better encouragement, to give him 300 acres of land "

A similar warrant was given to Lieut. Robert Troop for " services at Severn ;" and also to John Bayley, "son of John Bayley, late of our

---

[1] Act, 1777, C. 21.

Calvert, the Baron of Baltimore, became merged in the sovereignty of Maryland and vested in her citizens, and lands became allodial, subject to no feudal incidents and to no tenure, save allegiance to the State.[1]

---

said province, planter, who lost his life in our service in Anne Arundel county in the late war there."

The allusions to expeditions to distant parts of the colony are frequent, but unfortunately no details are given.

A strange warrant was given to John Abbington, Gent., "to hunt wild cattle and keep an Indian."—Baltimore Sun, Feb. 9, 1894.

1 10 G. & J. Maryland Reports, p. 444.

CHAPTER V.

The Land Tenure of Colonial Maryland.

THERE was no legally established system of transferring land in the earlier history of Maryland, and the records are replete with examples of the inconveniences felt and the losses sustained in consequence of it.

In the absence of a better method, it was usually done by writing the transfer on the back of the patent, or on a separate sheet of paper and delivering it to the grantee, or by placing the grantee in possession of the land by livery of seizin.[1]

The latter—a mode of conveyancing at common law—was accomplished by the actual or constructive entry of the grantor and grantee on the land, which was then symbolically delivered in the presence of witnesses from the neighborhood, thus giving notoriety to the the transaction and making known the change of owners.[2] In 1663, a more uniform system of conveyancing was adopted. By this Act, transfers,

---

1 Kilty, Appendix, p. 36; Bozman, p. 58.   2 Blackstone.

On Saint Gabriel's Manor (now Point Lookout) Martin Kirk, in 1656, was given seizin of a part of the Manor "by the rod", which was done by the steward and said Kirk each taking hold of an end of the rod, and the former saying, in the presence of witnesses, "the lord of this manor, by me, the steward, doth hereby deliver you seizin by the rod, and admit you as tenant of the premises", and the said Kirk, "in full court", "having done his fealty to the lady of the manor (Miss Margaret Brent) is thereof admitted tenant".—Bozman, p. 581.

by bargain and sale, of real estate were to be in writing, indented and sealed, and recorded within six months, either in the Provincial Court, or in the Court of the County in which the land lay.[1]

To this was added, in 1671, the necessity for the acknowledgment of deeds, to be made either before a Judge of the Provincial Court, two members of the Privy Council, or two Justices of the Peace of the County in which the land was situated, the acknowledgment of married women to be taken privately, and out of the hearing of their husbands.[2]

These Acts, however (which were re-enacted in 1692, when the government of the Province was assumed by the Crown), did not apply to conveyances of land made by Lord Baltimore, and were confined in their application, as between other persons, to deeds of "bargain and sale" only[3]—a deed in which the grant is made for a valuable consideration, as distinguished from a feoffment—a deed of gift, accompanied by formal delivery of the property.[4]

As enrollment took the place of livery of seizin, the latter became unnecessary after 1715, in case the deed was recorded; but, as no deeds could be recorded, except deeds of "bargain and sale", this ancient custom still continued in practice, to

---

1 Archives Act, 1663, p. 489.

Bozman says a system was adopted in 1639, but this is an error. A bill for that purpose was introduced, but did not pass. Bacon intimates that the Act of 1663, did not pass, but this is an error also. See Archives (Ass. Pro. 1663) p. 487, and same 1666, p. 46.

2 Archives, Act, 1671, p. 305.

3 2 H. & McH. Maryland Reports, p. 279.

4 If, however, the owner of the property was a non-resident, but a "trader" in the Province, before the deed or conveyance became effective, the person to whom it was made had to give bond, approved by the Chancellor, to pay and satisfy all debts of the grantor due and owing to any person or persons living in the Province, to the extent of the value of the land conveyed.—Act 1753, C. 36.

give efficacy to other species of conveyancing, and it was not until 1766, when provision was made for the ackowledgment and enrollment of all kinds of deeds, that it was formally abolished.[1] After 1766, deeds took effect from the date of their execution, and not from the date of enrollment, as the law had hitherto provided they should.[2]

The old custom of indenture—cutting the deed unevenly on the top and sides so as to make it correspond to a duplicate—was as indispensible to the validity of deeds in early Maryland as was the name of the grantor. And it was necessary too, for it to be *actually indented*, and not simply an indenture in name.

The last mentioned Act made this unnecessary as to feofments and other deeds to which it extended, but as it did not apply to deeds of "bargain and sale", then the most general in use, the indenting of that class of deeds continued to be necessary until 1794, when this requisite was declared no longer essential.[3]

A good possessory title to lands in Maryland, could be acquired under the Act of 1663, by an "undisputed, continuous, and uninterrupted possession" for the period of five years, except as against married women, infants, lunatics, and persons out of the Province, or of unsound mind, any of

---

[1] 10 G. & J. Maryland Reports, p. 443; Act, 1715, C. 47.

[2] Act, 1766, C. 14.

Under the Act of 1766, C. 14, deeds had to be acknowledged either in the Provincial Court, or before a Judge thereof; or in the County Court, or before two Justices of the Peace. If made before either of the two latter, and out of the county in which the land lay, the clerk's certificate to their official character was required. Deeds thus acknowledged could be enrolled either in the county in which the land lay, or in the Provincial Court, and, after 1776, in its successor, the General Court —2d H. & McH. Maryland Reports, p. 451.

[3] 2 H. & McH. Maryland Rep, p. 176; Act, 1766, C. 14; Act, 1794, C. 57.

G

whom could sue for the recovery of the lands within five years after the removal of such disability.[1] Nor did it apply to the Proprietary of the Province, as to his unpatented lands, though it did as to those he claimed by escheat, until he had formally repossessed himself of them.[2]

The Act of 1663, however, did not remain in force many years. It was superseded by the English statute (21 James I, ch. 16), and the one by which questions of possessory title are still determined in Maryland.[3]

The descent of lands in early Maryland was regulated by the English rules and canons of inheritance. By the Act of 1642, lands were to "descend to the heir who hath right by the law of England". If such heir was not in the Province, the heir next in succession was to hold it for his use, which possession, if undisturbed for seven years, ripened into actual ownership. The widow, in addition to one-third of the land, was entitled to the mansion house during her widowhood.[4] Among the curious bills introduced in the first Assembly held in the Province, but which, like all the others of that session, failed to become a law, was one which deprived a woman of lands descending to her, unless she married within the age fixed by law.[5]

Under the English rule, thus introduced in Maryland, males inherited to the exclusion of females, and of the male issue, the oldest son, in the absence of a will, succeeded to the entire estate. Custom followed close to the law, and even where wills were made, the oldest son generally received the "lion's share" of the estate.

---

[1] Archives, Act, 1663, p. 501.
[2] 3 H. & J. Maryland Reports, p. 507.
[3] 1 H. & J. Maryland Reports, p. 350; Venable, p. 23.
[4] Archives, Act, 1642, p. 157.   [5] Shea, p. 51.

This partial and unjust rule of "primogeniture", as it was called, had its origin in the feudal ages, when it was deemed important to keep the estate entire, and when the oldest son was supposed to be the one best capable of taking his father's place, and of performing the military services which were incident to the grant. Later, it was maintained in England as a means of supporting nobility and its titles. Its introduction in Maryland was not due to either of these reasons, though it did, in effect, help to sustain the leadership of the great Maryland families, but was most probably the result of the want of a better system, and the bondage of the people, at that day, to English traditions and institutions.[1]

At the time of the American Revolution, however, English ideas and customs were not so popular in Maryland, and in 1786, the General Assembly declared, "that the law of descent in Maryland, which originated in the feudal system and military tenures in England, was contrary to justice, and ought to be abolished". It was, accordingly done, and substantially the same rules of descent as those now in force, were adopted in its stead.[2]

The law of entailments, by which lands could be transmitted for generations in the line of a particular heir, was also practically swept away by the same Act, which declared, that

---

[1] There were, also, certain local modes of inheritance, which prevailed in England by custom, such as "borough English" and "ultimogeniture"—the former the right of the youngest son to the entire estate, and the latter the right of the youngest son to the homestead. These customs were predicated upon the theory that the oldest sons were provided for during the lifetime of the father, and that the youngest remained at home and cared for his parents in their old age and infirmity. They were never introduced in Maryland, but the latter of them did prevail in some of the New England colonies, and, it is said, still exists in some of the northern counties of New York.—Social Condition of the Colonies.

[2] Act, 1786, C. 45.

estates in tail general, should descend in *fee simple*, and to the same heirs at law, as fee simple estates.

An Act[1] had hitherto been passed, making it practicable to "bar" or "dock" entailments, by a simple conveyance of the property, and though neither of these, in terms, converted estates in fee tail into fee simple estates, they did so in effect, by vesting in the owner all the rights and powers incident to the ownership of fee simple estates.[2]

While entailments found a successful lodgement in Maryland, the restrictions surrounding them were too numerous and inflexible for popularity, and the records furnish repeated instances of efforts having been made to "dock" them by the old process known as "common recovery", long before the Revolution.[3]

Under the Maryland Charter, the Proprietary was expressly authorized to erect manors "according to English customs and usages", and in the exercise of this right, he directed that every distinct tract of two thousand acres, or

---

1 Act, 1782, C. 23.   2 21 Maryland Reports, p. 477.

The Act of 1786, providing for the descent of estates tail, applied only to estates of fee tail general—those limited to heirs of the body generally. This Act, as re-enacted in 1820, is the one now in force, and, as it does not embrace estates tail special—those limited to particular heirs of the body—the latter class, it would seem, can still be created and exist in Maryland, but subject always to the possibility of being barred by the tenant in tail conveying the property as provided by Act of 1782, which applies to all classes of entailments, and which makes the grant of the tenant in tail, operate to convert the entailment into a fee simple estate.

3 It is curiously recorded of one of the patriarchs of Colonial Maryland, that, when importuned by his sons to break the entailment upon his estate, replied. "If one of you inherit the whole estate, I shall be responsible for the production of one fox hunter; if I divide it, I shall make as many fox hunters as I make heirs", thus illustrating the prevalence of this sport among the landed gentry of that day.

—Old Maryland Manors, p. 11.

more, might be erected into a manor, under such name as the owner desired.¹

While many of the larger tracts in Maryland were called manors by reason only of the quantity of land they contained, there were a large number of manors, formally erected in the Province and invested with all the "royalties and privileges usually belonging to manors in England", among them the right of the lord of the manor to establish and hold Courts Baron and Court Leet.² This clause in the grant of Maryland manors, was not a mere "high sounding sybol", but meant the practical introduction into Maryland of the English system of manorial holdings, with all the customs, powers, and emoluments, as well as the halo of importance and dignity attached thereto.

The bestowal of this privilege upon the first Baron of Baltimore—one which was at that time denied the great feudal Barons of England—indicates the high favor in which he was held by the Crown, and its incorporation in the Maryland Charter shows that he possessed a keen perception of its practical bearing on his Maryland enterprise. Through the system he not only made provision for the government of the larger landed communities by which they would be kept under control, and yet he be relieved of settling their local affairs, but it placed him in a position to gratify the strong demand of the times for local self-government, and at the same time check any undue growth of that spirit and prevent it reaching dangerous proportions.³

---

1 By the first Conditions of Plantation, tracts of one thousand acres, or more, might be erected into a manor, but after 1641, the right to erect manors was restricted to tracts of not less than two thousand acres.

2 For an account of the Manorial Courts in Maryland, see Chapter, The Judicial System of Colonial Maryland.

3 Local Institutions in Maryland.

On the Maryland manors, generally resided the lord of the manor and his tenants, among whom the land was divided into small farms.[1] Some of the tenants were mere renters from year to year; others held under leases for life or a term of years, while others purchased and owned the land on which they lived, but subject to all the duties and customs of manors in England. Among these, were rent, escheat, forfeiture, fines for selling or devising the tenament, or a change in the ownership by death of the tenant intestate, attendance of all between the ages of twelve and sixty years upon the Manor Courts, and the oath of fealty to the lord of the manor.

To the lord of the manor also belonged all escheats and forfeitures accruing from the land leased or sold, the former extending not only to cases in which the tenant died without heirs, but to those also, in which the tenant was in arrear in rent, and did not have sufficient personal property on the premises to pay it by distraint, and the latter to cases of rebellion. Instances are furnished in which both of these rights were exercised upon Governor Leonard Calvert's manors, the escheats being for non-payment of three years' rent, and the forfeitures for participation in Ingle's rebellion.[2]

In addition to the large number of manors laid out for private individuals, the Proprietary had at least two, of not less than 6,000 acres each, surveyed in every county, and set apart for his own use.[3] Many of these were still in his possession at the time of the Revolution, and were subject to the Maryland Act of confiscation, among them the one of 10,000

---

[1] In Maryland, the demesne (the part occupied by the manor house, etc.) was the sixth part of the manor, that had to be distinctly set apart, and which could not be alienated, separated, or leased for a period longer than seven years.—Kilty, p. 39.

[2] See details of these proceedings in Kilty's, p. 103.

[3] Kilty, p. 63.

acres lying westward of Fort Cumberland, erected in 1764, and which, with other lands, was divided into "military lots" after the Revolution, and awarded to the officers and soldiers of the Maryland Line.[1]

There were, also, large manors laid out for the Indians, the principal one, perhaps, being Calverton Manor, containing about 10,000 acres, and located, says the order directing it, on "a tract of land at the head of Wicocomico River, called Choptico". It was erected in 1651, for the "six nations", who wanted to be placed under the protection of the Maryland government. This scheme of colonization, however, of making copyhold tenants of the Indians, seems to have been abortive, at least, so far as instituting a confederacy of the different tribes is concerned, as in 1692, the only one of them apparently living on the manor was the Chopticons.[2]

The gradual decline of the manorial system in Maryland, was not due to adverse feeling against the institution of manors and manorial customs, but to the introduction of slavery. When labor from that source became abundant and cheap, land could be worked more profitably with slaves than by tenants. The former, therefore, gradually supplanted the latter, and the "Maryland manor" became in time a "Maryland plantation", cultivated by slaves, either in its entirety or as separate estates.

It has been charged that it was Baltimore's plan to found in Maryland an order of nobility, based on baronial

---

[1] Ibid, pp. 332-350.   [2] Archives (Cl. Pro. 1692) pp. 3-36.

There were also large tracts laid out on the Eastern Shore, for the Choptank and Nanticoke Indians (Kilty, pp. 351-355)—these tribes were the remnants of the *Kuskarawoaks*, once famous as the great makers of *peake* and *roanoke* (Indian money). *Peake* was more valuable than *roanoke*, but they both consisted of shell—the former of the *conch*, the latter of the *coekle*—wrought into the shape of beads.—Day Star, p. 111.

holdings. It is true, the Charter[1] expressly provided that dignities and titles could be conferred, and incidentally, that a provincial peerage might be established, and that among the bills transmitted by Baltimore to the Assembly, in 1637 (but which, with the others sent, was rejected), was a "Bill for Baronies". It is, however, also true that after the bill which was subsequently passed, substantially as prepared by him,[2] he vetoed it,[3] either from political reasons, growing out of the claim he was at that time making that *he*, and not the Assembly, had the right to initiate legislation, or from prudential motives which prompted a reconsideration of his original plan of founding "Baronies" in the Province.

Be this as it may, it is highly probable that the "Bill for Baronies", as introduced by him, was a proposition, not for an order of nobility, but for the creation of political subdivisions, such as are still known in Ireland as "Baronies", and where Baltimore was then engaged in the enterprise of colonization.[4]

At the session of 1639, two bills were introduced, but not passed, constituting the lords of manors a privileged class; the one providing, that they should only be tried by a jury composed of lords of manors, if so many could be procured, and, if condemned to capital punishment, they were, unlike the body of people, to be executed by being beheaded, and not by hanging; the other, that lords of manors should be eligible, like members of the Council, to seats in the Assembly without election by the people,[5] but it nowhere appears that Baltimore was interested in the passage of either of them, or responsible for their introduction.

---

1 Section 14.   2 The Foundations of Maryland, p. 40.
3 Ibid; Bozman, 11, p. 67.
4 Bozman, 11, p. 67; The Foundation of Maryland, p. 42.
5 Archives (Ass. Pro. 1639) pp. 51-74.

THE LAND TENURE

Yet, whatever his intention may have been as to the creation of an order of nobility in Maryland, certain it is, that a genuine aristocracy did spring up and develop into a prominent feature of the colony, as the natural evolution of his land system. Nothing could have contributed more, indirectly, to the development of an aristocracy, as well as in moulding the character and habits of the people, than the land tenure of Colonial Maryland. Under its influences, both economic and political, land soon came to be esteemed the highest source of wealth in the Province, and, a little later, its ownership became a mark of distinction and an element of power.

In early Maryland there was a property qualification for voters, the right of the elective franchise being restricted to freemen who had not less than fifty acres of land, or a "visible personal estate of £40 sterling within the County"; the same qualification being required of delegates to the Assembly,[1] and only the landlords and employing classes were subject to taxation, which was rated according to the number of productive persons under their care—a system, purely aristocratic both in its intention and tendency.

From the class recognized as gentlemen, the County Court Judges, High Sheriffs, and Upper Magistrates, and, indeed, State and county officials generally, were selected, and as rural life was then esteemed the most honorable, those of this class were all expected to be owners of landed estates. They were entitled to be addressed as Esquires, the small freeholder and tenant being called Master or Mr.[2]

These, among other distinctions, between the freeholders and those who were landless, and between small landlords and the great landed proprietors of the Province; the importance attached to the lords of manors, by reason of their vast

---

[1] McMahon, pp. 445, 449.   [2] Scharf, II, p. 50; Day Star, p. 116.

possessions and judicial powers, and the strong support which the system received from the law of primogeniture and entailment, were powerful elements in the development of an aristocracy.

The isolation, too, of those vast estates, separated as they were, by such wide distances, and the solitary life of the planters who resided on them, necessarily made their proprietors rely on their own resources for entertainment, and made it also essential that each manor or plantation—being a community within itself—should be wholly self-sustaining, and wholly independent—a condition they shortly attained.

Co-operation was not an element of such a society, and the absence of this deprived the body of the people of the facilities for education which that closer community of feeling and association of interests—prevailing in some of the New England colonies—afforded, and which, for more than a century, practically restricted education to the sons and daughters of the wealthy planters, who could resort to colleges and seminaries. This condition intensified the consciousness of inferiority in the former class, while it excited in the latter, a sense of increased pride in their possessions, and a feeling of superiority in their surroundings and station in life.

And thus it was that the great landlords of the Province—political powers of the land and the educated element of the community—living upon their vast estates, independent and within themselves, possessing wealth without riches, dispensing that abounding hospitality, and cherishing that spirit of self-reliance and invincible independence, for which the society the soldiery, and the statesmanship of Maryland became renowned.

CHAPTER VI.

The Judicial System of Colonial Maryland.

THE Palatinate jurisdiction conferred on the Baron of Baltimore, over the Province of Maryland, as well as the powers expressly given by the seventh section of the Provincial Charter, are the corner-stones of the judicial system of Colonial Maryland. These accorded to him the full and sole authority to ordain judges, establish courts, and define their jurisdiction, and the manner and form of their proceedings.

This right he first exercised by commission, the earliest one extant being that of April 15th, 1637, by which he appointed Governor Leonard Calvert, Chief Justice and Chancellor of the Province, and invested him with full power to award process, hold pleas, and to hear and finally determine all civil actions, suits, and demands, both in law and equity, as well as all criminal causes, except that where a life, member, or freehold were involved, at least two members of the Privy Council were to sit with him.[1] Causes were determined by the common law of England, except where superseded by a provincial statute, and except, also, where life, member, or freehold were concerned, which could only be taken away by

---

[1] Archives (Cl. Pro. 1637) p. 49

an express law of the Province.[1] This, in 1642, was extended to persons who were outlawed or fined more than 1000 ℔s. of tobacco.[2]

Baltimore, however, soon submitted the General Assembly to regulate the perfunctory matters appertaining to the administration of justice in Maryland, such as the time, place, and manner of holding courts, and also to define their jurisdiction and the compensation of their judges, but the right to appoint the judges he always retained and exercised himself, or through his representative, the acting Governor; and he also required that all courts should be held, and that all process should issue and run in his name, and not in the name of the King or of the Province.[3]

The first exercise of this privilege by the Assembly, was in 1638, O. S., when an Act was passed vesting jurisdiction throughout the Province, in all civil, as well as criminal causes, in the Governor; in the Commander of the Isle of Kent (within that Island), and in the Privy Council, in cases in which the Governor was a party; except that in crimes extending to life or member, the offender was first to be indicted and then tried by at least twelve freemen.[4]

Successive Acts were, from time to time, passed,[5] under which the judicial system was gradually developed, and which will be noticed in detail, under the head of the several courts of the Province.

---

1 McMahon, p. 113; Act, 1642, C. 4; Act, 1646, C. 2.

2 Archives (Ass. Pro. 1642) p. 184.   3 McMahon, pp. 156, 157.

4 Archives (Ass. Pro. 1638) p. 83.

5 In 1638, an Act was introduced providing for a specific arrangement of the judicial system of the Province, but it did not reach its third reading, and was not passed.—(Archives, Ass. Pro. 1638, p. 39.) Bozman, however, devotes much space in explaining the tenor of this Act, which is misleading unless critically read, as the courts therein named were not established.

The first judicial officers appointed for Maryland, except the commission to the Governor and Council of 1637, before referred to, were Justices of the Peace.[1]

As early as January, 1637, O. S., one was commissioned for Saint Mary's County, and in February of the same year, three were commissioned for Kent.[2] The jurisdiction of these Justices was defined by their commissions, and was more comprehensive than that given to those subsequently appointed who were only constituted conservators of the peace, and with the powers and duties incident to the office of justice of the peace in England.[3]

In 1715, they were given jurisdiction, concurrently with the County Court, in all civil causes within their respective bailiwicks, in which "the real debt or damage doth not exceed 400 lbs. of tobacco, or 33 s. and 4 d. in money",[4] but this, apparently, did not apply to controversies with the Indians, as two years later an Act was passed, in which, after reciting the inconvenience of having such matters brought before the Governor and Council, Justices of the Peace were authorized to try and determine disputes between the "English and Indians", not exceeding 20 s. sterling.[5]

The first time Justices of the Peace were given jurisdiction exclusive of the County Courts, was in 1753, and at that time it was also increased to 600 lbs. of tobacco or 50 s. currency.[6] From their decision an appeal would lie to the County Court,

---

[1] The Court of Piepoudre, or market court, authorized by the charters of the cities of Saint Mary's and Annapolis, while a part of the system of Maryland jurisprudence, yet, being so circumscribed in territorial jurisdiction, are not treated here. For a brief notice of these courts, see Chapters ; The First Capital of Maryland.

[2] Archives (Cl. Pro. 1637) pp. 60, 62.   [3] Ibid, 1661, p. 422.
[4] Act, 1715, C. 12.   [5] Act, 1717, C. 14.
[6] Act, 1753, C. 13.

which at first applied to all cases, but in 1763, the right of appeal was limited to cases in which the amount involved exceeded 400 lbs. of tobacco, or 33 s. and 6 d. in money, and to stay execution pending the appeal, a bond had to be filed in double the amount of the judgment.[1] The constables were the executive officers of the Justice's Court.[2]

Two Justices of the Peace could take the acknowledgment of deeds,[3] and a single Justice could take the probate of any account,[4] and administer the oath of office to all government officials[5] and public inspectors.[6]

Justices of the Peace were appointed by the Governor, were usually the leading men of the county, and constituted, with those known as Justices of the Quorum, the County Court.

The first County Court held in Maryland, of which there is any record, met at Saint Mary's, on the 12th day of February, 1637, O. S. It was presided over by the Governor and two members of Council. A grand jury of twenty-four freeman was impaneled and sworn, and several indictments found,[7] but by a singular coincidence they were for offences which the Court, by the express terms of its commission, could only determine by a statute of the Province for such cases made and provided, and Baltimore having vetoed all Acts passed by the Assembly up to that time, the Court found itself in the unique position of having before it, prisoners arraigned and no laws by which to try them.[8]

But the General Assembly, which was then in session, did not propose to let the offenders go unwhipt of justice, and

---

1 Act, 1716, C. 5. 2 Act, 1763, C. 21.
3 Act, 1715, C. 15. 4 Act, 1715, C. 47.
5 Act, 1729, C. 20. 6 Act, 1763, C. 18.
7 Archives (Pro. Ct. 1637) p. 21. 8 Ibid; Bozman, pp. 60, 575.

believing itself equal to emergency, and not bound by the restrictions imposed upon the Governor and Council in their judicial capacity, resolved itself into a high court of justice, assumed jurisdiction of the cases, and, with the acting Attorney General, John Lewger, tried and convicted the prisoners of murder, the crime for which they were indicted.[1]

This Court, however, while called a County Court, was not such, as they were subsequently organized, but was the Provincial Court, sitting as a County Court, which it continued to do for the County of Saint Mary's until new counties were erected, and which had, until its limits were thus curtailed, embraced the whole of the western shore, as distinguished from Kent, on the eastern shore. For the latter, a special Court was at first instituted, with a Chief Judge and two Associates, and with jurisdiction over civil causes to the extent of 1200 ℔s. of tobacco, and over all crimes and offences not punishable with loss of life or member.[2]

The earliest reference to a County Court, among the legislative proceedings in Maryland, was in 1638, when an Act was introduced, but not passed, "for the erecting of a County Court".[3] The next, is the Act of 1642, which refers to them as existing tribunals, from which it may be inferred that the Proprietary had, in the meantime, instituted them. This Act fixed the terms of court, and provided the oath for the Justices, the order of trials, method of appeal, and the manner of drawing the jury, and of selecting the Sheriff,[4] the latter being done by the Court placing three suitable persons in nomination, from whom the Chief Judge appointed the

---

1 Archives (Ass. Pro. 1637) pp. 16, 17, 18.
2 Archives (Cl. Pro. 1637) p. 62.
3 Archives (Ass. Pro. 1638) p. 47.   4 Ibid, 1642, pp. 147-152.

Sheriff of the County for the ensuing year.[1] This method of selecting the Sheriffs of the several counties, continued until 1662, when, upon the nomination of three persons by the County Court, the Governor, and not the Chief Judge, made the appointment.[2]

In 1676, the right to nominate the Sheriffs was taken away from the County Courts by the repeal of the Act of 1642,[3] after which the power of appointment was exercised by the Governor alone. In 1692, their term of office was extended to two years, and in 1699, to three years,[3] on which basis it continued until the Revolution.[4]

The Clerks of the County Courts were appointed by the Secretary of the Province,[5] this being one of the prerogatives belonging to that office. In 1691, the question of depriving the Secretary of this privilege was agitated, but it resulted in no change, the decision, however, being that the office "ought not to be sold",[6] but, as the Secretary had to give security for the "good behavior" of the County Clerks, he was allowed to receive one-tenth of the fees and emoluments of the office.[7] They were appointed at will, but generally held office during good behavior,[8] and besides keeping the Court records, they

---

1 Ibid.   2 Ibid, 1662, p. 45..

3 Bacon, Act, 1676, C. 2.

4 The duties performed by the Sheriffs in early Maryland, were very similar to those incident to the office of Sheriff in England. Besides serving writs and processes, imprisoning criminals, and inflicting punishments, it was also incumbent upon them to proclaim at the County Courts, the late Acts of the Assembly; to collect county and parish rates or dues; to supervise the return of taxables; and to perform such other duties as were incumbent upon the Sheriffs in England, and which the Governor, the Assembly, or the Courts might, from time to time, order and direct.

5 Archives (Cl. Pro. 1671, pp. 23, 136.

6 Act, 1692, C. 25; Act, 1699, C. 26.

7 Archives (Cl. Pro. 1691) pp. 289, 293.

8 Ibid, Sharpe, Cor. p. 6; Ibid, Cl. Pro. 1671, p. 136.

were the keepers of the County Seal,[1] and the records of all births, marriages, and deaths of white persons within their respective counties.[2]

Each County Court had a Crier and a Bailiff.[3] The County Courts were presided over by Justices of the Peace or Commissioners, who were appointed by the Governor, and a reference to their names shows them to have been among the most prominent men in the Province. A distinction was made between the Justices of the Quorum, who were presumed to possess higher qualifications, and the other Justices in the Commission, the presence of one or more of the Quorum Justices being necessary at each session of the court to give it legality. The Justice of the Quorum first named in the Commission was the Chief Judge, and in his absence the one next named presided.[4]

The number of Justices varied in the several Counties from six to twelve, four of whom being necessary to constitute a legal session of the court.[5] But to prevent a discontinuance of the court, two Justices, one being of the Quorum, could call and adjourn[6] it to a future day.[7]

The Justices of the County Courts were paid a per diem, each receiving 80 ℔s. of tobacco for each day of attendance,[8] and in order to insure their presence, they were subject to a fine of 100 ℔s. of tobacco for non-attendance, without good cause.[9]

The County Courts were Courts of Record,[10] and in their earlier history they held six terms a year, consisting of the

---

1 Archives (Ass. Pro. 1671) p. 294.   2 Ibid, 1691, p. 529.
3 Act, 1763, C. 18·   4 Archives (Ass. Pro. 1642) p. 183.
5 Archives (Cl. Pro. 1661) pp. 422, 424 ; Ibid 1675 pp. 65, 69.
6 A failure to meet or adjourn Court on the first day of the term, left its proceedings "without a return day"—a defect that could only be cured by Act of Assembly. See Archives, Act, 1794, p. 137.
7 Act, 1715, C. 14 ; 1756, C. 6.   8 Act, 1716, C. 11.
9 Archives (Ass. Pro. 1663) p. 497.   10 Ibid, 1678, pp. 70, 71.

first six successive days of every alternate month, but later they were reduced to four terms a year. They began for the Counties of Talbot, Baltimore, Saint Mary's, and Worcester, the first Tuesday in March, June, August, and November ; for Dorchester, Cecil, Anne Arundel, and Charles, the second Tuesday ; for Calvert, Kent, Somerset, and Frederick, the third Tuesday, and for Prince George and Queen Anne, the fourth Tuesday of said months.[1]

In 1663 the County Courts were directed to provide a pillory, ducking-stool, whipping-post, stock, and branding-irons for their respective Counties,[2] and in 1674, a Court house and Prison were ordered to be erected in each County, under the direction and supervision of the Justices of the several Counties, which order appears to have been promptly complied with.[3] They were also required to make court rules,[4] a copy of which had to be " kept sett up att the Court house doore ", and to purchase Keeble's Abridgments of the statutes of England, and Dalton's Justice, for the use of the County Courts.[5] Among the other administrative duties incumbent

---

1 Ibid, 1648, p. 232 ; Acts, 1715, C. 4 ; 1742, C. 19 ; 1748, C. 15.
2 Archives (Ass. Pro. 1663) p. 490.
3 Ibid, 1674, p. 413, Ibid, 1675, p. 447.
4 The first regulation of the County Court of Cecil, of the year 1721 reads : " When the Justices meet together at the Court house, to hold a court, one of them shall order the Crier to stand at the Court house door and make three " Oyeses " and say, all manner of persons that have any business this day at his Majesty's Court, draw near and give your attention, for the Court is now going to sit : " God save the King ". Rule 7 reads : " the plantiff's attorney standing up and direct himself to the court & then to the jury if any and open his client's case after the clerk's reading the Declaration * * * and when done he to sitt down and then the Defendant's Attorney to stand up and answer him as aforesaid & not to speak both together in a confused manner or indecently ". Rule 9 prescribed that no one presume to keep his hat on in court except " any of the Gentlemen of his Majesty's Honerable Council ".—Johnson's History of Cecil County, p. 244 & 246 ; Local Institutions in Maryland, p. 89.
5 Archives (Ass. Pro. 1678) p. 70.

upon the County Courts were, to levy county taxes,[1] assess parish rates,[2] and fix their boundaries,[3] and to appoint the keepers of weights and measures,[4] road supervisors,[5] constables, and press masters.[6]

The Sheriff selected and summonsed the grand and petit jury for the County Court, which had to be done at least ten days before court convened.[7] Those exempt from jury service were, delegates, magistrates, coroners, schoolmasters, overseers of highways, and constables, and no one was eligible as a petit juror who had any cause depending for trial at that term of the court.[8] The jury thus summonsed were compelled to serve, unless excused, under penalty of 500 ℔s. of tobacco.[9] The same penalty was attached to witnesses, summonsed before the County Court, and not attending, besides being liable in damages to the party injured by the loss of their testimony.[10]

The compensation allowed grand jurors was within the discretion of the court, but could not exceed 500 ℔s. of tobacco a piece per term, and was paid by the County.[11] The petit jury received 15 ℔s. of tobacco a piece for each day of attendance, out of the County levy, and 120 ℔s. of tobacco to the panel in every case in which they were sworn, to be taxed as a part of the costs of the case.[12]

The right, however, to trial by jury, was limited to crimes affecting life or member, until 1642, when it was, for the first time in Maryland, extended to all cases, civil and criminal, the party demanding it giving security to pay the cost of the jury,

---

1 Archives (Ass. Pro. 1671) p. 273 ; Acts, 1704, C. 34 ; 1748, C. 20.
2 Act, 1729, C. 7. 3 Act, 1713, C. 10.
4 Archives (Ass. Pro. 1671) p. 281. 5 Act, 1704, C. 21.
6 Act, 1715, C. 15 & 43. 7 Act, 1715, C. 37. 8 Ibid.
9 Ibid. 10 Ibid. 11 Ibid. 12 Act, 1719, C. 3.

except that in criminal cases affecting life or member, the demand could be made without furnishing such security.[1]

Witnesses before the County Court were entitled to 30 ℔s. of tobacco per day, to be taxed with the costs of the case. In criminal cases these fees, and indeed the fees of all the court officials, including the sheriff and jailer, were paid by the County, but only in case they could not be made out of the traveser, by way of execution or servitude.[2]

The jurisdiction of the earlier County Courts, the records do not cleary define, the reason for which, perhaps, being that until 1650, there were but two civil divisions in the Province, whose judicial affairs were administered as before stated.

In the proclamation erecting Charles County in 1658, the jurisdiction of the County Court for that County was limited in civil cases to 3000 ℔s. of tobacco, and in criminal causes, to those not affecting life or member.[3] This, while applicable to a single County, serves to show the idea then entertained of the scope and character of their jurisdiction. Three years later, when justices of the County Courts were appointed, apparently for the first time for all of the Counties then erected, their jurisdiction was the same as that prescribed in 1658 for Charles County.[4]

---

1 Archives (Ass. Pro. 1642) p. 151.   2 Act, 1715, C. 26,—37.
3 Liber, P. C. R. p. 52, 54, Maryland Historical Society,
4 Cl. Pro. 1661, p. 422.

The oath administered to Judges, after the allegiance and fidelity clause, was as follows: "To none will I delay or deny right. Reward of none will I take for doing justice. But equal justice will I administer in all thing to my best skill, without fear, favor or malice, of any person, according to the laws of this Province, so help me God". Liber C. and W. H., p. 6.

The following curious oath was administered to Judges of the County Courts, during the reign of George 1st: "The subcriber, Do truly and sincerely acknowledge profess and testify and declare in my conscience before God and the world that our Sovereign Lord King George is

The jurisdiction of the County Courts was concurrent with the Provincial Court until 1692, when they were given an exclusive jurisdiction in civil cases to the extent of 1500 ℔s. of tobacco and cask,[1] which in 1714, was increased to £20 sterling, or 5000 ℔s. of tobacco, and their concurrent jurisdiction extended to £100 sterling or 30,000 ℔s. of tobacco.[2] But they could not hold plea where the debt or damage did not

---

Lawfull and rightfull King of Great Brittain and all other the Dominions and Countries thereunto belonging and I Do Solomnly and sincerely Declare that I do believe in my conscience that the person Pretended to be Prince of Wales During the Life of the Late King James and since his Decease pretending to be and taking upon himself the stile and title of King of England—by the name of James the third or of Scotland by ye name of James the eighth or the stile & title of King of Great Britain hath not any right or title whatsoever to the crown of the Realm of Great Brittain or any other the Dominions thereunto belonging, and I do renounce, refuse, and âbjure any allegiance or obedience to him and I do swear that I will bear faith and true allegiance to his Majesty King George and him will defend to the utmost of my powers ag^t all Traitors Conspiracies and attempts whatsoever wh^c shall be made ag^t his p^{son} cro^n & Dignity and I will do my utmost endeavour to disclose & make known to his matic & succ^{rs} all treasons and traitorous Conspiraces wch I shall know to be ag^t him or any of them and I do faithfully promise to the utmost of my power to support maintain and defend the succession of ye Cro^w ag^t him ye Ld James and all other p^{son} whatsoever which succession by an act intitled an act for the further Limitacon of the Crown and better securing ye rights and Liberties of the subjects is and stands limited to the Princess Sophia Electress and Duchess Dowager of Hanover and the heirs of her body being protestants & all these things I do Plainly and sincerely acknowledge and swear according to the Express words by me spoken and according to the plain and common sence and understanding of the same words without any equivocation mentall evasion or secret reservasion whatsoever & I do make this Recognition acknoleagment abjuracon renouiciacon & promise heartily willingly and truly upon the true faith of a christian, so help me God.

I do likewise Declare that I Do believe that there is not any transubstantiation in the Sacrament of the Lords Supper or in the Elements of Bread and Wine at or after the Consecration thereof by any person what. soever. Taken from Charles County Court Records, Liber, 32, 1729—33 folio 3.

---

1 Archives (Ass. Pro. 1692) p. 447.   2 Act, 1714, C. 4.

exceed 600 lbs. of tobacco or 50 s. currency, those cases being determined exclusively by a single magistrate, from whom an appeal would lie to the County Court, where the amount involved exceeded 33 s. 4 p., or 400 lbs. of tobacco.[1] In 1773 they were given exclusive jurisdiction in all civil cases in which they before had jurisdiction and concurrent jurisdiction with the Provincial Court in all other cases. The same act gave them jurisdiction, concurrently with the Provincial Court, in all criminal matters whatsoever.[2]

The County Courts also had jurisdiction, concurrent with the Provincial Court, in all matters testamentary within their respective Counties until 1673, when the Perogative Court was established, which however, still left them with jurisdiction over guardians and orphans, and of the estates of orphans, with full power to protect the latter from waste or loss.[3] It was especially incumbent upon them to see that orphans were educated, and if their estates were insufficient to admit of this, they were to be apprenticed. The June term was known as the "orphan's term", at which it was made the duty of the Court to ascertain whether orphans were being maintained and educated according to their estates, and whether apprentices were being taught their trade and properly treated, and to correct any misconduct or dereliction of duty on the part of the guardians or those with whom the apprentices were placed.[4]

In 1773 the County Court were given jurisdiction in equity, concurrently with the Court of Chancery, in actions not exceeding £20 sterling or 5,000 lbs. of tobacco.[5]

---

1 Act, 1763, C. 21.   2 Act, 1773, C. 1.
3 Archives (Ass. Pro. 1654) p. 354; Ibid, 1663, p. 493.
4 Act, 1715, C. 39.   5 Act, 1763, C. 22.

Either as a matter of practice or by rule of court, persons were prohibited from suing out writs when plaintiffs, and appearing and confessing judgment when defendants, except through an attorney.

THE JUDICIAL SYSTEM

From the judgment of the County Courts, an appeal would lie to the Provincial Court. At first the right of appeal was without limitations, but in 1692 it was restricted to causes in which the debt or damages amounted to not less than 1,200 lbs. of tobacco,[1] which, in 1713, was made equivalent to £6 sterling.[2]

Upon this footing the County Courts remained until the revolution, after which they were reorganized and the several Counties laid off into districts to be presided over by a "Chief Judge, learned in the law, and two associates of integrity, experience and knowledge",[3] and thus they became merged into the more comprehensive tribunals known as the County Court of a specified judicial district, and subsequently as the Circuit Court of a specified judicial circuit.

It is recorded that the first Court held on the Eastern Shore of Maryland—the one erected for Kent in 1637—was a Court Leet,[4] but the commission[5] by which the Justices of that court were named, and its jurisdiction defined, indicates that it was not a manorial Court Leet, but was a tribunal similar to the County Court as subsequently erected.

That Manorial Courts, however, had practical existence in early Maryland, has been incontestably established[6] and the discovery of the valuable and unique records of St. Clements

---

This being represented to the General Assembly "as a great grievance" an Act was passed making it "lawful for all persons within the Province to order out process in their own names without any titling from an attorney"; and also that they should have the right "to appear and imparle till next court, or to confess judgment to any action" brought against them.—Act, 1716, C. 20.

1 Archives (Ass. Pro. 1692) p. 444. 2 Act, 1713, C. 4.
3 Act, 1790, C. 23. 4 Bozman, p. 39, note.
5 Archives (Cl. Pro.) p. 62.
6 See Johnson's interesting monograph "Old Maryland Manors".

Manor, not only show the method of holding them, but also the scope and character of their jurisdiction. This record, which is carefully preserved in the Maryland Historical Society, and which is believed to be the only one of its kind extant, though heretofore published, is here reproduced in the following note :[2]

---

2   RECORDS OF THE
COURT LEET AND COURT BARON
OF ST. CLEMENT'S MANOR, 1659-72.

Sr CLEMENTS ⎫   A Court Leet & Court Baron of Thomas Gerard Esq$_r$
MANOUR   ⎬ ss there held on Thursday the xxviith of October 1659 by Jn$_o$ Ryves gent Steward there.

CONSTABLE: Richard ffoster Sworne.

RESIANTS: Arthur Delahay: Robt^e Cooper. Seth Tinsley: Willm at Robt^e Coles: Jno Gee Jno Green Benjamin Hamon Jno Mattant.

FFREHOLD^{RS}: Robt^e Sly gent: Willm Barton gent: Robt^e Cole: Luke Gardiner: Barthollomew Phillips: Christopher Carnall: Jno Norman: Jno Goldsmith.

LEASEHOLDERS: Thomas Jackson: Rowland Mace: Jno Shankes: Richard ffoster: Samuell Harris: John Mansell: Edward Turner: ffrancis Sutton with Jno Tennison.

JURY AND ⎫ Jno Mansell   ⎫   Jno Tennison   ⎫
HOMAGES ⎬ Bartholl: Phillips   ⎪   Jno Goldsmith   ⎪
            Jno Shankes   ⎪   Jno Mattant   ⎪
            Jno Gee   ⎬ Sworne   Sam: Harris   ⎬ Sworne
            Edward Turner   ⎪   Jno Norman   ⎪
            Seth Tinsley   ⎭   xofer Carnall   ⎭

ORDT AGT SAM: Wee the aboue named Jurors doe p^{r}sent to the Cou^{rt}
    HARRIS   that wee finde how about the 3^d day of octob^r 1659 that:

Jmprimis wee p^{r}sent that about the 3^d of October 1659 that Samuell Harris broke the peace wth a Stick and that there was bloudshed comitted by Samuell Harris on the body of John Mansell for wch hee is fined 40l tob wch is remitted de gratia dni.

    Wee doe find that Samuell Harris hath a license fro' the Gou'no^r & wee conceive him not fitt to be p^{r}sented.

ORD^R AGT ROBT^R Jtem wee p^{r}sent Robert Cole for marking one of the
    COLE   Lord of the Manno^{rs} hoggs for wch hee is fined 2000l Tobco affered to 1000l.

    Jtem wee p$_r$sent Luke Gardyner for catching two wild hoggs & not restouring the one halfe to the Lord of the Manno^r wh^{ch} he ought to haue done & for his contempt therein is fined 2000^l Tobco affered to 200l of Tobco.

Considering the large revenues that accrued to the lord of manor from the manorial courts, and the dignity incident to the exercise of the judicial powers attached to them, it may be safely assumed that they were held where ever the right to

---

Jtem wee p^rsent that Cove Mace about Easter last 1659 came to the house of John Shancks one of the Lord of the Manno^rs tenants being bloudy & said that Robin Coox & his wife were both vpon him & the said John Shancks desired John Gee to goe wth him to Clove Maces house & when they the s^d John Shancks & John Gee came to the said Cloves his house in the night & knocked att the dore asking how they did what they replyed then the s^d John Shancks & John Gee haue forgotten But the s^d John Shancks asked her to come to her husband & shee replyed that hee had abused Robin & her and the said John Shancks gott her consent to come the next morning & Robin vp to bee freinds wth her husband & as John Schanks taketh shee fell downe on her knees to be freinds wth her s^d husband but hee would not bee freinds wth her but the next night following they were freinds and Bartholomew Phillipps saith that shee related before that her husband threatened to beate her & said if hee did shee would cutt his throat or poyson him or make him away & said if ever Jo: Hart should come in agayne shee would gett John to bee revenged on him & beate him & hee heared the said William Asiter say th^t shee dranke healths to the Confusion of her husband and said she would shooe her horse round & hee the said Bartholomew Phillips heard the said Robin say if ever hee left the house Cloves should never goe wth a whole face. Jt is ordered that this businesse bee tranferred to the next County Co^rt according to Law.

Also wee present John Mansell fore entertayning Beniamyn Hamon & Cybill his wife as Jnmates Jt is therefore ordered that the s^d Mansell doe either remove his Jnmate or give security to save the pish (parish) harmless by the next Co^rt vnder payne of 1000^l Tobco^r.

Also we p^rsent Samuell Harris for the same and the same order is on him that is on John Mansell.

Also wee present the Freeholders that have made default in their appearing to forfeit 100^l Tobco apeice.

Wee doe further p^rsent that our Bounds are at this p^rsent unpfect & very obscure. Wherefore wth the consent of the Lord of the Manno^r Wee doe order that every man's land shall bee bounded marked and layed out betweene this & the next Co^rt by the p^resent Jury wth the assistance of the Lord vpon payne of 200^l Tobco for every man that shall make default.

do so existed, and where conditions suited ; though they appear to have given way to the early County courts at a comparatively early date.

ST. CLEMENTS MANNOR } sst At a Court Leet & Co^{rt} Baron of Thoms Gerard Esqr there held on thursday the 26th of Aprill 1660 by John Ryves Steward there

CONSTABLE Richard ffoster.

RESIANTS Robert Cowx William Roswell John Gee John Green Beniamin Hamon.

FREEHOLDERS: Robert Sly gent Will'm Barton gent Robt Cole Luke Gardiner Christopher Carnall John Norman John Goldsmith.

LEASEHOLDERS Thom's Jackson Richard ffoster Samuell Norris John Mansfeild Edward Turner John Shancks Arthur Delahy Clove Mace John Tennison

JURY AND HOMAGE
} Christopher Carnall
John Tennison
John Gee
Edward Turner
Beniamin Hamon
John Greene

Richard Smith
John Norman
John Love
George Harris
Willm Roswell
Walter Bartlett

Wee the above named Jurors doe p^{r}sent to the Co^{rt} Luke Gardiner for not doeing his Fealty to the Lord of the Manno^r Jt is ordered therefore that he is fined 1000^l of Tobcoe

Wee p^{r}sent fower Jndians, vizt
for breakinge into the Lord of the Manno^{rs} orchard whereof three them were taken & one ran away & they are fyned 20 arms length of Roneoke.

We p^{r}sent also two Jndian boys for being taken wth hoggs flesh & running away fro' it & they are fined 40 arms length.

Wee p^{r}sent also a Cheptico Jndian for entringe into Edward Turners house & stealinge a shirt fro' thence & hee is fined 20 arms length if he can be knowne

Wee p^{r}sent also Wickocomacoe Jndians for takeinge away Christopher Carnalls Cannowe fro' his landing & they are fyned 20 arms length if they bee found.

Wee p^{r}sent also the King of Cheptico for killing a wild sow & took her piggs & raysed a stock of them referred to the ho^{ble} Gounor.

Wee concieve that Jndians ought not to keepe hoggs for vnder p^{r}tence of them they may destroy all the hoggs belonginge to the Mannor & therefore they ought to bee warned now to destroy them else to bee fyned att the next Court   Referred to the ho^{ble} the Gou'no^r.

We reduce Luke Gardiners fyne to 50^l of Tobcoe

THE JUDICIAL SYSTEM

Before the Manorial Courts—the Court Leet and Court Baron—controversies between the residents of the manor and all important business relating to the manor, were determined.

Wee am'ce the fower Jndians to 50 arms Length of Roneoke & the Jndian that had his gun taken fro' him to bee restored agayne to the owner thereof

The Jndian boys wee am'ce 40 arms Length of Roneoke as they are above am'ced

Wee am'ce the Cheptico Jndian for stealing Edward Turners shirt to 20 arms length of Roneoke

Wee am'ce also Wickocomacoe Jndians for takeinge away Christopher Carnalls Cannowe to 20 arms Length of Roneoke

Memorand that John Mansfeild sonne of ——— Mansfeild deceased came into this Co——— did atturne tent to the Lord of this Mannor

St CLEMENTS \
MANNOR } A Court Leet & Court Baron of Thomas Gerrard esquire there held on Wednesday the Three & Twentieth of October 1661. by Thomas Mannyng Gent Steward there for this tyme

BAILIFF William Barton Gent.
CONSTABLE Raphael Haywood Gent
RESIANTS Mr Edmond Hanson George Bankes ffrancis Bellowes Tho: James John Gee Michaell Abbott.
FFREEHOLDERS Robt Sly Gent Will Barton Gent Luke Gardiner Gent, absent Robt. Cole Gent. Raphael Haywood Gent Bartho Phillips Gent.

JURY	Rich: ffoster		Robt Cole
	Edward Conoray		Bartho Philips
	Edward Runsdall		Edward Conovay
	John Shankes		Edward Ransdell
	John Knape		Gerett Brenton
	Gerett Brenson	JURY AND	Clobe Mace
	Clove Mace	HOMAGE	Edmond Hanson
	Robt Cooper		Robt Cooper
	Arthur De La huy		Arthur De La hay
	John Tenison		Wm Rosewell
			Tho; James
			Mich. James

[Several leaves of the record missing]

The Court adiorned till two of the Clocke in the afternoone.

John Gee and Rich. foster sworne

The Jury presents that Bartho: Phillips his Landes not marked and Bounded Round

The Jury Likewise present that the Land belonging to Robt Cooper and Gerett Breden is not marked and bounded Round

The Court Leet, was the court of the people. The steward of the manor presided, and the jury and officers were chosen from the residents of the manor, the attendance of all of whom, between the ages of twelve and sixty was required. It had jurisdiction over the police regulations of the manor, and

---

The Jury Presents Robt Cooper for Cutting of sedge on St Clements Jsland and fowling wthout Licence for wch he is Amerced 10^l of Tob. Affered to 10^l of Tob.

The Jury Present that Edward Conoray while he was Rich fosters servant did by accident worray or Lugg wth doggs on of the L^d of the mannor^s Hoggs and at another tyme Edward Conoray going to shoot at ducks the dog did Run at somebodys Hoggs but we know not whose they were and did Lugg them for wch the Jury doe Amerce Rich: ffoster 50^l of Tob Affered to 20^l of Tob

The Jury presents Mr Luke Gardiner for not appearing at the Lords Court Leet if he had sufficient warning

St Clements Manno^R ss A Court Leet of Thomas Gerard Esqr. there held on Thursday the eighth day of September 1670. by James Gaylard gent steward there.

Essoines: Benjamin Salley gent James Edmonds Richd Vpgate Capt Peter Lefebur these are essoined by reason they are sick and cannot attend to their suit.

ffreeholders: Justinian Gerard gent, Robt^e Sly gent, Thom Notley gent, Capt Luke Gardiner, Benjamin Salley gent, Robert Cole, Barthollomew Phillipps, Jno Bullock Wm Watts, James Edmonds, Richard Vpgate, Simon Rider, Jno Tenison, Rich^d ffoster, Edward Connory, Jno Shankes, Jno Blackiston,

Leaseholders: Robt^e Cowper Capt Peter Lefebnr, Henry Shadock, Richd Saunderson Jno Hoskins, Thomas Catline.

Resiants: Rich$_d$-Marsh, Joseph ffowler Roger Dwiggin Thom Casey, Jno Saunders, Henry Porter, ffrancis Moudeford Wm Simpson Wm Georges George B———es Wm West, Wm Cheshire, Jno Paler, Robte ffarrer George Keith, Joshua Lee James Green, Thom oakely, Jno Turner, Maunce Miles, Jno Dash W^m ffelstead Jn$_o$ Chauntry:

Jury	Rich^d ffoster		Jno Blackiston	
	Jno Tenison		Jno Stanley	
	Edward Connory	Sworne	Richd Saunderson	Sworne
	Robte Cowper		Jno Bullock	
	Thom Cattline		Thom oakely	
	Wm Watts		Jno Paler	

Bayliff Jno Shankes & Sworne.

offenses of a criminal nature, except those punishable with loss of life or limb, among them "such as have double measure, buy by the great and sell by the less; such as haunt taverns and no man knoweth whereon they do live; such as sleep by day and watch by night, and fare well and have nothing". It

---

PRESENTM^{TS}: Wee p^{r}sent that Barthollomew Phillips his land was not layd out according to order of Court formerly made wherefore he is fined one hundred pounds of tobacco & caske unto the Lord.

We p^{r}sent John Tenison for suffering his horse to destroy John Blakiston's Corne field.

We p^{r}sent that Jno Stanley and Henry Neale killed three marked hogs vpon the Lords Mano^r wch Capt Gardiner received wch hogs were not of Capt Gardiner's proper marke which is transferred to the next Provinciall Court, there to be determined according to the Law of the Province.

We p^{r}sent that Edward Connery killed or caused to be killed five wild hogs vpon the Lords Manor this was done by the Lords order and Liscense

We p^{r}sent that the Lord of the Manno^r hath not provided a paire of stocks, pillory, and Ducking Stoole Ordered that these Jnstrum^{ts} of Justice be provided by the next Court by a generall contribution throughout the Manor

We p^{t}sent That Edward Convery's land is not bounded in

We p^{r}sent that Thomas Rives hath fallen five or sixe timber trees vpon Richard ffosters land within this Mano^r referred till view may be had of Rives his Lease

We p^{r}sent That Robert Cowper's land is not bounded according to a former order for which he is fined 100^l tobco.

We p^{r}sent that Jno Blackiston hunted Jno Tenisons horses out of the sd Blackistons corne field fence which fence is proved to be insufficient by the oathes of Jno Hoskins and Daniell White

We p^{r}sent Richard ffoster to be Constable for this Mano^r for the yeare ensuing who is sworne accordingly.

We p^{r}sent that Jno Bullocks land is not bounded.

We p^{r}sent Mr Thomas Notly, Mr Justinian Gerard & Capt Luke Gardiner, ffreeholders of this Mano^r: for not a appearing to do their suit at the Lords Court wherefore they are amerced each man 50^l of tobacco to the lord

Jt is ordered That every mans land w^{thin} this Mannor whose bounds are vncertein be layd out before the next Co^{rt} in p^{r}sence of the greatest part of this Jury according to their severall Grants vnder penalty of 100^l tobco for every one that shall make default.

also exercised supervision over the trade on the manor," fixed the price of bread and ale ", and enforced its game laws and ordinances against the sale of impure food. It could not punish by imprisonment, but could impose fines, all of which went to the lord of the manor.

AFFEIR Thomas Catline } Sworne.
Willm Watts

S^T CLEMENTS } ss A Court Leet & Court Baron of Thomas Gerard
MANOR Esqr there held on Monday the 28th of October 1672 by James Gaylard gent Steward there,

ESSONIES

FFREEHOLDERS. Justinian Gerard gent Gerard Sly gent Thomas Notley gent Benjamine Sally gent Capt Luke Gardiner Robt^e Cole Bartholomew Philips Jno Bullock. Wm Watts James Edmonds Richard Vpgate Simon Rider John Tennison Richard ffoster Edward Connory Jno Shankes Jno Blackiston Thomas Jourdaine.

LEASEHOLDERS Capt Peter Lefebur Henry Shaddock Richard Saunderson Jno Hoskins Thomas Catline

RESIANTS Joseph ffowler Roger Dwiggin Henry Porter Wm Simpson William Georges Wm West Wm Cheshire Jno Paler Joshua Lee Maurice Miles Jn_o Dash W^m ffelstead Richard Chillman Robte Samson Henry Awsbury Jno Hammilton Wm Wilkinson Abraham Combes Willm Harrison Jno Rosewell Vincent Mansfeild Edward Williams Marmaduke Simson Nicholas Smith Humphry Willey James Traske Derby Dollovan Jno Vpgate Thomas Rives Michaell Williams Jno Sprigg Charles Rookes ffrancis Knott Richard Hart Willm Polfe Thomas Attaway James Green Jno Ball Thomas Liddiard Edward Bradbourne Jno Suttle Jno Lee Jno Barefoot ffrancis Wood.

JURY   W'^m Watts   } Sworne   Jno Bullock   } Sworne
       Jno Tennison   Thom oakly
       Jno Rosewell   Thom Jorden
       Jno Stanly   Jno Hoskins
       Richard Saunderson   Jno Paler
       ffrancis Knott   Vincent Mansfeild

Edward Bradbourne complaineth agt Jno Tennison that he unjustly deteineth from him 200^l tobco to the contrary whereof the s^d Tennison having in this Coart taken his oath the s^d Bradbourne is nonsuited.

We prsent Jno Dash for keeping hoggs & cattle upon this Mannor for wh^{ch} he is fined 1000^l tobco.

We prsent Henry Poulter for keeping of hoggs to the annoyance of the lord of the Mano^r. Ordered that he remove them within 12 days under paine of 400^l tobco & cask.

THE JUDICIAL SYSTEM 135

The pillory, ducking-stool, and stocks were the usual instruments of punishment. It would also make by-laws for the government of the manor, and elected the manor bailiffs, constables, assessors, and ale-tasters.

The Court Baron was the court of the freeholders, the jury being selected from that class exclusively, and before it were tried all matters in dispute between the lord of the manor and his tenants, as well as all questions of title, trespass, and bebt, between the tenants, and all other matters of a civil nature, relating to the general welfare of the manor.

We p^rsent the s^d Henry Poulter for keeping a Mare & foale upon this Mano^r to the annoyance of Jno Stanly ordered that he remove the s^d mare & foale wthin 12 daies vnder paine of 400^l of tobco & caske

We p^rsent Joshua Lee for injuring Jno Hoskins his hoggs by setting his doggs on them & tearing their eares & other hurts for which he is fined 100^l of tobco & caske

We p^rsent Humphry Willy for keeping a tipling house & selling his drink without a License at unlawfull rates for wch he is fined according to act of assembly in that case made & provided

We p^rsent Derby Dollovan for committing an Affray and Shedding blood in the house of the s^d Humphry Willy Ordered that the s^d Dolovan give suretys for the peace.

We p^rsent Wm Simpson for bringing hoggs into this Manor for which he is fined 3^l of tobco And ordered that he remove them in 10 days vnder paine of 300' of tobco & caske

We p^rsent Rob^{te} Samson & Henry Awsbury for selling drinke a^d unlawful rates for which they are each of them fined according to Act of Assembly.

We p^rsent Simon Rider for keeping an under tenant contrary to the teno^r of his Deed referred till view may be had of the s^d Deed.

We p^rsent that Raphaell Haywood hath aliened his ffreehold to Simon Rider upon wch alienacon there is a reliefe due to the lord.

We p^rsent an alienacon from James Edmonds to Thomas Oakely upon wch there is a Reliefe due to the lord and Oakely hath sworne fealty.

We p sent that upon the death of Mr Rob^{te} Sly there is a Releief due to the lord & that. Mr Gerard Sly is his next heire who hath sworne fealty accordingly

We p^rsent an alienacon from Thomas Catline to Anne Vpgate.

The extinction of Manorial Courts in Maryland, it has been suggested, was due to the introduction of slavery, with whom mannors could be made more profitable than with tenants, and with whom the system of private jurisdiction was no longer necessary.

"The Court Baron and Court Leet, having served their turn were cast aside. If they played no great part in the history of the State, they are interesting as an extinct species * * * connecting the life of the present with the life of the past".[1]

The Prerogative Court was the court for the probate of wills and for the administration of all matters testamentary. Until 1673, these were within the jurisdiction, concurrently, of the Provincial Court and the County Courts, but in that year Baltimore created the office of Commissary General, "for the probate of wills and granting of letters of administration

---

We p^rsent that upon the death of Richard Vpgate there is a Releife due to the lord & [Annie] Vpgate his relict is next heire.

We p^rsent Mr Nehemiah Blackiston tenant to the land formerly in possession of Robert Cowper Mr Blackiston hath sworne fealty accordingly

We p^rsent an alienacon from Wm Barton to Benjamine Sally gent upon wch there is a Releife due to the lord & Mr Sally hath sworne fealty to the lord.

We present an alienacon from Richard ffoster of pt of his ffreehold to Jno Blackiston upon which there is a Releife due to the lord

We p^rsent a Stray horse taken upon this Manor and delivered to the lord

We p^rsent Robte Cole for not making his appearance at this Court for which he is amerced 10^l of tobco affeired to 6^l of tobco.

We p^rsent Edward ———uder to be Constable for this yeare ensuing Sworne accordingly.

AFFEIRO^{RS} Wm Watts } Sworne.
          Jno Bullock }

1 "Old Maryland Manors", from which most of the data relating to Manorial Courts was obtained.

For an account of the manorial system in Maryland, see chapter, "The Land Tenure of Colonial Maryland."

within the whole Province", and with full power to adjudge and decree upon all matters and causes incidental thereto.[1] The Clerk of the Secretary of the Province was at the same time directed to deliver to the Commissary General, all records and papers relating to the testamentary business within the Province, which was accordingly done, and, in April, 1673, the Prerogative Court was formally opened.

It was a prototype of the old English court of that name, over which the Archbishop presided, it being his "prerogative" to take charge of all matters testamentary.

The Commissary General was required to hold court once in two months, or oftener, if necessary ; to conduct the proceedings "according to the laws of England, where no law of the Province prevailed", and he was invested with the same powers to enforce his orders and decrees as was possessed by the High Court of Chancery.[2]

It was also incumbent upon him to appoint a Deputy Commissary for each county who could probate wills, grant letters of administration in their respective counties, and pass accounts not exceeding £50 in money,[3] which, in 1763, was extended to £150 currency,[4] though, by special commission from the Commissary General, they could pass accounts without limitation as to amount.[5] They could not, however, decide any question in controversy, either as to the right of administration or the passing of accounts, all of which had to be submitted to the decision of the Commissary General.[6]

The Deputy Commissaries were required by rule of court, to make their returns to the Commissary General every two months, with a list of every paper filed within that period, and to transmit annually, a full list of all administrations granted,

---

1 Archives (Cl. Pro. 1673) p. 24.   2 Act, 1715, C. 39.   3 Ibid.
4 Act, 1763, C. 18.   5 Ibid.   6 Act, 1715, C. 39.

I

wills probated, and accounts passed, in their respective offices, as well, also, a "list of alienations of land", consisting of an abstract of each of said wills, giving the name, quantity, and location of the lands devised, and the name of the devisees.[1]

It was the practice, also, for the Deputies, after recording the wills probated in their respective counties, to transmit them, together with inventories, accounts, and distributions appertaining to the settlement of each estate, to the Commissary General, who placed them on record in the general office. As a result of this practice, owing to the destruction of the testamentary and other records in so many of the counties, the records of the Prerogative Court are among the most valuable in the Archives of the State.

The Commissary General was in turn required to transmit, within three months after final distribution, a copy thereof to the County Court of the county in which the estate was located, in order that such part of it as belonged to orphans could be under the supervision of that court.[2]

The Court held six terms a year, commencing on the second Tuesday of January, March, May, July, September, and November,[3] and it was supported by the fees of the office.[4]

From the decisions of this Court, an appeal could be taken within thirty days, to a Court of Delegates, appointed especially for the purpose, and whose decree was final.[5]

The Prerogative Court did not survive the Revolution, one of the earliest acts of the infant republic being to declare that under "the form of government assented to by the freemen of this State", it was intended that the Prerogative Court should be abolished. This was accordingly done, and an

---

1 Deputy Commissaries Guide, pp. 154, 155.
2 Act, 1715, C. 39.   3 Dep. Com. Guide, p. 154.
4 Act, 1763, C. 18.   5 Act, 1726, C. 9.

Orphans' Court, with a Register of Wills for each county, was instituted in its stead.[1]

The High Court of Chancery was not organized until 1661,[2] prior to which time the Governor and Council had exercised jurisdiction over all matters in equity. The Court was presided over by one judge, denominated Chancellor, who was appointed by the Proprietary.[3] Two associates, called Masters in Chancery, were appointed, as in England, to sit with him, until 1721, when that feature was abolished, after which the office of Master appears to have merged into that now known as Examiner.[4] The clerk of the court, called the the Register, was appointed by the Secretary of the Province.[5]

The Chancellor was made keeper of the Great Seal, and, as such, sealed all patents, commissions, writs, and other public instruments.[6] The emoluments of the office consisted of fees for each and all of his official acts, and which rendered it one of the most lucrative in the Province.[7]

In its earlier history, the Court held only four terms a year, but after 1719, it was, like the High Court of Chancery in England, presumed to be always open.[8]

The Court of Chancery had exclusive jurisdiction over all matters in Chancery, where the amount involved exceeded 1200 ℔s. of tobacco, or £5 in money,[9] and was co-extensive with the Province, but, after 1763, the County Courts had concurrent jurisdiction where the amount did not exceed £20 sterling, or 5,000 ℔s. of tobacco.[10] It also had exclusive jurisdiction over trust estates,[11] and was the only tribunal through

---

1 Act, 1777, C. 8.   2 Archives (Cl. Pro. 1661) p. 439.
3 Ibid, 1673, p. 12.   4 Bland, 2, pp. 54-60.
5 Archives (Cl. Pro. 1673) p. 24,   6 Ibid, 1677, p. 161; Act, 1763, C. 18.
7 Act, 1763, C. 18.   8 Bland, 1, p. 624; Ibid, 2, p. 59.
9 Act, 1715, C. 41.   10 Act, 1763, C. 22.   11 Act, 1773, C. 7.

which alimony was recoverable, though not until a late period did it have authority to decree a divorce.[1]

Decrees of the High Court of Chancery were subject to the same stay of execution for six months as judgments of the Courts of Common Law, when superseded in the same manner.[2]

While the Court of Chancery was established in Maryland from an early date, it was a long time before any provision was made looking to an appeal from its decisions, during which time its decrees, like those of the High Court of Chancery in England, originally, were final and conclusive.

Acts of Assembly were passed, from time to time, regulating appeals from the Courts of Common Law, but they were confined to appeals from those courts, and it was not until 1721, that provisions were made for an appeal from the Court of Chancery.[3] This Act restricted the right to appeal from "any decree of the Chancery Court", and did not extend to appeals from orders or decisions,[4] a right, indeed, which did not exist by virtue of any legislative enactment, until after the Revolution.[5]

Appeals from the Court of Chancery were to the Court of Appeals,[6] and were subject to the same rules and limitations applicable to the Courts of Common Law,[7] under which no appeal would lie to the Court of Appeals, unless the amount involved exceeded £50 sterling, or 10,000 ℔s. of tobacco.[8]

It was a remarkable fact, that none of the Acts of Assembly, regulating appeals in Chancery, prescribed any method for staying execution pending the appeal, the terms upon which the appeals might be granted, or the manner of

---

[1] Bland, 2, p. 566; Maryland Ch., 4, p. 293.
[2] Act, 1721, C. 4.
[3] Act, 1721, C. 14.
[4] Ibid; Cl. Pro. P. L. p. 595.
[5] Act, 1785, C. 72.
[6] Act, 1721, C. 14.
[7] Act, 1729, C. 3.
[8] Act, 1713, C. 4.

making up the record, as to all of which, before the revolution, the Court seems to have been governed by the rules and practice of the High Court of Chancery in England,[1] which in every particular it closely resembled.

Upon the adoption of the State Government, in 1777, the Court of Chancery was given constitutional recognition,[2] and under which, also, the Chancellor continued to be the keeper of the Great Seal of Maryland.[3]

A Court of Admiralty was erected in Maryland, in 1684. The order directing it, provided that it should consist of not less than four Judges, appointed by the Governor, and who were invested with full power, to try and condemn all ships or vessels found within the Province "transgressing against his Majestie's laws of navigation, and other laws relating to customs". The Court appointed its own clerk, and it was also authorized to appoint appraisers and summon juries.[4] It also had a Marshall, who, with the Judges and all other officials of the Court, were paid by fees[5] The Court of Admirality was continued after the revolution, but it consisted of one Judge only, a Register and Marshall, and sat at such places as the Court deemed most convenient for the trial of the cases before it.[6]

As early as 1732, Courts of Oyer, Terminer, and Gaol delivery, or as more commonly known, Courts of Assize, were established for the several counties of the Province, for the trial of crimes and offenses,[7] but in 1766, these were superseded by two Courts of Assize for the entire Province, one for the eastern and one for the western shore ; these Courts were

---

1 1 Bland, p. 15. 2 Constitution, Sec. 40.
3 Ibid, 36. 4 Archives (Cl. Pro. 1684) p. 360
5 Act. 1763, C. 18. 6 Hanson, Act, 1781, C. 29.
7 1st H. & McH. Maryland Reports, p. 83.

each presided over by a Justice appointed by the Governor, from the Judges of the Provincial Court ; one being appointed from each side of the Chesapeake Bay, and sat twice a year, in every county within their respective districts, for the trial of causes arising in said county.[1] The Justices were directed to make all necessary rules of Court and to enforce them by reasonable fines. The Sheriff of the county in which the court was being held was its executive officer. Fifty freeholders were summonsed, ten days before the court met, to serve as grand and petit jurors, who were subject to the same rules as those respecting jurors in the Provincial Court.

The jurisdiction of the Assize Courts was concurrent with the criminal jurisdiction of the Provincial Court, and extended to all crimes and offenses not cognizable in the County Courts, and to such, also, as were removed from the County Courts, a right specially given in criminal cases.[2] From their decisions an appeal would lie to the Provincial Court, upon bill of exceptions, which latter, unlike appeals in criminal cases, from other courts, was expressly granted in appeals from the Court of Assize.[3]

The Judges in the Assize Courts each received 7,000 ℔s. of tobacco for their compensation.[4]

The law under which these Courts were organized, was allowed to expire, in 1769,[5] and does not appear to have been revived before the revolution.

---

1 Act, 1766, C. 5.   2 Ibid.
3 Ibid ; 1st H. & Mc. H., Maryland Reports, p. 83.
4 Act, 1766, C. 5.   5 Hanson.

CHAPTER VII.

The Judicial System of Colonial Maryland.

THE Provincial Court of Maryland was, from the time of its organization to the American Revolution, the chief *nisi prius* court, and, for a long time, the chief appellate tribunal of the Province, and possessd all the powers of the highest English common law courts. It did not owe its origin to legislative enactment, but to commission from the Proprietary, by which the judges, in its earlier history, were appointed and its jurisdiction defined.[1] But the commission did not bestow upon it the name, nor did any Act of Assembly do so. The Court was simply established, and it was apparently called the Provincial Court, because its jurisdiction was co-extensive with the Province, and in distinction to the County Court, which was limited to a single county. The General Assembly indeed, thus referred to it, and so called it as early as 1642.[2] A plausible suggestion has been made, that, as it was at first, the Supreme Court of the Province; courtesy and common parlance bestowed upon it the name of the Provincial Court.[3]

The Justices of the Provincial Court, at first, were the Governor and the Council of the Province—the former being Chief Justice, and in his absence, the member of the Council, who stood next in commission to the Governor, presided.[4] It

---

1 Archives (Cl. Pro. 1637) p. 49.
2 Archives (Ass. Pro. 1642) pp. 147 to 152.
3 Bozman II, p. 304, note.   4 Archives (Cl. Pro. 1637) p. 53.

sometimes happened that, the Lord Proprietary was himself present, and on such occasions acted as Chief Judge of the court.[1]

Under the earliest commission, of which there is any record, the Governor, in most cases, could sit alone, it being necessary to have the council associated only in causes which involved a freehold, and in crimes which extended to life or member,[2] but after 1642, the Council constituted a part of the Court, in all cases, civil and criminal.[3] A quorum consisted of three Judges, including the Chief Judge,[4] or the one next in commission, though the records show that the attendance of the members of the council was usually large, due perhaps, in part, to the fact of their compensation being a per diem.

In 1692, the Provincial Court was organized as a distinct tribunal from the Governor and Council, and a Chief Judge with eight associates, constituted the bench. The first Judges under the new organization were commissioned by the Crown,[5] but subsequently they were appointed by the Governor, and held their office during good behavior, though nominally, its tenure was at will.[6] At a later period, it was strongly urged, that the bench of the Provincial Court, be reduced to a Chief Judge and four associates, and also that they be appointed, exclusively, from those learned in the law,[7] but this was not carried out, the reason assigned for the latter being, that "gentlemen of the law", could not be induced to serve, owing to the meagreness of the compensation attached to the office.[8]

---

[1] 4th, H. & McH Maryland Reports, p. 477.
[2] Archives (Cl. Pro. 1637) p. 53.
[3] Archives (Ass. Pro. 1642) p. 147.
[4] Archives (Cl. Pro. 1637) p. 53.
[5] Archives (Cl. Pro. 1692) p. 307.
[6] Archives, Sharpe's Cor. p. 7, 11.
[7] Ibid. [8] Ibid, p. 334.

While, however, not always learned in the law, the bench of the Provincial Court uniformly, had on it the best available talent within the Province, and steadily maintained a distinguished rank for dignity, character and sound administration of justice. Among the noted justices who were long associated with it, may be mentioned the names of Chief Justices Calvert, Brice and Hayward, and associates Addison, Brooke, Tench, Courts, Golbsborough, Henry, Mason, Darnall, Hall, Hooper, Weems, Bordley, Jennifer, Hands, Hepburn and Leeds.

The Provincial Court commonly sat at Saint Mary's while it was the seat of government, though, as a matter of public convenience, sessions of the court were sometimes held in other parts of the Province, but in 1699, Annapolis was made the seat of the court and the place also, where all of its writs and processes were returnable.[1] The Court was convened by the beat of a drum, until 1681, when a bell was procured for that purpose, and for convening the General Assembly.[2] The Clerk of the Provincial Court was appointed by the Secretary of the Province,[3] and the Sheriff of the County was its executive officer, both of whom, together with the Crier and Bailiff of the court, were paid by fees.[4] The justices of the Provincial Court were required to make all necessary rules for the proper government of the court, and to purchase for its use, the Statutes of England and Dalton's Justice.[5]

The jury for the Provincial Court was taken from the whole Province, every county being required to furnish two grand and three petit jurors, for each term of the court, who were selected and summonsed by the sheriffs of their respective

---

1 Act, 1699, C. 19.
2 Archives, Act, 1681, p. 144.
3 Archives, Cl. Pro. 1671, p. 23—136.
4 Act, 1763, C. 18.   5 Act, 1715, C. 41.

counties, and who were entitled to twenty days' notice.[1] In all other respects, the manner of selecting the jury of the Provincial Court, as well as the questions of disqualification and exemption from jury service, were determined by the same rule as those which prevailed in the County Courts, except that the penalty for failure to serve was larger—being 1,000 ℔s.[2] of tobacco—as was, also, their compensation, which, in the case of the grand jury, while within the discretion of the Court, might have been as much as 3,000 ℔s.[3] of tobacco a piece, per term, subsequently increased to 6,000 ℔s.,[4] and 48 ℔s. a piece for itinerant charges.[5] The petit jury received the same itinerant charges,[6] and 30 ℔s. of tobacco a piece, for each day of attendance,[7] subsequently increased to 48 ℔s.,[8] besides the 120 ℔s. allowed to the panel in each case in which they were sworn,[9] but later reduced to 96 ℔s.,[10] all of which was paid out of the public levy,[11] except the allowance to the panels of petit juries, which, as in the County Courts, was taxed as a part of the costs of the case.[12]

The law relating to witnesses before the Provincial Court, was the same as that applicable to them in the County Courts; except that their compensation was larger, being 40 ℔s. of tobacco per diem, and itinerant charges, collectable as witness fees in the County Courts;[13] except also, that before they could be amerced for failure to attend, their reasonable charges had to be tendered;[14] but fees of witnesses whom the Court deemed unnecessary, could not be taxed as a part of the

1 Act, 1715, C. 37.   2 Ibid.   3 Ibid.
4 Act, 1760, C. 16.   5 Ibid.   6 Ibid.
7 Act, 1715, C. 37.   8 Act, 1760, C. 16.
9 Act, 1719, C. 3.   10 Act, 1760, C. 16.
11 Act, 1715, C. 37.   12 Ibid ; Act, 1719, C. 3 ; Act, 1760, C. 16.
13 Act, 1715, C. 37.   14 Act, 1692, C. 16.

costs of the case, and in no instance could fees be taxed of more than three witnesses upon any one question of fact.¹ The Justices of the Provincial Court were also paid a per diem, their compensation being 140 ℔s. of tobacco and itinerant charges for each day of attendance, which was paid out of the public levy of the Province.² The terms of court were probably prescribed by rule of court, as no Act of Assembly or order of the Proprietary appears to have been passed for that purpose. Its terms were April, May, July, September, and October.³

Under the acts regulating practice in the Courts of the Province, continuances could not be allowed, unless stayed by injunction, beyond the fourth term after the appearance term, and should the case not be disposed of by that term, if through default of the plaintiff, it was to be dismissed with costs; if through default of the defendant, judgment was to be awarded to the plaintiff, and if through the counsel on either side, the attorney in default was subject to a forfeiture of 5,000 ℔s. of tobacco and the costs of the suit;⁴ but later this time was extended, when the court was sitting as an appelate tribunal, to the period of two years from the end of the appearance term.⁵ Where the plaintiff was desirous of a more speedy trial, and had a copy of the declaration and writ served upon the defendant twenty days before the appearance term, the court was required to compel the defendant to proceed to trial at that term, and upon failure to do so without sufficient cause, to enter judgment for the plaintiff.⁶

---

1 Act, 1760. C. 16.   2 Act, 1716, C. 11.
3 1st H. & McH. Maryland Reports; 4th Ibid Appendix.
4 Act, 1721, C. 14.
5 Act, 1730, C. 16.   6 Act, 1763, C. 23.

Causes were to be determined according to the "very right of the cause", and without regard to such ommissions and errors as are usually taken advantage of by special demurrer, but this did not apply to the writ or declaration in civil, or to the indictment and other process in criminal causes.

Attorney's fees were also regulated by the judicature Acts of the Province, the maximum fees for prosecuting cases in the Provincial Court, being 400 ℔s. of tobacco; in the Court of Appeals, Admiralty Court, and Court of Chancery, 600 ℔s., and in the County Courts, 100 ℔s., unless the judgment recovered exceeded 2,000 ℔s. of tobacco, in which case the sum of 200 ℔s. of tobacco could be charged.[1] The penalty for demanding or receiving larger fees than those prescribed by law, was disbarment.[2]

---

1 Act, 1715, C. 14.   2 Ibid.

No Attorney could practice before the Provincial Court or the Court of Chancery, prior to 1715, except those who were "admitted, nominated and sworn", by the Governor of the Province. They could, however, practice before the County Courts upon being admitted by the Judges thereof. After 1715, the right to admit to practice in the higher courts was no longer limited to the Governor, but was vested in the Judges of the several courts. The Courts were very exacting in requiring Attorneys to be regular and punctual in their attendance, and the records furnish repeated instances in which they were fined for failure in either respect. Under an order of the High Court of Chancery, any Attorney who failed to be in "Court by 8 of ye clock in Summer and 9 in Winter", was subject to a fine of ten shillings sterling for the first default; twenty, for the second, and disbarment for the third. (Archives Ass. Pro. 1674, p 467; Act, 1715, C. 48; Chancery Records, May 24th, 1697, p. 355.) The State's Attorneys, or his "Lordships Attorneys", as they were called, were appointed by the Attorney General of the Province, subject to confirmation by the Council, and frequently represented more than one county. Those appointed by Attorney General Robert Carville, in 1688, were, William Dent, for Saint Mary's, Charles, and Calvert; George Parker, for Anne Arundel; John Meriton, for Baltimore; Robert Smith, for Kent and Talbot; William Nowell, for Cecil; Thomas Pattison, for Dorchester, and James Sangster, for Somerset.—Archives (Cl. Pro. 1688) p. 18, 30.

If a plaintiff was defeated, or discontinued the action, he was subject to amerciament of 50 ℔s. of tobacco, if in the Provincial Court, to be applied as the Governor and Council saw fit, and 30 ℔s. of tobacco, if in the County Courts, to be applied to county charges. A like penalty was imposed upon every defeated defendant after imparlance (demanding time to plead), but this did not apply to defendants where the judgment was rendered at the appearance term, nor did it apply to executors, administrators, and minors, whether plaintiff or defendant.[1] Judgments obtained in the Provincial Courts, like judgments of the other Courts of the Province, were subject to a stay of execution for six months, provided the debtor furnished two sufficient suretors, who confessed judgment for the debt and costs.[2]

The Provincial Court was invested with both an original and appellate common law jurisdiction, and, until 1661, when the Court of Chancery was erected, it had jurisdiction, also, over the equity business of the Province. In its earlier history, it had original jurisdiction in all matters criminal and civil, and which was co-extensive with the Province.[3] This was entertained concurrently with the County Courts and the Assize Courts (as long as the latter continued to be a part of the judicial system), to the extent of the jurisdiction of those respective courts;[4] but, after 1692, the Provincial Court could only hold plea in cases in which the amount involved exceeded 1,500 ℔s. of tobacco,[5] and, in 1714, this limit was extended to £20 sterling, or 5,000 ℔s. of tobacco.[6]

In all other common law civil cases, its original jurisdiction was exclusive. Thus it stood, until 1773, when its original

---

[1] Act, 1722, C. 12.   [2] Acts, 1715, C. 33; 1721, C. 4.
[3] Archives (Cl. Pro. 1637) p. 49.
[4] Ibid, 1661, p. 22; Act, 1766, C. 5.
[5] Archives (Ass. Pro. 1692) p. 447.   [6] Act, 1714, C. 4.

jurisdiction was still further curtailed by being limited to cases involving not less than £100 sterling, or 30,000 ℔s. of tobacco, and the County Courts, at the same time, were invested with a general concurrent jurisdiction in all cases, civil and criminal.[1] The County Courts being so much more accessible, this Act, in effect, resulted largely in making them the Courts of first instance throughout the Province, except in cases of greater magnitude or of deeper gravity, and in correspondingly increasing the volume of business before the Provincial Court as an appellate tribunal. It was in its latter aspect that it stood out most conspicuously as the great central figure in Maryland's early judicial system.

For more than half a century the Provincial Court was the sole and exclusive appellate tribunal of the Province, except for appeals from Justices of the Peace and the Prerogative Court, and indeed, throughout its entire history, the records of its judicial work show that a large volume of business, for that period, was before it in its appellate capacity.

It is true, there was established during the protectorate in Maryland, and that it remained a permanent institution, the tribunal known as the Court of Appeals, presided over by the Governor and Council, and which was given exclusive jurisdiction over appeals from the High Court of Chancery;[2] but its common law jurisdiction was limited to appeals from the Provincial Court, when sitting as a court of first instance, and in which the amount involved exceeded £50 sterling, or 10,000 ℔s. of tobacco,[3] and as the County Courts appear to have been the active *nisi prius* courts of the Province, particularly after the enlargement of their jurisdiction from time to time, for civil, and the Assize Courts for criminal business, and over

---

1 Act, 1773, C. 1.   2 Act, 1713, C. 4; Act, 1721, C. 14.
3 Act, 1713, C. 4.

the decisions of which Courts the Provincial Court alone had appellate jurisdiction, the common law appeals before the Court of Appeals were necessarily limited in number.

It is here worthy of note, that the fact that the Court of Appeals, whose terms were February, May, July, September, and October,[1] heard cases during the sessions of the General Assembly, has led to the impression that the Legislature of Maryland also possessed appellate judicial powers, but this is an error, growing, perhaps, out of the fact that the Governor and Council constituted both the Upper House of Assembly and the Court of Appeals, and that when the terms of the two conflicted, the business of the Court was transacted during the term of the Assembly.[2]

The proceedings of the Provincial Court, as reported in the two volumes of the Maryland Archives, entitled "Provincial Court, 1636 to 1658", were cases which were before it as a court of first instance only, the latter date being the period at which it commenced to exercise its appellate jurisdiction,

---

[1] 1st and 4th H. & McH. Maryland Reports.

[2] The early records also furnish a few instances in which there was a further appeal to the King in Council, but while this right clearly existed by virtue both of Act of Assembly and proclamation, only a few cases are to be found in which it was exercised, owing, perhaps, to the complex rules governing such appeals and the costs incident thereto. This right was limited in civil causes to those in which the amount involved exceeded £300 sterling, and, in criminal cases, to those in which the fine imposed was above £200 sterling. The mode of ascertaining the value of the thing in controversy was regulated by rules established by the King. The appeal could only be from the court of last resort, and had to be taken within fourteen days and prosecuted within a year after the judgment or decree was rendered. A bond had, also, to be given to pay costs and damages in case the decision should be affirmed. On all reaching the English Court, the case was referred to the "Committee on Appeals from the Plantations", who appointed the time and place of hearing, and reported its decision to the King in Council, by whom it was formally ratified.—Bland, 1, p. 570, note; 1st H. & McH. Maryland Reports, pp. 57, 91; 2d Ibid, pp. 324, 346.

its proceedings as such having been largely reported in the first and fourth volumes of Harris and McHenry's Maryland Reports. And, in this connection, it should also be noted that to Maryland belongs the distinction of possessing the most ancient series of reported cases on this side of the Atlantic, the next oldest being Jefferson's Virginia Reports, Dallas' Pennsylvania, and Quincey's Massachusetts Reports, and which begin, respectively, in 1730, 1754, and 1763.

The earliest Act relating to appeals in Maryland, was in 1642, under which the right of appeal was without limitation, the appellant being simply required to give security to prosecute the appeal and to abide by the decision of the superior court.[1] It did not, however, seem to encourage the exercise of the right, since the Court could award "double damages" to the party aggrieved, if it found "no cause of appeal",[2] though no cases are of record in which such damages were awarded.

The next, was the Act of 1678, and which required the appellant to first file a bond in double the amount of the judgment, not only to prosecute the appeal, but to pay the judgment, if affirmed, together with such damages as the Court should award for the delay.[3] The bond served the further purpose of staying the execution pending the appeal. This Act also provided the easy method of appeal by a simple transcript of the record, under the hand of the Clerk and Seal of the Court—the one in practice in Maryland to-day—as contradistinguished from the more complex system by writ of error, though the latter method was also allowed.

The Act of 1692 imposed the first limitation upon the right of appeal, and which restricted it to cases in which

---

[1] Act, 1642, C. 6.   [2] Ibid.
[3] Archives (Ass. Pro. 1678) p. 71.

the amount involved was equal to, or exceeded 1200 ℔s. of tobacco.¹ In 1713, provision was made for the first time for appeal from the Provincial Court, in the exercise of its original jurisdiction, to the Court of Appeals. The Act provided for the right of appeal from the County Courts to the Provincial Court, where the debt or damages amounted to £6 sterling, and from the Provincial Court to the Court of Appeals, where the debt or damages amounted to £50 sterling.² This Act of 1713, and which continued in force until the Revolution, repealed all former Acts regulating appeals from the courts of common law, but reenacted the provisions contained in them relating to the method of appeal and the appeal bond. But these, it was held, did not apply to criminal causes, which could only be reviewed by the Superior Court upon the common law writ of error,³ except that bills of exception were allowed in appeals from the Assize Courts, for which provision was expressly made.⁴ The time in which an appeal could be taken was, presumably, fixed by rule of court, the Acts of Assembly being silent upon the subject.

Under the Constitution of 1776, the Provincial Court was abolished, and the Court known as the General Court, and presided over by three Judges of "integrity and sound judgment in law",⁵ the terms of which were April and September, for the Eastern, and May and October, for the Western Shore,⁶ was established in its stead.

The General Court was, in turn, abolished in 1805, when, upon the reorganization of the courts of the State, the County Courts were given its original, and the Court of Appeals, its appellate jurisdiction.⁷

---
1 Archives (Ass. Pro. 1692) p. 444.   2 Act, 1713, C. 4.
3 5th H. and J. Maryland Reports, pp. 234, 329 ; 9th G and J. p. 76.
4 1st H. and McH. p. 83 ; Act, 1766, C. 5.   5 Const., Art. 56.
6 Act, 1777, C. 15.   7 Act, 1805, C. 16.

J

Thus was swept away, by the waves of Revolution, that ancient monument of Maryland's Colonial Judicial System. For more than a century and a quarter, the Provincial Court was the chief judicial tribunal of the Province, and which, amid all the political fermentations and religious turmoils of its time, steadily went on in the even pathway of duty, performing the high functions committed to it, without fear and without reproach, exploring and marking throughout its domain in the new world, the great highways of the law, and building up a code of jurisprudence as a bulwark of security to Maryland and her people, both as a colony and as a State.

This treatise cannot be better concluded than by subjoining the following extracts from the admirable paper of the Honorable Charles E. Phelps, Judge of the Supreme Bench of Baltimore City, read before the State Bar Association, in 1897, entitled "Some Characteristics of the Provincial Judiciary":

Perhaps the first impression made upon the mind of the lawyer who looks through the old (Maryland) reports is the entire absence of anything like judicial reasoning. The conclusion reached by the court is uniformly expressed in the briefest formula, with no attempt at what is called an opinion. This remark is applicable not only to the cases decided by the Provincial Court, but also to cases in the Court of Appeals, and to the few probate cases appealed from the Commissary General or Prerogative Court to the Court of Delegates. This absence of judicial reasoning leads to the suspicion that the judges of that day were not lawyers by profession.

There exists direct evidence to this effect in the observations of the celebrated Daniel Dulany, upon the judgment of the Provincial Court, in the case of West vs. Stigar, 1 H. & McH., 247 (1767). The dissatisfied counsel in that case, pending, or in anticipation of a writ of error, applied to Mr.

Dulany, the great oracle of the day, for his opinion, and elicited a very full one, beginning as follows:

"On perusing the record, I am strongly of the opinion that the judgment of the Provincial Court ought to be reversed, but what may be the opinion of the Court of Appeals I should be more confident in predicting, if the judges were lawyers by profession, than I am on consideration that they are not." * * * *

From the circumstance which indirectly suggested this digression, the non-professional character of the provincial judges, it might be inferred that their decisions upon general principles have not been regarded as entitled to the same authority as those upon the construction of provincial statutes or customs. The same was the case in Virginia, where, as we learn from Mr. Jefferson, in the preface to his reports, the General Court consisted of the "King's Privy Counsellors only, chosen from among the gentlemon of the country for their wealth and standing, without any regard to legal knowledge". He remarks that their decisions on English law were not as authorative as those on the peculiar laws of Virginia. "As precedents," he adds, "they established the construction of our own enactments, and gave them the shape and meaning under which our property has ever since been transmitted, and is regulated and held to this day." * * * *

A less attractive feature of the provincial judiciary than even their want of legal learning, was their lack of official independence. Like all other provincial incumbents, the provincial judges, from the highest to the lowest, held their positions at the pleasure of the appointing power, the Proprietor, or his deputy, the Governor, for the time being. They were, consequently, looked upon as his creatures, or as Mr. McMahon expresses it, as his "satellites", "the mere breath of his nostrils".[1] In all controversies in which the interests of the Proprietor, or even the private interests of his dependents or favorites were involved, they occupied a weak and most unfortunate position. Whether justly or not, they were always liable to the suspicion of influence and favoritism. This habitual and suspected attitude of the Provincial Judges as minions of power could not fail to make a deep and lasting impression upon Maryland public opinion. All eyes were naturally turned to the jury as the real bulwark of public and private rights. Although summoned by sheriffs, who were themselves also removable at pleasure, jurors naturally shared the sentiments and reflected the opinions of the mass of the community from which they were drawn, and into which they were speedily to dissolve. Traditional confidence in the jury and jealousy of the court has in Maryland found organic expression in the provision, in sharp contrast with the federal jurisprudence of the United States, that "in the trial of all criminal cases the jury shall be the judges of law, as well as of fact".[2]

It has left other deep and permanent traces upon the daily practice in all our courts. The usage which prevails in England and in many of these States, both in civil and criminal cases, of a summing up of the evidence in a charge by the court has no existence in Maryland, where anything in the nature of a judicial balancing of evidence, or comment upon the weight of the testimony or the credibility of witnesses is scrupulously avoided. In criminal cases the court, as a rule, does not undertake to instruct the jury as to the law at all, even at the request of counsel, and when the court does advise

---

[1] McMahon, pp. 157, 309-311; Calvert vs. Eden, 2 H. & McH. pp. 345-360.

[2] Constitution, Art. 15, Sec. 5.

the jury, at their own request, such opinion is always carefully guarded by some expression to show that it is not to be taken as binding, but as advisory only.

Considering the length of time it has been under fire, and the storm of abuse which for many ages it has provoked from defeated litigants, the venerable palladium not only still lives, but may be congratulated on presenting a remarkably healthy and robust appearance.

While to the lessons of provincial experience can be distinctly traced, the trend of public opinion in Maryland, in securing the independence of the jury from the possible undue influence of the court, account is to be taken of the same provincial tradition, as a factor in the development of the peculiar sensitiveness of our people, as respects the independence of their judges from undue influence of power. In no State is the popular nerve more acute, or the popular instinct more alert to the danger and disaster incident to the possible prostitution of such delicate and far-reaching functions, as those necessarily confided to the courts of law and equity. * *

The two negative characteristics of the Provinciul Judiciary that have been referred to, their want both of professional training and of official independance, have left an affirmative stamp upon the organic law of Maryland in two well known provisions respecting the qualifications of judges.[1]

In like manner the provisions in the Declaration of Rights (Art 8) requiring the separation of the three departments of government, stands in sharp contrast with the fundamental policy of the provincial organism. Here we find a curious state of things, from the modern standpoint, powers legislative, executive, and judicial, confounded together and massed in the same man, or set of men.

---

[1] Declaration of Rights, Art. xxxiii; Constitution, Art. 14, Sec. 2.

The Governor and his Executive Council composed, at the same time, the Upper House of the General Assembly. They had, in addition, the exclusive legislative power in certain cases. The Governor was (in the very early history of the Province) at the same time Chief Justice and Chancellor, as well as Lieutenant-General and Admiral. The members of the Council were at the same time judges of the Provincial Court, Judges of the Court of Appeals, and, in the infancy of the Province, Judges of the County Court of the oldest county. The Commissary General having, under the name of the Prerogative Court, probate jurisdiction with the appointment of a deputy in each county, was usually a councillor. From the councillors were generally appointed the Court of Delegates, a special and occassional Appellate Court of Probate. From the councillors were also commissioned in part, although not exclusively, the special and temporary Courts of Assize, of Oyer and Terminer, and General Gaol Delivery for the several counties. The Judges of the Land Office, when the tribunal was established, were often also councillors. In fact, above the rank of Justices of the Peace and County Commissioners, who held the County Courts, the whole body of the Provincial Judiciary served, at the same time, as Legislators and Executive Councillors.

Nor did this remarkable blending of powers stop here. The most important and lucrative fiscal and administrative functions were engrossed by the same body. They furnished the principal officeholders of the Province. It was natural and it was customary that the Proprietor's relatives and friends should be provided for in this way. All officials were supported by fees. For instance, the Chancellor's fee for sealing every decree was at one time fixed at two pounds currency, or four hundred and eighty pounds tobacco, and half as much for every injunction. The Secretary, who acted as Registrar of the Court of Chancery, was allowed forty pounds tobacco for every bill filed, and as much "for every court the same shall continue",[1] and so on.

The custom of the Proprietor to increase his revenue by exacting a bonus from the holders of lucrative offices, caused a constant tendency to the imposition of excessive fees along the whole line. This became a standing subject of complaint, and of frequent struggle between the two houses. The Upper House, composed of the beneficiaries of extortion, resisted as long as possible, the efforts of the Burgesses to accomplish the definite legal regulation of fees. When established by law, but exceeded in practice, appeals to the courts for redress often failed, from the fact that the Judges were themselves either the offending parties, or else closely allied with them.

Another grievance was found in the stubborn resistance, for some time interposed by the Upper House, to attempts at limiting a pecuniary minimum to the jurisdiction of the Provincial Court, and conferring upon the County Courts exclusive original jurisdiction in petty cases. It was, naturally, felt to be an altogether needless and oppressive hardship, that in such small cases, parties and witnesses should be compelled to travel long distances to obtain justice. But the Upper House was composed of the Judges of the Court whose emoluments were in question, and the self-interest of a privileged class for a long time prevailed over the public welfare.

These and similar causes of dissatisfaction and friction furnished an object lesson in the science of government which contributed more than the abstract speculations of Montesquieu, to the establishment, at the Revolution, of the wholesome principle which forbids the mischievous concentration in

---

[1] Archives (Ass. Pro. 1676) pp. 532-534.

the same hands, of powers, in their nature, distinct and independant.

They also furnish a practical commentary upon that provision in the Declaration of Rights (Article 33), which forbids a Judge from holding any other office, or receiving fees or perquisites.

It is as easy to trace these articles of the Declaration of Rights to the abuses mentioned, as it is to find in the peculiar Maryland prohibition of a poll-tax, (Art. 15) a direct origin in the exasperating provincial " forty per poll " levied for the support of the established church.

That these were serious defects in the scheme of government as practically worked out under the rule of the Proprietors, there can, of course, be no doubt. It was blemished by pluralism, by nepotism, by venality, by an undue susceptibility to influence in the administration of justice, by want of capacity in the judicial corps. These defects have received but scant notice from historians. They have been thrown into the shade by those far more familiar and fascinating features which have attracted so much admiring attention to early Provincial Maryland as the cradle of religious liberty, and to later Provincial Maryland as the nursery of civil liberty and of revolutionary heroes.

While, therefore, all proper weight is to be accorded to, and all necessary instruction derived from such criticism as may be well taken, no hasty judgment is to be pronounced upon the Proprietors. These faults were mainly those of the age, or those incident to the novel circumstances under which the experiment was made. The whole anomalous situation has been aptly summed up as an "aristocratic government overshadowing the sleeping germ of democracy".[1]

---

[1] McSherry's, p. 177.

THE JUDICIAL SYSTEM

Candor compels the reluctant confession that the record of the Provincial Judiciary System, in one important detail, compares favorably with the practical administration of criminal justice in some parts of Maryland upon the eve of the twentieth century.

There were, it is true, shortly after the original settlement, and before the regular tribunals were fairly in the saddle, some rather eccentric proceedings at old Saint Mary's, resulting in capital executions for piracy and murder. But these were conducted in solemn form, before the Assembly of Freemen, constituting itself a court, *pro hac vice*, and had none of the revolting marks of tumultuous and irresponsible mob violence. It is also true, that during the transition period of revolutionary overthrow of the Provincial Government, there did occur fierce political outbreaks which ceased however with the re-establishment of law and order under the Republic. * * * *

The Provincial Judges, if not lawyers, were, as a rule, at least men of worth and probity, of standing and substance, and of more or less liberal education. If they belonged to a priviledged class, they had at least the conscience, the generous impulses, and the self-respect of their class. We hear no charges of bald corruption even in the most excited manifestoes of insurrectionary violence. For one hundred and forty years, through stormy vicissitudes in State and church, the long procession of provincial judges moved on, dispensing justice to successive generations, if not with conspicuous learning and ability, at least with humanity, moderation, and good sense.

Their deficiency in technical knowledge was to a considerable extent supplemented by the efforts of the professional gentlemen who practised before them, and who have left not only traditional, but recorded evidence of their worthiness to head the long and illustrious line of the Maryland Bar. While the appointment of lay judges was the rule, the rule was not altogether without exceptions, as in the case of Lewger, Gerrard, Jenings, and of the two Dulanys, father and son. Such exceptional appointments have fortunately left a few brilliant names to illustrate the obscure annals of the Provincial Judiciary. If they handed down to the veneration of posterity no constellation of great names like those of Hale, Mansfield, Marshall, and Taney, the Maryland contemporaries of Scroggs and Jeffreys furnished at least no parallel to their bad fame. Their administration of individual justice appears to have been sufficiently impartial, and as between party and party, they may be assumed to have poised the scales with an even hand.

CHAPTER VIII.

Some Characteristics of the Maryland Establishment.

THE history of the Protestant Episcopal Church and church law in Maryland, falls naturally into three divisions: First, from the settlement of the Province to the English Revolution, of 1688; second, from the English Revolution, of 1688, to the American Revolution, of 1776; and, third, from the American Revolution, of 1776, to the present day.

In the first of these periods there was almost no church in the Province. In 1642, it is said there was not one Protestant clergymen in Maryland.[2] On May 25, 1676, the Rev. John Yeo, a clergymen of the Church of England, who

---

[1] This Chapter consists principally of the brief filed by the author and his associates (who have courteously consented to its use in this connection), in the Court of Appeals of Maryland, in the case of Saint Matthew's Parish vs. Rev. F. S. Hipkins, and reported in vol. 75, Maryland Reports, p. 5, etc. The associate counsel in the case, on the part of the parish, were the Honorable Henry E. Davis, Governor Wm. Pinkney White, and Henry Wise Garnet, to each and all of whom the fullest recognition is accorded and acknowledgment made, and particularly to the indefatigable Davis, to whose profound learning and logic, as displayed in the preparation of the brief, special credit and honor are due. Though a large number of the briefs were printed at the time, the demand was in excess of the supply, and the reproduction here of the historic parts of it has been strongly urged.

[2] Winsor's History of America, Vol. III. p. 531. Neil, the Founders of Maryland, pp. 96, 99, 100.

had arrived in Maryland the year before, wrote his well-known letter to the Archbishop of Canterbury, complaining that there were then in the Province "but three Protestant ministers of us that are comformable to the doctrine and discipline of the Church of England ".[1]

Yeo's letter was referred to the Bishop of London, who in turn, referred it to Lord Baltimore, with an application that some provision be made for a Protestant ministry. To this application Baltimore replied that the Act of 1649, concerning religion, tolerated and protected every sect, and added that four ministers of the Church of England were in possession of plantations which offered them a decent subsistence, and that from the various religious tenets of the members of the assembly it would be extremely difficult, if not impossible to induce it to consent to a law that should oblige any sect to maintain other ministers than its own.[2] The privy council, however, directed that some provision should be made for the ministry of the Church of England, but nothing was done, although Baltimore returned to Maryland in 1680.[3]

The situation thus revealed shows how much use Baltimore was disposed to make of the power given him by his charter, the fourth section of which granted him "the patronages and advowsons', of all churches which should be built in the Province," together with license and faculty of erecting and founding churches, chapels, and places of worship * * * and of causing the same to be dedicated and consecrated

---

[1] Neill, p. 148.

[2] But then there were at this time three Protestant churches, one on Trinity (now Smith's) creek; Saint Georges church, now Poplar Hill; and one on Saint Paul's creek, now Church Run, on Saint Clement's Manor. The first permanent minister, however, of the Church of England—Rev. William Wilkinson—did not arrive until 1650. Allen, "Who were the early settlers of Maryland "; " Day Star ", p. 145.

[2] Neill, p. 151.   [3] Winsor, p. 547.

THE CHURCH ESTABLISHMENT 165

according to the ecclesiastical laws of our Kingdom of England ".

Nor was there any church law save the "Toleration Act", the purport of which was only to guarantee religious liberty. The Province had made none, and the English ecclesiastical law never had a place in Maryland's church system.

In a word, then, there was in Maryland prior to the Revolution of 1688, neither church nor church law worthy of consideration. But the events of 1688 in England had a direct and almost immediate effect upon the Maryland church, resulting, first, in the recognition of William and Mary (1692, chap. 1), and, secondly, in the passage of the Act of 1692, chap. 2. (The different views taken of the causes and purpose of this latter Act do not now concern us, but the curious on the subject may consult with interest Browne's Maryland, pp. 185, 190 *et seq;* Doyle's English Colonies in America, first volume, pp. 319-320; Lodge's English Colonies in America, pp. 119 *et seq;* Davis' Day - Star, pp. 87 *et seq:* McMahon's Maryland, 237 *et seq*).

The Act of 1692, chapter 2, which may be said to mark the beginning of the second of the periods above indicated, is entitled " An act for the service of Almighty God and the establishment of the Protestant religion in this Province."

Bacon says of it : " This Act laid the first foundation for the establishment of the Protestant religion in this Province and contains many notable particulars relating to parochial rights obtained under it ". He proceeds to give an abstract of its provisions, of which those material to our inquiry are as follows :

"(1). That the Church of England, within this Province, shall have and enjoy all her Rights, Liberties and Franchises as now is, or hereafter shall be, established by law :

And, also, that the Great Charter of England be kept and observed in all Points.

"(3). The County Justices to meet, by Appointment, at their respective County Court-Houses, giving Notice to the principal Freeholders to attend them, * * * * and there, with the advice of the said principal Freeholders, lay out their several Counties into Parishes, * * * * to be entered upon record. * * * *

"(4). The several Parishes being thus limited, the Freeholders of each parish to meet, by Appointment of the Justices of the County Courts, and make choice of six Vestrymen, who shall have a clerk to take Accounts, &c., and with the first Tobaccos, Wares, Goods, &c., by this Act, or any other Ways or Means whatsoever, given, granted, raised or allowed to the use of the Church or Ministry of the said Parish to which they belong, shall erect and build one Church, &c., in the Parish (such Parishes as have already Churches and Chapels built in them excepted). * * * *

"(5). Forty per Poll, deducting 5 per Cent. for the Sheriff's salary, on all Taxables; which Tobacco so raised (after building a Church or Chapel within Each Parish) to be appropriated and applied by the Vestrymen, to the Use and Benefit of the Minister. But if no Minister be Inducted, then to be laid out for the necessary Reparation of the Churches, or other pious Uses, at the discretion of the Vestry.

"(6). The Vestry were impowered to take Possession of Any Bequests, Grants, &c. by any Persons piously inclined, * * * and apply the same to the Use and Intent of the Donor or Donors.

"(7). The Vestries impowered to prosecute and maintain any Actions whatsoever, real, personal or mixed, for the Recovery of all or any of the Premises aforesaid, from any

Persons detaining any Goods or Chattels, Tenements or Hereditaments given and granted, and otherwise appointed to the uses aforesaid, and for any Damages, Tresspasses, &c., as amply as a Body Politic, or Corporate, might or could do, for recovering and preserving the Premises aforesaid : The principal Vestryman, with other of the Vestrymen, to be mentioned in the Writ and Declaration, and other Proceedings.

"(8). On Death or Removal of any Vestryman, the other Vestrymen, at their next Meeting, were impowered to chuse another in his Room, &c."[1]

An Act, entitled "An Additional Act to the Act for Religion", was passed October 18, 1694, and another, with the same title, was passed May 22, 1695. Bacon gives none of the provisions of either of these Acts, stating that both were repealed by Act of 1696, chapter 18.

This Act of 1696, bears the same title as that of 1692, and purported to repeal the latter as well as the Act of 1695. The Act of 1694 is not mentioned, probably because it was, in terms, limited in its operation to the period of three years.

The King dissented to the Act of 1696, on November 30, 1699, assigning as a reason that "therein is a clause declaring all the laws of England to be in force in Maryland ; which clause is of another nature than that which is set forth by the title in the said law".[2]

---

[1] The Vestry acted for the State in the erection and care of church buildings, and as preservers of the peace within the limits of the church and church yard. Later, other functions were added, such as choosing of counters to prevent the excessive production of tobacco, the nomination of inspectors of tobacco for the warehouses within their parishes, and of reporting persons liable to be taxed as bachelors. Vestrymen and church wardens were subject to a fine for refusing to act.—Church Life in Colonial Maryland.

[2] Bacon.

The objectional clause provided as follows:

"That the Church of England, within this Province, shall Enjoy all and Singular her Rights, Priviliges and Freedoms, as it is now, or shall be, at any Time hereafter, established by Law in the Kingdom of England: And that his Majesty's Subjects of this Province shall enjoy all their Rights and Liberties, according to the Laws and Statutes of the Kingdom of England, in all Matters and Causes, where the Laws of this Province are Silent."

On the King's dissent to the Act of 1696, and within six months thereafter, namely, on May 9, 1700, another Act was passed, entitled, "An Act for the Service of Almighty God and Establishment of Religion in this Province according to the Church of England".[1] This Act was likewise disapproved by the King, and was returned, as Bacon says, "with amendments proposed which were accepted, and an Act, pursuant thereto, passed the 25th of March, 1702, whereby this Act was repealed".

The Act of 1702,[2] is entitled "an Act for the establishment of religious worship in this Province, according to the Church of England, and for the Maintenance of Ministers". It is printed in full by Bacon, and contains twenty-two sections. Its material provisions are as follows:

"That the Book of Common Prayer and Administration of the Sacraments, with other Rites and Ceremonies of the Church, according to the use of the Church of England, the Psalter or Psalms of David, and Morning and Evening Prayer therein Contained, be solemnly read by all and every Minister or Reader in every Church which now is, or hereafter shall be settled and established in this Province; and that all Congregations and Places of Public Worship, according to

---

[1] 1700, Chapter 1.   [2] Chapter, 1.

the Usage of the Church of England, within this Province, for the Maintenance of whose Ministers and the Persons officiating therein, any certain Income or Revenue is, or shall, by the Laws of this Province, be established and enjoined to be raised or paid, shall be deemed settled and established churches ".[1]

" That a Tax or Assessment of Forty Pounds of Tobacco per Poll be yearly and every Year successively levied upon every taxable Person within each respective Parish, * * * * which said Assessment, of Forty Pounds of Tobacco per Poll, shall always be paid and allowed to the Minister of each respective Parish, having no other Benefice to officiate in, *presented, inducted, or appointed by his Excellency the Governor, or Commander in Chief, for the Time being.*[2] * * * *

" That Marriages forbidden by the Table of Marriages of the Church of England be not performed, under penalty, and that no marriage be performed by a layman in any Parish where a Minister or Incumbent shall reside.[3]

" That the Sheriff shall collect the Forty per Poll and pay over the same to the Minister or Incumbent in each respective Parish.[4]

" And the better to promote the execution of the good Laws of this Province, so far as concerns the respective Parishes, and for the more easy Dispatch of Parish business, * * * * that there be select Vestries in each Parish of this Province, and that the several Vestrymen of the several Parishes within this Province, that now are, or hereafter shall be chosen by such select Vestry, of which Vestry the Number shall always be six at least, except upon Death or Resignation, or other Discharge of any of them according to the Provision herein made to that Purpose ; and in such Case of Death or

---

[1] Act, 1702, C. 1, Section 2.
[2] Ibid, Section 3.
[3] Ibid, Sections 4, 5.
[4] Ibid, Section 6.

Resignation, or other legal Discharge from serving, the remaining Part of such Vestries shall, with all Convenient Speed, summon and appoint a general Meeting of all the Inhabitants of the said Parish, who are Freeholders within the same Parish and contribute to the Public Taxes and Charges of the said Parish. who shall, by Majority of Voices, elect and choose one or more sober and discreet Person or Persons, Freeholders of each respective Parish, to supply such Vacancies.[1] * * * *

"That two new Vestrymen shall be annually chosen, in the Places of two others, who shall be left out; to which Purpose, all the Inhabitants of every Parish, being Freeholders within the same Parish, and contributing to the Public Taxes and Charges thereof, or such of them as shall think fit to attend, shall repair to their respective Parish Churches, every Year successively upon Easter Monday, and there, by their free choice, declare what two Persons shall be discharged from their being Vestrymen, and choose two others, qualified according to this present Act, in their Stead and Room; who taking the Oaths and performing all other Thing required by this present Act, or other Laws of this Province, for Vestrymen, shall be deemed and taken to be Members of the said Vestry, to all Intents and Purposes: *Provided always*, That in every Parish where any Minister or Incumbent is, or shall be lawfully, *according to the Laws and Usages of this Province* appointed *and in Possession of any Living, invested with the Forty Pounds per Poll, and residing therein*, he shall *during the Continuance aforesaid*, and no longer, be one of the Vestry of such Parish, and Principal of such Vestry, although there be the number of Six Persons, or more, besides".[2]

---

[1] Ibid, Section 7. The remainder of the section prescribes the vestrymen's oaths. [2] Ibid, Sections, 8, 9.

THE CHURCH ESTABLISHMENT

"That each Vestry shall appoint a Register to make due entry of Vestry Proceedings, Births, Marriages, and Burials, &c., and provide Books accordingly, under penalty.[1]

"That each Vestry shall meet once a month, &c., under penalty.[2]

"That tables of Marriages be set up in the several Parish Churches.[3]

"That the said Vestrymen, and the rest of the Inhabitants of every Parish, being Freeholders within the same Parish, and contributing to the Public Taxes and Charges there, do once every year, upon Easter-Monday, Yearly, make choice and appoint two sober and discreet Persons, Freeholders

---

[1] Ibid, Sections 10, 11.

The following is the decision in the Saint Margaret's Vestry case, Annapolis, Maryland, involving the interesting question of the rights and duties of a Parish Register in Maryland, decided January 29, 1894, by Revell, J.

"The petition in this case was filed on the 11th of February, 1893, alleging in detail that the relator had all the necessary qualifications entitling him to enrollment on the parish books and to the right of suffrage in the election of vestrymen of the parish; that the enrollment was necessary to enable him to participate in the election of vestrymen at the next election, to be held on Easter Monday following, April 3, 1893; that the register was fully informed of the qualifications of the relator, but refused an application made February 9, 1893, to enroll him, in denial of his rights and in violation of the plain duty of the register, and prayed for the writ of mandamus.

"The Vestry Act of 1798, chapter 24, section 2, provides that 'every white male citizen of this State above twenty-one years of age, resident of the parish where he offers to vote six months next preceding the day of election, who shall have been entered on the books of said parish one month at least preceding the day of election as a member of the Protestant Episcopal Church, and who shall contribute to the charges of said parish in which he offers to vote such sum as a majority of the vestry in each parish shall annually, within ten days after their election, in writing, make known and declare, not exceeding $2, shall have a right of suffrage in the election of vestrymen for such parish.'

---

[2] Ibid, Section, 12.   [3] Ibid, Section, 13.

of their respective Parishes, to be Church Wardens for that year; all the inhabitants of every Parish, being Freeholders within the same Parish and contributing to the Public Taxes and Charges thereof, having Liberty also to vote in the Choice of Church Wardens.[1]

"That the Church-Wardens and Vestry pay the Parochial Charges and Repairs of Churches, etc., "out of such Gifts, Goods, or Chattels as shall come to their hands for the Church or Parish Use"; that the penalties, etc., prescribed by the Act be levied by the Church-Wardens and applied to the Parochial charges; and in case of insufficient effects to pay the Parochial charges, etc., the County Courts on application of the Parish Vestry and Church-Wardens, to assess the respective Parishes, not exceeding ten Pounds of Tobacco per poll in any one year.[2]

"Section 3 provides that it shall be the duty of the register to enroll any person of the Protestant Episcopal Church who shall apply for the purpose on the books of the parish, under penalty, etc.

"Section 5 makes a majority of the vestrymen who shall attend judges of the qualification of voters and of the qualification of the parishoners proposed to be elected as vestrymen.

"The vestrymen under section 6 and the register of the parish, section 18, are required to take and subscribe the oath of support and fidelity and for the faithful execution of their respective offices.

"Now, in this case", continues the court, "what was the duty of the registerer which he was bound to perform, not only under penalty but under the sanctity of an oath? Was it the mere mechanical act of enrolling the name of any person of the Protestant Episcopal Church applying to him for that purpose on the books of the parish? Were this all, then his duty would be plain and he would have to enroll any person, black or white, male or female, belonging to said church who made application. But there were other and important qualifications of the applicant to be considered. He must be a white male citizen of this State, above twenty-one years of age, a resident, etc.

"The judges of this court well know the difficulty in determining the perplexing questions of residence and citizenship under the registration law of this State from the numerous appeals arising from the action of the officers of registration which the court has been called upon to

---

1 Ibid, Section, 14. 2 Ibid, Section 15.

THE CHURCH ESTABLISHMENT 173

"That no Minister or Incumbent shall at one Time hold more than two parishes; nor two unless by the desire or Agreement of the Vestry of the said adjacent Parish and consent of the Vestries where he resides and Appointment of the Ordinary."[1]

That Vestries may appoint Lay-Readers in certain cases, such Readers "procuring License from the Ordinary"; that the first Tuesday in Every Month shall be Vestry day, without notice; that Vestrymen may be removed in certain cases, their successors to be elected by the parishioners; that the Vestry books may be inspected by the parishioners, who may appeal from any Vestry proceedings to the Governor in Council and thence to the Crown; that protestant dissenters shall have the benefit of the Acts of Toleration; and, that the Act of 1700, Chapter 1, be repealed.[2]

By the Act of 1704, Chapter 34, further provision was made for the levying of the "ten per poll" for parochial charges, etc.

And the Act of 1730, Chapter 23, provides for the election by the Vestry, of Vestrymen to serve in the place of those elected who may decline to serve; provides a penalty for those

---

decide, involving delicate and difficult questions of law and fact. The register must also determine whether the applicant lives within the limits of the parish, whether he is a member of the church, and other questions may arise by no means free of difficuly, all of which involve the exercise of discretion or judgment. Discretion is but freedom to act according to one's judgment—the prompting and exercise of judgment, cautious discernment, discrimination.

"It has been argued", adds the court, "that a denial of relief in this case 'would be a wrong without a remedy; that a vestry in collusion with a register could exclude parishoners from all participation in the church government and perpetuate their powers indefinitely.' This condition must assume a corrupt vestry. Were this so, such a vestry being under section 5 of the vestry act, judges of the qualification of voters and

---

[1] Ibid, Section 16.   [2] Ibid, Sections 17-22.

declining to serve; prescribes that the two eldest Vestrymen shall be annually left out and not liable to service again for three years, and provides for the collection of penalties imposed by the Act of 1702.

Such remained the "Establishment" down to the American Revolution, except as affected by the Acts of 1763, 1771, and 1773, to be noticed hereafter.

What was the character of this "Establishment", and what its government, laws, and usages? There is current with some, a general and vague conception that in some way the English ecclesiastical system — the English "Established Church", if you please—lies back of the American Church, and in some undefined way furnishes its rules of conduct and government. That this is not so, is, we venture to think, abundantly shown by what is above set forth.

The "English Ecclesiastical Law could have been of no force in a colonial church in this country, until adopted by it, and such adoption could only be by express enactment, or by general *usage* for so long a period of time as to ripen into law"; for, "if *disuse* is not to be regarded as proof that a law was inapplicable to the condition of a colony, then it follows, that for more than one hundred years prior to the

---

of the qualification of the parishioners proposed to be elected as vestry men, could strike down as disqualified any one offering to vote for vestrymen or offering himself as a candidate, notwithstanding the register had enrolled every man offering himself as a voter.

"But an applicant offering himself to the register as a qualified voter in said church is no worse off than a registered voter under the laws of this State offering his ballot at an election for President of the United States and being refused by the judge of election, and as the learned counsel says: 'What is he going to do about it' but enforce the penalty prescribed by law and sue for damages? The election is over. His great freeman's right of suffrage is denied, and he is without other relief. I shall sustain the demurrer upon the ground and for the reasons above assigned."

Revolution, the Colonial Churches were necessarily subjected to foreign law without reference to their consent or wishes. Surely this was never the condition, either in Church or State, of any English colony ''.[1]

That it was never the condition of Maryland is beyond peradventure. It would be threshing very old straw to go over the question of the English law in force in Maryland. Kitty's Report on the Statutes, bringing to approximate settlement a matter long open, is testimony to one phase of the question, how much English law was adopted in Maryland; while the judicial decisions are conclusive that nothing of English law was ever in force unless adopted by legislative acts, judicial decisions, or constant usage.[2]

But let us examine the Maryland "Establishment" and the Church in Maryland, with this conception in view. And to do this adequately we must first glance at the English establishment.

What this English establishment was and is, will be thoroughly understood only by a consideration of the following matters: 1, The parishes of the church; 2, The property and support of the church in each parish; 3, The government of the church; and, 4, The appointment of rectors, their rights and tenure.

1. A parish is that circuit of ground which is committed to the charge of one parson or vicar, or other minister having care of souls therein.[3] The time when England was first divided into parishes is unknown, nor is it material to our inquiry.[4]

---

[1] Andrews, pp. 42, 43.
[2] See opinion of Chase, judge, in United States vs. Worrall, 2 Dall. p. 384; McMahon, C. 3.
[3] Blackstone, Comm. 1, pp. 111-113.
[4] Earl of Selborne's Defense of the Church of England against Disestablishment, pp. 115, 138.

2. The property of the church in each parish consisted of the parish church and chapels, a "manse", or house of residence for the incumbent, with a glebe or portion of land attached to it, the fittings, furniture, and ornaments of the church and chapels, and the tithes.

As respects the glebe and other lands of the church, the source thereof was as follows :

"Originally, the land was the property of some lay person, which, when the rectory was formed, was dedicated to the church, and conveyed by him to the rector. Thus the freehold was vested in the rector, and he was entitled to the land, including the grass, herbage, and everything else, as fully as the original owner had been ; but, as the land had been set apart by consecration for the church and churchyard, the right which the rector, as the owner of the freehold, had in the profits was proportionately diminished, because he could not desecrate it, or use it for any purpose which was inconsistent with the object of its consecration. Nevertheless, the enjoyment of the property, so far as it could be exercised by one holding a sacred office, belonged to the rector, as the owner of the freehold ".[1]

But some of the founders, as they are called, were ecclesiastical corporations, and some of them kings ; in every case, however, the effect of the foundation being the same.[2]

The fittings, etc , were, as a rule, the offerings of "individual piety or munificence ", or " provided by private contributions ".[3]

Tithes were paid by the parishioners. Originally, says Blackstone, " every man was at liberty to contribute his tithes to whatever priest or church he pleased, provided only, that

---
1 Greenslade vs. Darby, L. R. 3 Q. B. p. 421.
2 Selborne's Defence, p. 114.   3 Ibid, p. 116.

he did it some ",[1] and in the absence of specification they were distributed by the bishop in his discretion. But in the time of Edgar, about the year 970, it was ordered that all tithes should be given to the mother church of the parish; subject, however, to certain provisions for the support of chapels within the parish.[2]

"The lords, as christianity spread itself, began to build churches upon their own demesnes or wastes * * * * and, in order to have divine service regularly performed therein, obliged all their tenants to appropriate their tithes to the maintenance of the one officiating minister, instead of leaving them at liberty to distribute them among the clergy of the diocese in general; and this tract of land, the tithes whereof were so appropriated, formed a distinct parish. * * * * Thus parishes were gradually formed, and parish churches endowed with the tithes that arose within the circuit assigned".[3]

3. The government of the Church of England, was in accordance with the ecclesiastical division of the kingdom, which was as follows: Provinces, of which there were two, Canterbury and York, and of each of which the archbishop was the head; dioceses, into which each province was divided, and of which the bishops were the respective heads; archdeaconries, into which each diocese was divided, and over which the archdeacons respectively ruled, within the limitations of their authority; rural deaneries, each of which had its "rural dean"; and, finally, parishes, into which every deanery was divided.[4]

The archbishop, who was also called the Metropolitan, had general authority over the clergy throughout his province, besides having a diocese of his own in which he exercised Episcopal jurisdiction.

---

[1] Blackstone, Comm. 1, p. 111.
[2] Ibid, p. 112.
[3] Ibid, p. 113.
[4] Ibid, p. 111.

"The power and authority of a bishop, besides the administration of certain holy ordinances peculiar to that sacred order, consists, principally, in inspecting the manners of the people and clergy, and punishing them in order to reformation, by ecclesiastical censures. To this purpose, he has several courts under him", as also his dean and chapter as his council. "It is, also, the business of a bishop to institute and to direct induction to all ecclesiastical livings in his diocese".[1]

A parson had full possession of all the rights of the parochial church; and in each parish there might also be a curate, an officiating temporary minister, being, as Blackstone says, of "the lowest degree in the church".

A title very common in the English ecclesiastical system is that of the "ordinary", who is defined as being "one possessing immediate jurisdiction in his own right and not by special deputation;" as, "a bishop, archbishop, or other ecclesiastic or his deputy, in his capacity as an *ex officio* ecclesiastical judge".[2]

Each parish also had its vestry, church-wardens and parish clerks and sextons. Of these the church-wardens were the guardians or keepers of the church and representatives of the body of the parish. They were sometimes appointed by the minister, sometimes by the church, sometimes by both together, as custom might direct. They were deemed for some purposes a corporation, having a property in the goods and chattels of the parish and could bring actions in relation to them. They also levied fines, kept order in church, etc.

Vestries, as we understand them, were not in existence. Properly speaking, the vestry was "the assembly of the whole

---

[1] Ibid, p. 377.   [2] Century Dictionary.

parish met together in some convenient place for the dispatch of the affairs and business of the parish ". Every parishioner who paid his "rates" had a right to come to these meetings, over which the parson presided, "for the regulating and directing this affair". "From the practice of choosing a certain number of persons yearly to manage the concerns of the parish for that year" grew up what were known as select vestries. But neither vestries, in the proper sense of the word, nor select vestries had any powers necessary to be noticed.[1]

4. As already noted, every rector or person, in order to procure a benefice, had first to be presented, that is, offered to the bishop of the diocese to be instituted. The presentation was made by the patron, as he was called, of the cure, the person having the right of advowson. "The founders of parish churches had power, when parishes were first formed and endowed, to determine in whom the right of 'advowson' (*i. e.*, of presentation to the benefice when vacant) should be vested". This right was a heritable right, passing, on death or alienation, to the heirs or successors in estate of him having the right.[2]

Upon presentation, the bishop, if he had no objection to the person presented, instituted him ; that is, put him in " care of the souls of the parish ". Then followed induction, by virtue of which, the parson was in possession of the temporalities of the benefice.

At common law, to become a parson, says Blackstone— and, as he declares, "the appellation of *parson* (however it may be depreciated by familiar, clownish, and indiscriminate use), is the most legal, most beneficial, and most honorable that a parish priest can enjoy ", there are four requisites necessary:

---

[1] Burn, Ecclesiastical Law.   [2] Selborn, p. 123.

holy orders, presentation, institution, and induction. Presentation, he says, is the offer of the proposed incumbent to the bishop for institution. Institution is " a kind of *investiture of the spiritual part* of the benefice", but induction is something of more importance.

" Upon institution, the clerk may enter on the parsonage house and glebe and take the tithes ; but he cannot grant or let them or bring an action for them until induction.

" Induction is performed by a mandate from the bishop to the archdeacon, who usually issues out a precept to other clergymen to perform it for him. It is done by giving the clerk corporal possession of the church, as by holding the ring of the door, tolling a bell, or the like ; and is a form required by law, with intent to give all the parishioners due notice and sufficient certainty of their new minister, to whom their tithes are to be paid. This, therefore, is the *investiture of the temporal part* of the benefice, as institution is of the spiritual. And when a clerk is thus presented, instituted, and inducted into a rectory, he is then and not before, in full and complete possession, and is called in law *persona impersonata*, or parson *imparsonee*."

And one might cease to be a parson in one of several ways only :

1. By death ; 2, by cession, in taking another benefice ; 3, by consecration to a bishopric ; 4, by resignation, accepted by the ordinary ; and, 5, by deprivation, which might be by sentence ecclesiastical, "for fit and sufficient causes allowed by the common law " or *ipso facto* in certain cases, "in pursuance of divers penal statutes." [1]

It thus appears that at the common law there was no such thing as a " severance of the pastoral relation " for differences

---

[1] Blackstone Comm. 1, p. 384-392.

between parsons and their congregations. The parson, once in, had a freehold in the glebe, and the right to tithes, etc., and could not lose his rights, except by ceasing to be parson, as above indicated. In other words, if not deprived, and if he did not resign or accept another cure, or become a bishop, his tenure was for life.

Contrast with this order of things in the English Church, the Maryland "Establishment".

1. The parishes in Maryland, as mere territories to be committed to the clergy, were well enough provided for by the Act of 1692; that is to say, the directions of that Act, if carried out, would sufficiently have carved the State into parishes.[1] And, in the main, this was sufficiently done for all practical purposes. We find throughout, however, that new parishes were being constantly formed: whether by the division of old ones;[2] or the erection of new ones:[3] or by the consolidation of two or more already existing.[4] And it was not unnatural that the boundaries of the several parishes should thus become confused, so as to make necessary an Act for ascertaining the boundaries of all.[5]

---

[1] Under this Act the Province was divided into thirty parishes, and which in 1694, in respect to churches and ministers, stood as follows: Saint Mary's, two parishes, three churches and one minister; Kent, two parishes and two churches, but no minister; Anne Arundel, four parishes, two churches and one minister; Calvert. four parishes, three churches and two ministers; Charles, three parishes, two churches and one minister; Baltimore, three parishes, two churches and no minister; Talbot, three parishes, four churches and two ministers; Somerset, four parishes, one church and one minister; Dorchester, two parishes, one church and no minister; Cecil, two parishes, two churches and one minister. (Allen," Who were the early Settlers of Maryland.") Two years later three more churches had been built, and nine additional ministers had come in, making in all eighteen. (Ibid). In 1720, the number of parishes had increased, to thirty-eight, and in 1760 to forty-two, and there

[2] Act, 1704, C. 96.
[4] Act, 1722, C. 3.
[3] Act, 1706, C. 4.
[5] Act, 1713, C. 10.

2. But, when we come to consider the property and support of the church in each parish, we find a radically different state of things from that in England.

Some gifts of land there were, but gifts were not the rule. Prior to 1704, "several pious and well-disposed persons" had "granted unto the respective parishes whereto they [did] belong, certain parcels of ground for the use and benefit of a church and church-yard", but, through the neglect of the vestries selected under the Act of 1696, no deeds to such lands had been taken. Wherefore, by Act of 1704, Chapter 38, provision was made for confirming the titles of such lands to the respective parishes, the grand juries being authorized to make inquiry in the matter, etc., and where lands had been given, but the quantity not mentioned, the vestry was authorized to "take of such lands, for the use of the church, and thereto adjacent, two acres and no more".

---

were forty-one ministers. (Hawks "History P. E. Church, p. 170; Allen, "Who were the early Settlers in Maryland".) A majority of these clergymen were of English birth, but a large number of them were Scotch and a few of them Irish. In 1720, it was estimated that there were "between ten and eleven thousand families of Episcopalians in the Province", (Hawkes, p. 170.) According to the report of the Governor of Maryland, in 1696, from items furnished, on his requisition, by the Sheriff's of the several counties, made to the Bishop of London, there were in Maryland at that date also, eight Roman Catholic churches, five priests and two lay brothers, limited to the Counties of Charles and Saint Mary's; three Presbyterian churches and two ministers, limited to the County of Somerset; and eight Quaker meeting houses, three meetings in private houses and two preachers, limited to the Counties of Kent, Anne Arundel, Calvert and Talbot. (Allen, "Who were the early settlers in Maryland".) But in justice, it should here be noted, that the meagreness of this report as to Roman Catholic Priests and places of worship was perhaps due to the fact that they were in Maryland, at that time under "proscription", as the number of Roman Catholics in the Province a few years thereafter—1708—was reported to be 2974, and located as follows: Anne Arundel, 161; Baltimore, 53; Calvert, 48; Prince Georges, 248; Charles, 709; Saint Mary's, 1238; Cecil, 49; Kent, 40; Queen Anne, 179; Talbot, 89; Dorchester, 79 and Somerset, 81. (London Pub. Rec. Office, Maryland, B. T. Red No. 4, H. p. 79; Scharf, vol 1, p. 370.

Similar provision was made by the Act of 1722, Chapter 4, for confirming lands devised for the use of the church; and, in some cases, special Acts were passed, vesting in the vestry, special gifts of lands.[1]

Generally, these gifts and devises were to the vestry or parish, but in one instance, at least, the gift or devise was to the rector and his successors.[2]

Another source of acquisition of lands was by gift or grant of public lands; as in the case of certain lots in Annapolis,[3] the "Old Stadt-house in St. Mary's city, in St. Mary's county, and the lot whereon the same stands",[4] and a tract of two acres, "parcel of fifteen acres laid out for public uses at the town of Vienna, Dorchester county".[5]

But by far, the chief source of acquisition was in provision of law, mostly in specific instances, authorizing the vestries to buy lands, and levying a tax of tobacco or money to pay therefore and to erect churches thereon.[6] The Acts of this class are practically innumerable and were passed as lately as 1774. In some cases the expression "to make a glebe", or "to be made a glebe",[7] was used. Besides, the vestries were empowered, with the aid of commissioners, to acquire lands by condemnation;[8] in all cases the lands and churches to be paid for by tax.

As respects the fittings, etc., of the churches, there were some few gifts of these, but in the main they were provided out of the "forty per poll" and the "ten per poll", provided for by the act of 1702.[9]

---

1 Act, 1700, C. 5; 1701, C. 5. 2 Act, 1719, C. 6.
3 Act, 1718, C. 8. 4 Act, 1720, C. 4.
5 Act, 1725, C. 9. 6 Act, 1727, C. 10.
7 Act, 1750, C. 17; 1751 C. 6. 8 Act, 1704, C. 38; 1747, C. 18.

9 It has been said that the "art of keeping warm is of modern invention", and eminently was the absence of this art seen in the house

The tenure of the land acquired in the several ways indicated, whether in the rector (as was the case in very rare instances), or in the vestry (as was the rule), seems to have been such that neither rector nor vestry could make any disposition of them without authority of the legislature. Thus we find acts enabling the rector to sell or the vestry to sell, or to lease or to exchange lands. These Acts clearly show that the vestries were treated as mere trustees, holding the church properties for the one purpose, "the use and benefit of the church".

3. As for government, the church had none. The "ordinary" was mentioned in the legislation on the subject, but there was no ordinary; and throughout the period we are considering there was no bishop, the first bishop, Claggett, not being elected until 1792.[1]

Respecting the government of the Church during this period, Hawks says:

"Theoretically, the Bishop of London was the diocesan: spiritual jurisdiction therefore, including the important particular of discipline. belonged to him, and the clergy had all along been accustomed so to think. But they were embarassed because they found that the matter of jurisdiction was in some mode or other in the hands of the proprietor also * * * * Thus Lord Baltimore selected a clergyman in England, and appointed him to a living; the Bishop of London gave him a license; the Governor of the Province inducted him; if he did wrong, the commissary tried him, if they happened to be a

---

of God. For until abont two generations ago, the churches of Maryland had no fires in them, or means provided for making fire. There was a fire in the Vestry house, a detached building, but at church time access to it was prevented by the doors being closed and locked.—Church life in Colonial Maryland, 120.

1 Hawks, p. 310.

commissary ; and when convicted, no power punished him ; for *after induction*, even his Lordship, the Proprietor, could not remove him ; and the Bishop of London, nominally his diocesan, could neither give nor take away the meanest living in the Province ".[1]

"As long as no clergyman could have a living in Maryland without Lord Baltimore's assent ; as long as the Governor had the sole right of induction, on his own or his Lordship's presentation and as long as *the legal effect of induction* was to fasten the incumbent on a parish for life, no matter what might be his conduct ; it is perfectly plain that to talk of the jurisdiction of bishop or commissary was a mere farce ".[2]

4. Passing now to the appointment of rectors, their rights and tenure, it is first to be observed that there were no patrons in Maryland, in the sense in which there were in England. All the livings were in the gift of the Lord Proprietary, a right of which he was to the end tenacious. How a rector got his benefice has just been shown by the extract from Hawks. And what his rights were after getting his place may be stated in few words : he got the use of the glebe and parsonage, if any, and his " Forty per poll ". These he enjoyed, at first, for life ; for so much of English conception of the rights and privileges of a rector seems to have been adopted by Maryland as to give to the formality of induction the same legal consequence in Maryland as in England.

That it was the formality of induction which was supposed to work the life tenure is made clear by the above extract from Hawks. And Eden, the last of the Proprietary Governors, saw the matter in the same light : "at present", said he, speaking in 1769 or 1770, "when a clergyman is *inducted*, he

---

[1] Hawks, p. 189.   [2] Ibid, p. 193.

becomes quite unaccountable and independent ".[1] It is important to bear this in mind ; for after the American Revolution induction ceased. As Hawks says, in 1807, when the question of the canon on that subject was under consideration, "of the Maryland clergy, not one had been inducted, nor was one likely to be ".[2]

Such being, in general, the character of the Maryland "Establishment", it is necessary in order fully to understand it and its effects, to consider briefly the character of the clergy created by the system, and the attitude of the people of the Province toward them.

It is a sad story ; that of the Maryland clergy under the "Establishment". But it is, unfortunately, only too true. The testimony on all sides is in one direction only.

Dr. Hawks, an esteemed clergyman of the Church and once a candidate for the Bishopric of Maryland, cannot be called a hostile witness. Hear him :

"It is not wonderful that the clergy, thus secure in their livings after induction, and with but feeble powers over them for punishment when they did wrong, should sometimes exhibit but a sad example to their parishioners * * * * It must be remembered that it was too much the fashion to send to all these colonies the refuse of the English clergy, insomuch that our wonder is less that the Church in many places did not grow than that it was not utterly extinguished ".

"The people looked around among the clergy and saw every man doing just what he thought best ; they sought for a power to protect their spiritual interests by punishing the faithless agents of the government in things spiritual, and they found that power—nowhere ".[3]

---

[1] Hawks, p. 255.   [2] Ibid, p. 363.
[3] Ibid, pp. 191, 235.

The pages of Hawks are replete with matter to the same effect. We are not surprised to see him write :

"No wonder that such a bastard establishment as that of Maryland was odious to so many of the people ; we think their dislike is evidence of their virtue. It deserved to be despised, for it permitted clerical profligacy to murder the souls of men ".[1]

Yeo's letter, above mentioned, written before the " Establishment ", reveals a bad enough condition of things :

But the clergy of that day were saintly in comparison with those of the period we are now considering. A less friendly, and, therefore, perhaps a more just critic of the clergy, writes :

"The church which finally drove Catholicism to the wall was, perhaps, as contemptible an ecclesiastical organization as history can show. It had all the vices of the Virginian Church, without one of its safe-guards or redeeming qualities * * * * A clergymen, writing in 1714, describes the disregard of holy things as universal ; the sacraments as neglected and sometimes not celebrated at all ; the manners of all classes as dissolute ; and the laws of marriage despised * * * * Maryland, like Virginia, had also the misfortune of not receiving ministers through the Society for the Propagation of the Gospel. The patronage was badly administered, unworthy men were frequently appointed, and the whole organization closely resembled a corrupt civil service * * * * It is not easy to conceive the utter degradation of the mass of the Maryland clergy. Secure in their houses and glebes, and the tax settled by law and collected by the sheriffs for their benefit, they set decency and public opinion at defiance. They hunted, raced horses, drank, gambled, and were the parasites and boon companions of the wealthy planters."[2] * * * *

---

[1] Ibid, p. 236.   [2] Lodge, p. 120.

Truly a shocking state of things; which is here revealed, not because the picture is pleasant to dwell upon, but because it is necessary to enable us to understand the legislation presently to be noticed. Small wonder that the clergy "were not only despised, but they were bitterly disliked", and that they were constantly opposed by government and people.

Indeed, the patience of the people seems to have been phenomenal. It was not until 1763[1] that the "Forty per Poll" was seriously interfered with, and it was then done only as part of an enactment for amending the staple of tobacco.

In 1771,[2] however, a significant Act was passed. It was limited in effect to seven years, before the end of which time the American Revolution was on and the "Establishment" a thing of the past. By this act it was, among other things, provided as follows :

"Upon a complaint in writing, by a majority of the vestrymen and wardens, exhibited to the Governor and Council, setting forth that the incumbent hath willfully neglected to officiate, or hath been guilty of scandalous immorality, the Governor, by the advice of his Council, may appoint three beneficed ministers, and three laymen, in conjunction with himself, or with the first member of the Council who shall be of the Church of England, if the Governor be not of that church, to inquire into the grounds of the complaint, by taking depositions in writing. And the sentence of this tribunal may be to admonish, to suspend, or to totally deprive; and, at discretion, they may further award the offender to pay costs. In case of a suspension, the Governor is authorized to appoint a minister to officiate in the party's stead, and to receive the income and profits".[3]

---

1 Act, 1763, Chapter 18.   2 Act, 1771, Chapter 31.   3 Hanson.

There is no more important act than this in the history of the Maryland Church. It is the first legislative declaration of the Maryland laity against a life-holding clergy, and was but the foreshadowing of what was shortly to come.

The last Act passed during the Establishment,[1] is also not without its significance. The Act of 1763, reducing the "Forty per Poll" to thirty, expired by limitation in 1770. Governor Eden thereupon took the ground that the "Forty per Poll" was restored. The question was taken up by the people, Daniel Dulany leading the Governor's side and Charles Carroll, of Carrollton, the other side. The election of 1773 turned largely upon the question and was decided against the Governor's party.[2]

In the course of this contest there developed another, being over no less a proposition than that the Act of Establishment of 1702 had never been law. The ground taken was that the Assembly which passed the law was chosen under writs of election in King William's name and convened March 16, 1701—'2, whereas the King had died eight days' before. The Revolution put an end to this question, but, says Hawks, had it not been so determined "it can hardly be doubted that this objection would so far have prevailed as to overthrow the establishment entirely": a striking illustration of the popular feeling towards the clergy and the "Establishment".[3]

---

[1] Act, 1773, C. 28.   [2] Brown, p. 266.

[3] This was probably the most noted political controversy within the annals of Colonial Maryland—more so even, perhaps, than that over the famous proclamation of 1770 to restore the "fee bills" as established by the Act of 1763—The controversy enlisted the most distinguished talent of the Province, and was characterized by a display of ability, learning, spirit and invective not often brought to bear upon any cause and which gave it unusual prominence. The spirit of resistance ran so high that in many cases payment of the tax was successfully resisted — notably in the case of Joseph H. Harrison, a representative in the House of Delegates, from

The Act of 1773, Chapter 28, mentioned, provided, "Thirty per Poll" for the clergy, but contained a *proviso* that it was "not to influence the determination of the question respecting the 40 per poll law".[1]

Thus stood the "Establishment" at the close of the period under consideration. We examine it in vain for evidence of the adoption of any feature of the English ecclesiastical law, save only as to the supposed legal effect of the induction of a rector. "Lord Baltimore did not found, build, or support the churches and chapels, either with or without license from the King. The people built and sustained them".[2]

Vestries and Church Wardens there were, but with powers and duties differing from those of similar officers in England, and all carefully prescribed by statute. There was no archbishop, bishop, nor church government of any sort. In short, there was no play for the English ecclesiastical law. And the imperfectly understood incident of induction, which had been borrowed, in a blind sort of way, from the mother country, could not itself have found place, had the people and the Proprietary been at one, instead of being constantly at odds.

Charles County. He refused to pay the tax and was arrested. He then paid it under protest, to redeem his person, and sued Richard Lee, the Sheriff, for false imprisonment, the Act of 1702, under which the sheriff was proceeding, being as alleged, null and void. Though there was no actual imprisonment, such was the spirit and temper of the times and the state of public feeling upon the subject, that he was awarded damages to the extent of £60, the full amount claimed. Charles County Court Records, March 1774. — Essays relating to this controversy may be found in 1st Chalmers "Collection of Opinions", p. 303, 343 ; Maryland Gazette, December 31st, 1772 ; January 14th and 28th ; February 4th, 11th and 25th ; March 18th and 25th ; April 1st, 15th, 29th, and May 27th 1773.

[1] Hanson.   [2] Hawks, p. 258.

THE CHURCH ESTABLISHMENT

In 1774, Maryland, in effect, renounced allegiance to the mother country. A provincial government was then organized, and continued its sessions until the close of 1776, when the new State government had been provided.

On November 3d, 1776, the Declaration of Rights was adopted. By the thirty-third section of this it was declared, that no person ought "to be compelled to frequent or maintain, or contribute, unless on contract, to maintain any particular place of worship, or any particular ministry". But, proceeds the Declaration :

"The churches, chapels, glebes, and all other property now belonging to the Church of England, ought to remain to the Church of England forever. And all Acts of Assembly lately passed for collecting monies for building or repairing particular churches or chapels of ease, shall continue in force and be executed, unless the Legislature shall by Act supersede or repeal the same; but no County Court shall assess any quantity of tobacco or sum of money hereafter, on the application of any Vestry or Church Wardens; and every incumbent of the Church of England who hath remained in his parish, and performed his duty, shall be entitled to receive the provision and support established by the Act entitled, An Act for the Support of the Clergy of the Church of England, in this Province, till the November Court of this present year, to be held for the county in which his parish shall lie, or partly lie, or for such time as he hath remained in his parish, and performed his duty".

The third section of the Declaration continued in force existing laws, except as altered by the convention "or this declaration of rights".

These provisions destroyed the "Establishment", root and branch. There was no "Established Church" after the date of the Declaration, and no "Forty per Poll" after "November Court". More than this, there were no "patronages and advowsons", no "induction". The Church was left without law and without order. "The Rev. Jonathan Boucher and a third of the clergy sided with the Crown. Ultimately, quite all the churches were closed, and the clergy, for the most part, left the country".[1]

In 1779, the legislature acted on the subject of the Church for the first time since the Declaration of Rights. By Act of March, 1779, Chapter 9, select vestries in each parish were provided for. The sections of the Act, material to our inquiry, are the following :

"That the select vestries so to be chosen, and their successors, shall, as trustees of the parish, be vested with an estate in fee in all the glebe-lands, as also in all churches and chapels, and the land thereunto belonging, late the property of the people professing the religion of the Church of England, and also as trustees aforesaid, shall have full property in all books, plate, and other ornaments belonging to said churches and chapels or any of them".[2]

"That the said vestrymen, or the major part of them, shall have full power and authority to employ a minister or reader of the Church of England, to officiate in their respective churches or chapels for such time as may be agreed upon ; and may take in subscriptions from all persons willing to contribute towards the support of such minister or reader, and also for the support of a clerk to such minister, and giving a salary not exceeding thirty pounds, to the register of such vestries.[3]

"That the possession and free use of all glebe-lands shall belong to the minister of each parish, from the time of

---

[1] Bishop White's Memoirs, p. 34.
[2] Act, 1779, Section 15.   [3] Ibid, Section 16.

his having agreed with the select vestry as aforesaid, for and during the time he shall continue to remain therein as minister of the parish ; and he shall be entitled to all profits thereof during the time aforesaid, anything herein contained to the contrary notwithstanding ".[1]

By Act of November, 1779, Chapter 7, this Act was amended (as to Section 15), by vesting in the select vestries, all property of the church, in their respective parishes, including debts, etc., which, it was thought, the earlier Act might not cover.

But this Act failed to revive the church. The vestries complained of their limited control over the church property, and other objections, to the system created by the Act, were urged, with the result that the Act of 1798, Chapter 24, was passed ; which, with an alteration unimportant to our consideration,[2] remains law to this day.

The preamble recites the inadequacy of the earlier Act, to the exigencies of the church. The substantial changes made by it, which are material to our consideration, are as follows :

The number of the vestry is fixed at eight, in addition to the rector, who is to preside at all meetings and have a vote in case of a tie, but not in any matter "in which he is in any manner particularly interested ".[3]

The rector is to " have, except he may otherwise contract with the vestry, the possession, occupation, and free use of all the glebe-lands, houses, ground-rents, books and other property belonging to his parish, and be entitled to the benefit thereof during the time he shall officiate therein as rector ".[4]

The vestry is given a fee simple in all lands and a good title and estate in all other property of the church ; "and it

---

[1] Ibid, Section 17. [2] Act, 1828, Chapter 136, Section 3.
[3] Act, 1798, Chapter 24, Sections 2, 8. [4] Ibid, Section 8.

shall be lawful for such vestry so to manage and direct all such property as they may think most advantageous to the interests of the parishioners, and they shall also have the property in all books, plate and other ornaments belonging to said churches and chapels, or any of them ".[1]

The vestry is made a body corporate, with power to receive lands and goods, and to rent or lease the lands " in such a manner as they may judge most conducive to the interests" of the parish; but the vestry may not sell any of the property of the church without the consent of five at least of the body, of whom the rector shall be one.[2]

"That the vestry of each parish shall have full power and authority, from time to time, to choose one or more ministers or readers of the Protestant Episcopal Church (heretofore called the Church of England), to officiate in any church or chapel belonging to the parish, and to perform the other duties of a minister therein, for such time as the said vestry may think proper, and they may agree and contract with such minister or ministers, reader or readers, for his or their salary, and respecting the use of the parsonage-house, or any glebe or other lands, or other property, if any, belonging to the parish, and on such terms and conditions as they may think reasonable and proper, and their choice and contract shall be entered among their proceedings; and upon the expiration of such contract, the said vestry may, in their discretion, renew their choice, or make a new contract, but if they do not incline so to do, their former choice and contract shall remain until they declare their desire to make a new choice or contract ".[3]

Two important differences between these two acts are to be noted. By the earlier, the rector is given absolute possession

---

1 Ibid, Section 9. 2 Ibid, Sections 28, 29.
3 Ibid, Section 15.

of the glebe, etc., whereas by the latter, the vestry may, by the terms of its contract, keep him out of such possession. Again, by the earlier, provision is made only for one specific contract between rector and vestry, by agreement of the two parties, whereas, by the latter, the vestry is given power to choose the rector for such time as it may think proper, and if a time limit be set, the vestry may allow the same to pass without losing the right at any time thereafter, to "make a new choice or contract".

What, then, is the power of a Maryland vestry as to dissolution of the pastoral connection of a rector previously chosen?

It is shown that the ecclesiastical law of England is not and never was in force in Maryland. As matter of law, it has never been decided by any tribunal having proper jurisdiction that even the incident of induction above noted ever had place in the Maryland system. But it is conceded that during the "Establishment" the clergy claimed life-tenure as the "legal effect of induction", the same as in England, and that the claim was so far acquiesced in that no clergyman appears ever to have been removed against his will.

The important point is, that the claim to life-tenure was always based by the clergy upon induction. The case was the same in Virginia. "Without induction, the clergy was held to possess no freehold in his living, but was at any time liable to removal, at the pleasure of the vestry, without trial or even crime alleged against him. Under those circumstances, there were but few of the clergy who could consider their situations as permanent, for there were but few who could prevail upon their vestries to present them for induction. The general custom, therefore, was to hire the minister from year to year".[1]

---

[1] Hawks, Virginia, p. 88.

What was this induction, that it should work such a result? The very act of induction answers the question: It was the investiture of the parson with the freehold in the church lands, the tenure of which was, of course, for life. The ceremony was as formal as the old livery of seisin, performed before the eyes of all. It gave the parson a property interest with which neither vestry nor parish, neither patron nor ordinary, could interfere when once it was vested. The only way in which it could be lost involuntarily was by such conduct of the parson as would lead to deprivation.

The Maryland article of induction was a great improvement on the English. The rector got no freehold in anything, and went through no very formal ceremony, but when the Governor or Proprietary "inducted" him, he was in, so that no earthly power could ever get him out. Deprivations had no terrors for him.

This monstrous assumption produced its natural fruit: hostility to the church and worse than corruption in the clergy. The state of affairs above set forth, could have produced but one result, *i. e*, that when the laity should ultimately come to deal with the clergy and its tenure it would do thorough work. It was just this that happened. The Vestry Act of 1779 not only did away with the farce of induction; it did not even stop at giving the vestry the right to select a minister for the parish; but it gave the vestry the right to fix the term of the rector's incumbency. The rector was to be employed—note the offensive word—for such time as might be agreed upon.

Let it be remembered, too, that at the time this Act was passed there was absolutely no ecclesiastical authority in Maryland. There never had been a bishop, and the undefined, more than uncertain, claim of jurisdiction of the Bishop of London had wholly disappeared. Who was there to interfere between rector and vestry if they should agree? And what rector could get a living unless he agreed with some vestry?

There was no diocesan convention to keep a parish unrepresented in its meetings if it did not happen to meet the convention's views. In a word, the clergy and the vestries were at large, with all the power and advantage on the side of the latter.

The Act of 1798 made no change in those particulars except to intensify them. By its terms the vestry was to "choose" instead of to "employ" its minister, but the rights of the vestry are, if anything, strengthened: in this, that the vestry may make its contract and let it continue in force until it sees fit to change it. Under the Act of 1779 some question may have arisen whether by allowing the rector to remain over his time he had not acquired a fresh term of at least one year. Under the Act of 1798, no such question can possibly arise.[1]

---

[1] The following is the syllabus of the decision in that case of Saint Matthew's Parish vs. E. H. Bartlett, et. al.—75 Maryland Reports, p. 5.

1. Under the Act of 1798, Chapter 24, incorporating the Vestries of the Protestant Episcopal Church and vesting in them the title and possession of all lands and properties belonging to the Church, the vestry is not only authorized to "choose" or appoint a minister, but his tenure and the termination of his pastoral relations are the subject matter of contract between the vestry and himself.

2. That Title Second, Canon Fourth, of the Canons of the Protestant Episcopal Church is inconsistent with the Act of Maryland of 1798, and is therefore not in force in the State of Maryland.

3. That in this case the vestry engaged the rector in compliance with the Act of 1798, and under its provisions, having contracted to pay him a certain sum per year, no other reference to time being made, it was a contract for a definite time, i. e., from year to year, and if such contract had been made for an indefinite time it would have been one to be determined at the will of either party.

4. That in the case before the court, the vestry acted within their powers under the law, and the complainent, Hipkins, is no longer rector of the parish and his bill is dismissed.

The Act of 1798 is not to be found, it is true, in the code. But the code is a codification of the public general laws and the public local laws.

Thus did the Acts of 1779 and 1798 settle the question of "severing the pastoral connection" in Maryland. The great principal of life tenure had been broken in upon. Maryland had had her full share of experience with a life holding clergy, and when she came to legislate upon the "new conditions", as created by the Revolution, she knew her mind on that subject quite as clearly as upon the subject of civil liberty.

But, to remain secure in the rights thus established, it was deemed necessary, at a later date, to also procure amendments to the general canon—canon of the "National Church" —on the subject.

As already stated, the English ecclesiastical law not being in force in this country, except as adopted; and, there being no ecclesiastical courts, or other authority to deprive a clergymay of his benefice, and the English law in that regard, being incapable of adoption; and, there being no statutes, penal or otherwise, governing the subject of deprivation, or "dissolution of the pastoral connection", it became necessary that some provision on the subject be made, either by the National Church, or by the churches in the several dioceses, or by both of them.

Now, it happened, as of necessity, that the National Church, or General Convention, was formed by the union of churches in various dioceses: at first, Connecticut, New York, New Jersey, Pennsylvania, Delaware, Maryland, and Virginia, and afterwards, Massachusetts and New Hampshire.[1] Without going into the subject in detail, it is matter of common knowledge that the National Church was modeled upon the

---

This Act is neither a public general law nor is it a public local law. It is a mere private Act incorporating the vestries of a particular religious denomination, *private corporations*, and being a private law it was not and could not properly be codified as part of the public general laws.

1 Andrews, pp. 24, 30.

Union of the States, with the familiar incidents of granted and reserved powers. Gradually, the constitution took form and the body of canons grew.[1]

Until 1804, however, there was no canon dealing with the dissolution of the pastoral connection. In the year mentioned, there was presented to the General Convention, the memorial of Trinity Church, New Jersey, respecting "an unhappy dispute between that parish and its rector".[2] The result—very much as it would have been in the Congress of the United States, in a political matter originally unprovided for—was a legislative provision, much deprecated by some, but thought necessary, and, therefore, advisable by the majority.

The object was to govern the matter of severance of the pastoral connection by general law. The original of the canon, "Title II, Canon 4", was the outcome. This canon took very much the form it now has, in 1832, and was finally put in its present form, in 1877.[3]

That canon professedly deals with the dissolution of the pastoral connection, and it prescribes a method for bringing about such dissolution. It enacts, in fact, that no rector shal be removed from his own parish against his will, except as provided by the canon. And it proceeds to provide that if the rector does not want to go, he may appeal to the bishop, or other proper ecclesiastical authority, who shall be "the ultimate arbiter and judge" in the matter. And if the bishop, should decide in favor of the rector, and the parish should not submit, the parish shall thereupon become disqualified "from representation in the convention of the diocese, until it shall

---

[1] See Bishop White's Memoirs, Bishop Perry's History of the American Episcopal Church ; Hawk's Ecclesiastical Constitutions.

[2] Bishop White's Memoir's ; Perry's Handbook, p. 104.

[3] Digest of Canons.

have been declared by the ecclesiastical authority to have given satisfactory guaranties for the acceptance of and compliance with the arbitration and judgment". But it provides also that it shall not be in force in any diocese with whose laws it may interfere.

From the very first, the right of the National Church, or General Convention, to make canons was very guardedly allowed and its exercise was most jealously watched by the several dioceses.[1]

In the same General Convention of 1804, there were adopted canons requiring the induction of ministers to entitle them to be considered as "regularly settled", and also providing for the "dissolution of the pastoral connection". Because the provisions of these canons interfered with the rights of certain of the dioceses under existing local law and usage they were so qualified at the very next convention, as to save all local rights.

Maryland was one of the dioceses affected by the canons mentioned. Says Bishop White, as to the requirment of induction:[2] "In Maryland the measure interfered directly with the vestry law". Hawks[3] says, in relation to the same matter: "This justly gave alarm to the Maryland Church. The vestry Act had settled the rights of ministers as parochial clergymen, and there was consequently some uncertainty, to say the least, as to the legal effect in Maryland of an induction * * * * In 1807, therefore, the delegates from the diocese to the General Convention were instructed, if possible to have the canon relating to induction reconsidered * * In 1808 it enacted that the canon should not be obligatory on the church in those States with whose usages, laws or charters it interfered".

---

1 Andrews, pp. 58, 59.   2 Bishop White's Memoirs, p. 231.
3 Hawks, pp. 363, 364.

In as full a sense and to as full an extent the canon relating to the "dissolution of the pastoral connection" encroached upon the rights of the Maryland Church and "interfered directly with the vestry law", which allowed the vestry to contract at pleasure with its minister. Accordingly, this canon was also, at the same time, similarly amended by the provision now contained in section four, to wit: That it shall not be in force in any State, with whose laws it may be inconsistent.[1]

That these canons are not in force in Maryland, is evidenced by another most significant consideration. The Convention did not like to make these amendments, and, in acting, used these words: "It is understood the church designs not to express an approbation of any laws which make the station of a minister dependent on anything else than his own soundness in the faith or worthy conduct".[2]

In the light of the Convention's protest, in amending the canons under consideration, what becomes of that loose, but not uncommon assertion, that life-tenure of the clergy is the universal underlying principle of the Protestant Episcopal Church? Hoffman's remarks upon the relations of rector and Vestry in New York, are not inappropriate here:

"In closing this important branch of the subject, I beg to remark that clergymen too often forget the new and peculiar relation in which they place themselves, when the church they belong to has been incorporated by the State. Whenever the provisions of such statutes expressly, or by necessary implication, govern his relations with a vestry or congregation, or otherwise, they form the absolute law for him".[3]

---

1 Hoffman, p. 122.   2 Ibid, p. 332.
3 Ecclesiastical Law of New York, p. 77.

M

Nothing can be plainer than that, view the case as we may, we are thrown upon the Maryland vestry law for a solution of the question at issue.

Under that law, the vestry may choose a minister for such time as it may think proper, and may agree with him as to salary on such terms and conditions as it may think reasonable and proper; and, upon the expiration of the contract, the vestry may renew it, but if not renewed, the vestry's choice and contract shall remain until it declares its desire to make a new choice or contract.

CHAPTER IX.

Some of Maryland's Early Churches.

IN 1692, the Church of England became, by law, the established Church of the Province. Provision was made for dividing the several counties into parishes, the election of vestrymen for each, and the imposition of a poll tax of 40 ℔s. of tobacco upon all the taxable inhabitants of each parish, for the support of the same.[1]

Under this Act, the counties of the Eastern Shore were divided into thirteen parishes, as follows: Kent, into Saint Paul and Kent Island; Cecil, into North Sassafras and South Sassafras; Talbot, into Saint Paul's, Saint Michael's, and Saint Peter's; Dorchester, into Great Choptank and Dorchester; and Somerset, into Coventry, Somerset, Stepney, and Snow Hill. The counties of the Western Shore were divided into seventeen parishes, as follows: Anne Arundel, into Saint Margaret's, Westminster, Saint Anne's, Saint James', and All Hallow's; Baltimore, into Saint George's, Saint John's, and Saint Paul's; Calvert into, All Faith, Saint Paul's, Christ Church, and All Saints; Charles, into William and Mary, Port Tobacco, Durham, and Piscataway or Saint John's; and Saint Mary's, into William and Mary, and King and Queen.[2]

---

[1] Act, 1692, C. 2.

[2] Archives (Cl. Pro. 1692) pp. 472-475; Perry's American Colonial Church; Old Brick Churches in Maryland, pp. 34, 127, 128.

The following is the record of proceedings for the laying out of Saint Mary's County into parishes :

"To his Excellency the Governor and Council.

"The bounds and limits of Saint Mary's County parishes laid out the 5th day of September, Anno Dom. 1692, by virtue of a late Act of Assembly thereunto directing, are as follows, viz : It was by the Justices and Freeholders of the said County, for the aforesaid end and purpose met at Newtown the day and year above said, and then and there agreed that Saint Mary's County be divided into two parishes, and that the same be divided between Newtown hundred and Clement's hundred by Mr. Langworth's (Saint Clement's) branch which leads to Pottuxen main road, the lower whereof to be called by the name of William and Mary Parish, and the upper, by the name of King and Queen Parish.

"Certified from the records of Saint Mary's County Court, this 2nd day of March, in the fifth year of their Majesty's Reign, Anno Dom. 1692.

"P. me Henry Denton, Cl."[1]

By this division, William and Mary Parish embraced all that part of the County lying between Saint Clements Bay and Point Lookout, its boundries being, the Potomac River, Saint Clement's Bay and River, the Calvert County line (then near Three Notched road to Pyne Hill Run, and with it to the bay), and the Chesapeake Bay to Point Lookout. And thus it continued, until Saint Andrew's Parish was erected in 1745, when the upper boundary was changed to Poplar Hill Creek, on the Potomac, and from thence by a line through Clifton Mills, (the Factory) to Legrand's Creek on the Patuxent. The records in which the boundaries of the Parishes of Saint

---

[1] Archives (Pro. Cl. 1692) p. 474.

Mary's County were recorded, perished when the Court House was burned in 1831, but the above mentioned line, separating William and Mary Parish from Saint Andrews, was ascertained and again defined in 1851, when William and Mary was divided into two parishes—Saint Mary's, all that part on the east side, and William and Mary—all that part on the west side of the Saint Mary,s River, the latter parish extending up the County to a line drawn from Poplar Hill Creek to Clifton Mills, and the former to a line drawn from Clifton Mills to Legrand's Creek on the Patuxent.[1]

The first Vestry of William and Mary Parish, elected 1692, was composed of John Campbell, Kenelm Cheseldine, Robert Mason, John Watson, Thomas Beall and John Llewellin.[2] Its first Parish Church was " Poplar Hill Church ", (now known as Saint George's), and which continued to occupy the same relation to the parish as it now does to that part of it which still bears the original name.

Of this venerable old edifice—erected as early as 1642, and the second Church of England built by the Maryland Colonists[3]—unfortunately, but little is known. Its location, however, is still susceptible of identification. It was a brick building, and stood about fifteen feet north of the present Poplar Hill Church, and, as indicated by its still visible outlines, its dimensions were about thirty-six by fifty feet.

The present church was erected, it is said, about 1750. The early records of the parish are no longer accessible; but, in the Whittingham Library, there are a few extracts taken from them, shortly before their destruction by fire, early in the present century. Among them, is the following order for some repairs to Poplar Hill Church :

---

1 See Proceedings, P. E. Convention, 1851.
2 Perry's American Colonial Church.
3 Who Were the Early Settlers of Matyland—Allen.

"At a Vestry held at Poplar Hill Church, April 10, 1721, the vestry agreed wth Mr. Josh Doyne to repair the windows of Poplar Hill Church. Viz$^{t.}$ To make four iron casements to be fitted to y^e middle light of y^e side windows, and to find glass for what is wanting. In consideration thereof, to allow the said Doyne 300 ℔s. of Tob^o for the iron casements, and for what glass is new, measured from end to end, each light at 12 ℔s. of Tob^o p^r foot. And for what is only mended by putting Paises of glass into the old lead, the lights to be measured and to be allowed 6 ℔s. of Tob^o p^r foot".

"Likewise, the same did agree with Mr. Josh Doyne to place a window in the west end of Poplar Hill Church, 6 foot square from out to out, and a new frame, the said Doyne to be allowed 400 ℔s. of Tob. for the same".

At this time, Messrs. Richard Hopewell, George Clark, William Harrison, Anthony Semmes, William Canoday, and James Waughop, appear to have been the vestrymen of the parish.

In the same library, is the following letter, from an early rector of the parish, which shows a cordial and liberal response of its parishioners to the appeal of Governor Sharp in behalf of the suffering people of Boston, consequent upon the destructive fire there, in 1760:

"MAY IT PLEASE YOUR EXCELLENCY:

"Since my letter of the 17th instant, I received last Sunday, at Poplar Hill Church, (quite unexpected) after divine Service, some more Money on Account of the Sufferers by the late dreadful Fire at Boston. I thought it incumbent on me to acquaint your Excellency of any further Sum that shou'd be collected; that thereby you may be informed of the Donations received by me. The Sum total now amounts to

Seventeen pounds eleven Shillings and four pence half penny, which I have paid the Sheriff in Obedience to your Commands, and am

"Sir, with the greatest Duty and Respect
"Your Excellency's Most obedient and humble Servant,
"MOSES TABBS.

"St. Mary's County
"June ye 25th 1760.
"To his Excellency."

In 1724, the Rev. Leigh Massey reported to the Governor that the parish contained two churches, about 500 parishioners and "an extraordinary glebe of 400 acres, but the house very indifferent".[1]

In the chancel of the old church was a horizontal slab, still in good preservation, containing the following inscription: "Near this place lyes inter'd the Rev^d Mr. Leigh Massey. He was educated at Oxford, Rector of this Parish, the darling of his Flock and Beloved by all who knew him. He dyed January 10, 1732-3; aged 29".[2] In the isle which led from the front door to the alter, is still to be seen another slab,

---

[1] Perry's American Colonial Church.

[2] The Rev. Leigh Massey, for many years the close friend and spiritual adviser of Washington, was the nephew of Mr. Massey, of Poplar Hill. He married the daughter of the distinguished lawyer and patriot of Virginia, George Johnston, and was the grand father of the late Major John T. Stoddert, of "Wicomico", Charles County, Maryland. He is said to have been a ripe scholar and a great wit. It is recorded of him that, he retired from the law, because his "conscience would not suffer him to make the "worst appear the better reason"; ceased preaching because of the "loss of his fore teeth"; withdrew from medicine, which he practiced without charge, because he was "sent for by everybody", and declined a judgeship, because it "took him too much from his family" He died in 1814, at the advanced age of eighty-six years.—See interesting letters about him from Major J. T. Stoddert, in Meades Virginia.

which is to the memory of Joseph Holt who died in 1701. Near these, was discovered in 1886, several inches below the surface, a rectangular slab, to the memory of the Rev. Francis Sourton. On it is engraved a curiously quartered shield, supposed to be his coat-of-arms, and an epitaph in latin, translated as follows : " Francis Sourtin Anglican of Devonshire, son of Francis minister of evangelic truth. He was sedulous in a life often afflicted, and was buried in 1679". The legend, also in latin, has been translated thus, " And thou reader living in the Lord Jesus Christ, keep the faith, and thou also, though dead, shall live ".[1]

In 1675, Robert Cager, of Saint Mary's, devised his property "for the maintenance of a Protestant ministry in Poplar Hill and Saint George's hundred. The following year the legislature confirmed the devise, and vested the title in the Mayor, Aldermen and Council of Saint Mary's City in trust for said purposes".[2] A part of this endowment—one of the earliest in Maryland—is the present glebe of Poplar Hill Parish (separated from William and Mary Parish in 1850) a tract of 400 acres, which still retains its original name " Itchcomb Freehold ". It is a curious coincidence that one of the executors of the will of Robert Cager was Mr. Francis Sourton,[3] of Devonshire, England. In 1701, Mrs. Elizabeth Baker also devised to the parish a tract of 100 acres, called "Town Land " and situated near Saint Mary's City.[4]

A few large, well bound and handsomely marked volumes of the old " Parish Library " established in 1701 by the Rev. Thomas Bray, Commissary of Maryland, have been preserved.[5]

[1] For data as to Trinity Church, on Trinity Creek, and the old State House at Saint Mary's, which was dedicated to public worship, and both within the limits of this parish.—See pp. 39, 40, 75, 76.
[2] Archives, Act, 1676, p. 531. [3] Ibid.
[4] Will, Will Record Saint Mary's County.
[5] In the possession of Mrs. Charles Grason.

THE EARLY CHURCHES

As the early records have perished, the names of the clergymen who officiated within the limits of the parish, before, as well as after its organization, and obtained from other sources, are here given.

As early as 1639, the Rev. Thomas White was at Saint Mary's, and while there married John Hallis and Restitua Tue,[1] servants of Cornwaleys, and which is believed to be the first protestant marriage ceremony performed in Maryland. In 1650, the Rev. William Wilkinson—the first permanent protestant minister in the Province — came to Maryland, located in Saint George's hundred and for thirteen years officiated at Poplar Hill and Saint Mary's.[2] He died in 1663, and was succeeded by the Rev. Francis Sourton. Mr. Sourton was probably in the parish as early as 1676.[3] He died in 1679.[4] In 1683, the Rev. Duel Pead was in the Parish, and in November of that year the Legislature passed a vote of thanks to him "for the learned sermon preached before the two Houses of Assembly on the 14th inst".[5] In 1689, the Rev. Paul Bertrand, who four years before had been sent from England to Calvert County, in response to the petition of Mary Taney,[6] was at Poplar Hill,[7] and in 1692, when the Parish was formally organized, the Rev. Thomas Davis was in charge.[8] He was succeeded in turn, by the Revs. James Crawford in 1694;[9] Peregrine Coney in 1696;[10] Benjamine Nobbs in 1700;[11] Joseph Holt in 1701;[12] Henry Jennings in 1706;[13] Leigh Massey in 1723 (died their in 1733);[14] Lawrence De Butts in 1735, (died

---

1 Rev. George A. Leakin, in Maryland Churchman, September, 1892; Neill, p. 78.
2 Day Star, p. 145.   3 See Will, Robert Cager.
4 See tombstone at Poplar Hill.   5 Arch. (Ass. Pro.) pp. 483, 562.
6 Gambrall, p. 67.   7 Rev. M. H. Vaughan.
8 Allen.   9 Ibid.   10 Scharf, 1 p. 352.
11 Ibid, p. 366.   12 Allen.   13 Ibid.
14 Act, 1723; Tombstone at Poplar Hill.

there in 1752);[1] Moses Tabbs in 1752, and served until his death, which occurred in 1777;[2] Rev. Joseph Messenger, of Saint Andrews Parish, officiated in William and Mary after the death of Mr. Tabbs and until 1786;[3] Rev. Benjamine Sebastine in 1786, from Christ Church, Calvert County;[4] Rev. James Simpson, from 1788 to 1793; Rev. Andrew Elliott in 1795; Rev. Charles Smoat, made Deacon by Bishop Claggett, June, 1793, Priest, November, 1795, (died there in 1805); Rev. Francis Barclay, from 1808 to 1810; Rev. James Jackson, from 1812 to 1816; Rev. John Brady, from 1816 to 1822 (died there in 1822); Rev. R. Kearny, from 1824 to 1828;[5] Rev. H. N. Hotchkiss, in 1829, during whose ministry the proposition to pull down the old State House at Saint Mary's was carried. He is said to have displaced the first bricks, died a few days thereafter and is buried in the Northwest corner of the lot upon which it stood.[6]

The interesting and valuable early records of King and Queen Parish, in Saint Mary's County, have been destroyed, and all that can now be obtained of its earlier history, must be gathered from scattered documents, references, and legislative enactments.[7]

When it was first laid out, it extended from Saint Clements Bay and Run to the extreme northern end of the county, as then defined, and which embraced within its limits, the territory known as "Newport Hundred", now a part of Charles County. Its boundaries were Saint Clements Bay

---

1 Maryland Gazette, July 9, 1752.   2 Allen.
3 Ibid; Saint Andrew's Records.   4 Allen.
5 Ibid.   6 Pilate and Herod, 13.
7 The substance of this sketch of King and Queen Parish, was given to "The Church Militant", the official organ of the Bishop of Washington, and was published by it in December 1898.

Run (the latter then called Langworth's Branch), the Calvert County line (then near the Three Notched Road) to the upper extremity of Newport Hundred, thence to the head waters of Wicomico River (now Zachiah Swamp) and with the Wicomico and Potomac Rivers to the beginning.[1]

In 1706, Newport Hundred was taken away, and united to William and Mary Parish, in Charles County,[2] but, in 1715, "it appearing that the severance had been obtained by misrepresentation", it was again united to King and Queen Parish,[3] where it remained until 1748. In 1744, an Act was passed to unite all that part of King and Queen Parish lying in Charles County, to Trinity Parish, in said County.[4] The Act went into effect in 1748,[5] thus making the dividing line between Charles and Saint Mary's, the upper boundary of the parish, as it is to-day. In 1745, the lower boundary of the parish was extended down to Bretton's Bay and Run, its easterly boundary, as established at the same time, being a line drawn, north 42½ degrees west, from Major Barnes' mill (on Bretton's Bay Run, about half a mile above the plank bridge), to the upper extremity of the county,[6] but, in 1748, on complaint to the General Assembly, that the latter line "did not leave to King and Queen Parish a proportionable number of taxable inhabitants", it was changed, and a line running north 36 degrees west, from Major Barnes' mill, was adopted in its stead,[7] and became the permanent dividing line between the Parishes of King and Queen and All Faith.

The first parish church was probably Newport Church, then located in about the centre of the parish. In 1735, the rector, vestry, and church wardens, were authorized by the General

---

1 Archives (Cl. Pro. 1674) p. 49.   2 Act, 1706, C. 7.
3 Act, 1715, C. 13   4 Act, 1744, C. 14.
5 Act, 1748, C. 9.   6 Act. 1745, C. 4.
7 Act, 1748, C. 4.

Assembly "to purchase two acres of ground to build a church on, in that part of the parish lying in Saint Mary's County, and to raise a fund, as well as to complete the said purchase and building, as to repair Newport Church within said parish".[1] The following year a special assessment was ordered for these purposes, and the freeholders of the parish were directed to meet "in order to choose a place to build the said church upon".[2] The place selected was Chaptico, and the church was completed in 1737. It is a capacious brick building, with steep roof, arched windows, and recess chancel. The ceiling, from front to rear, on both sides, is square to the outer lines of the chancel, and is supported by corinthian columns. From these square ceilings, an arched middle ceiling rises at a graceful angle, and, with the chancel ceiling, forms an arched ceiling through the entire middle of the building. It still stands, is in excellent preservation, and is an uncommonly handsome specimen of colonial church architecture.

In 1750, an Act was passed for the erection of "a chapel of ease in King and Queen Parish, in which the minister is to officiate every third Sunday".[3] This chapel was a frame building; was called All Saints, and was located on the site of the church still bearing that name, but built within the present century, and said to be the third in order erected on that site.

A little below All Saints, on Saint Paul's Creek, stood the little Episcopal Church of Saint Clement's Manor, erected as early as 1642—the third Protestant church built by the Maryland colonists.[4] The land for the site of this church, and a glebe, was given by Thomas Gerrard, the lord of Saint

---

1 Act, 1735, C. 9.   2 Act, 1736, C. 13.
3 Act, 1750, C. 21.
4 Who Were the Early Settlers of Maryland, p. 29.

Clements Manor. He was a Roman Catholic, but his wife, Susannah, a sister of Justinian Snow, was a Protestant,[1] and under her auspices the chapel was built. How long this little memorial of English church life in early Maryland stood, is not known. In 1696, the Council ordered the vestry of King and Queen Parish "to have the bounds settled of the one hundred acres of land given to the church by Thomas Gerrard".[2] No mention is made of the chapel at that time, and, as another one had been built elsewhere, it may be assumed that it had disappeared.

The latter chapel was at Wicomico (between Plowden's Wharf and Bluff Point), the stream on which it stood still being known as "Church Run". In 1696, Captain Gerard Slye complained to the Council "that the chapel built for the parish at Wicomico was on his land",[3] and asked that it be removed. This, however, was not done, and the chapel was still standing in the early part of the present century. It was erected in 1694. On July 30th, of that year, it was reported to the Council "that it was then going forward to be built nigh Captain Coades"[4]—the Bluff Point estate before mentioned.

In 1750, the vestry was authorized to sell the glebe land given by Thomas Gerrard, and to purchase a glebe nearer the centre of the parish.[5] In 1654, William Marshall gave "three heifers", from which a stock of cattle was to be raised "for the maintenance of a minister which is to be in the now known neck of Wicomico".[6] This, and the donation of land by Doctor Gerrard, are worthy of mention as the first church endowments in Maryland. That part of the parish in which

---

1 Day Star, p. 55.
2 Archives (Cl. Pro. 1696).
3 Ibid.
4 Cl. Pro. 1694.
5 Act, 1750, C. 17.
6 Archives (Pro. Ct.) p. 393.

the several chapels above referred to were located, is now within the limits of All Saints' Parish, carved out of King and Queen, and erected in 1893.

Among the fragmentary extracts from the early records of the parish, preserved in the "Whittingham Library", is a reference to the purchase in 1770 of "one silver Chalice Cup and cover", "a marble font and pedestal, two Baskerville's Bibles, two Royal Common Prayer Books, with Psalms, and two pulpit cushions". Whether the handsome communion service and marble font now in use at Chaptico church were a part of this purchase, has not been definitely ascertained. A tradition prevails that they were presented to the parish by Queen Anne, and that the service and font purchased in 1770, were for All Saint's Chapel. Be this as it may, it is susceptible of proof that a separate communion service and font were in use at the chapel from an early date, and the further fact that there is no evidence extant of the purchase of any other service for the parish, lends color to this much cherished tradition.[1] In 1773 an organ, said to have been a superior instrument for that day, was purchased for Chaptico Church. The following year the General Assembly authorized an annual levy of five pounds of tobacco per poll, to be made for the support of an organist.[2] This is one of the few instances in Maryland in which a church organist was paid by a general taxation. In 1813, the British broke into Chaptico Church, and in addition to other depredations, completely destroyed this old organ.

---

[1] Ridgely, in her excellent work, "The Old Brick Churches of Maryland", says: the "design of this church, simple but in perfect harmony, is attributed to no less a personage than Sir Christopher Wren, the architect of St. Paul's Cathedral, London" As Sir Christopher Wren died in 1723, this error must have proceeded from an uncertainty of the date at which the Church was erected—1735.

[2] Act, 1774, C. 7.

THE EARLY CHURCHES

The first vestry of King and Queen Parish (1692) was composed of Nehemiah Blackston, Richard Clouds, John Dent, Philip Briscoe, John Coade and John Bartcroft.[1] At the commencement of the American Revolution the vestry consisted of John Eden, William Thomas, Hanson Briscoe, Zachary Bond, John Dent, Thomas Bond and John Briscoe.[2]

The first minister in the parish, after its organization as such in 1692, was the Rev. Christopher Platts.[3] In 1715, the Rev. John Donaldson was inducted rector of the parish. In his report to the Governor in 1724, he stated that he had been in the parish nine years, and that it contained two churches, a glebe and two hundred families,[4] that "the Parish is 36 miles long and about 7 miles wide". Mr. Donaldson remained rector of the parish until his death, which occurred in 1747.[5] He was succeeded by the Rev. Richard Brown. In 1761, it was proposed that the Rev. Mr. Swift of Port Tobacco and the Rev. Mr. Brown of King and Queen, exchange parishes. In writing Lord Baltimore on the subject, Governor Sharpe took occassion to say,"that the Parishioners of Port Tobacco Parish have nothing against Mr. Swift except that he is a very poor and heavy preacher, and in that respect they would be no better off with the Rev. Mr. Brown".[6] The exchange was not made, and Mr. Brown remained in the parish until 1773, when he resigned. His successor was the then Curate, the Rev. George Goldie,[7] who continued to fill the position as rector of the parish until the revolution. There is some evidence, indeed, tending to show that he remained in the parish until the time of his death, 1791, with the exception of

---

1 Perry's American Colonial Church.   2 Hanson.
3 Scharf, 1, p. 366.   4 Perry's American Colonial Church.
5 Bacon.   6 Archives, Sharpe's Correspondence, p. 529.
7 Extract in Whittingham Library.

the year 1776, but this has not been definitely ascertained. Mr. Goldie was licensed by the Bishop of London in February, 1766, and had been Curate to the Rev. Thomas Bacon in All Saint's Parish, Frederick County.[1]

Formerly there was situated on the the northerly side of the church, and near the front, a frame vestry-house, surmounted by a belfry, and which was used also as a school building. At the rear of the church, and immediately beyond the chancel is the Key vault, over the entrance to which is a stone bearing the family coat-of-arms.

The record of the proceedings for the laying out of All Faith Parish is as follows: " At a Court held at Benedict—Leonardtown, the 14th day of February, in the year of our Lord God, 1692, and in the fifth year of the reign of our sovereign Lord and Lady, King William and Queen Mary, by the grace of God, King and Queen of England; Scotland, France and Ireland, defenders of the faith, etc., by the justices therein, authorized and appointed, together with the most principle freeholders thereunto called for the laying out of Parishes on the east side of the Patuxent River, in Calvert County, being in obedience to an Act of Assembly, entitled an Act for the service of Almighty God, and for the establishment of the Protestant Religion in this Province, made at the City of St. Mary's, the 10th day of May, Anno Dom. 1692, present, Mr. Thomas Tasker, Mr. Thomas Holliday, Mr. John Bigger, Mr. Francis Hutchins, Mr. James Keech, Mr. William Parker, and Mr. Francis Freeman, commissioners * * * * It is concluded and agreed on by the justices above named and by the principal freeholders at the time and place above said, met together: that from the main branch of

---

[1] History, Western Maryland, 1, p. 505.

THE EARLY CHURCHES 217

Swanston Creek to the lower part of Harvey Hundred, be in one parish, the church of the said parish being already built, standing by the fork of Trent Creek, called by the name of All Faith Church. The vestrymen appointed and chosen by the principal freeholders, met together at the time and place above said, being Capt. James Keech, Mr. John Smith, Mr. Richard Sotheron, Mr. John Gillam, Mr. Charles Ashcom, Mr. Richard Gardner. Very Copia pr Henry Jowles, Clk. of Calvert County ".[1]

In 1695, the territory embraced within the limits of All Faith Parish, lying between Indian Creek and the lower part of Harvey hundred, was annexed to Saint Mary's County,[2] and in 1744 that part of the parish lying north of Indian Creek, was united to Trinity Parish in Charles County,[3] thus leaving the whole of All Faith Parish within the domain of St. Mary's County.

The first westerly boundary of the parish, was the original dividing line between Saint Mary's County and Calvert County, and this continued for many years and until the new dividing lines between All Faith and King and Queen Parishes, fully described in sketch of the latter parish, were established. The southerly boundary of the parish, was in 1745, changed from the lower part of Harvey Hundred to Bretton's Bay run, the line as thus adopted, extending from Major Barnes' mill to Coles Creek on the Patuxent River.

In 1765, the Justices of Saint Mary's County were directed by the Assembly to make a levy of 120,000 ℔s. of tobacco for the use of the vestry of All Faith Parish, who were authorized to "build a new church where the old one stands" and also to "purchase from Mr. Thomas Reeder an acre of the land

---

[1] Archives (Pro. Cl. 1692) p. 473.
[2] Act, 1695, C. 13.
[3] Act, 1744, C. 14.

whereon John Knott formerly lived, and to contract for building thereon a chapel of ease ".[1] The old parish church was pulled down and a handsome brick edifice, still in excellent preservation, was erected on the same site.

The land upon which All Faith Church stands was donated it appears, by Mr. John Price, who gave one acre of ground for that purpose, and to enlarge the lot, Mr. James Keech, in 1734, gave an additional half acre.[2]

The one acre of ground for the "Chapel of Ease" provided for in the Act of 1765, was purchased and the Chapel erected. It was known as the "Red Church" and stood on the west side of the public road leading from Saint Josephs to Oakville, about fifty yards from the road, and about two hundred yards below the fork made by the conjunction of the Patuxent road with it. This little chapel has long since disappeared, and lives only in the memory of a few, but its site, and that of the adjoining graveyard, although sadly neglected, and now covered with a wild and luxuriant forest growth, are still discernible.

There had been a Chapel of Ease in the parish from a much earlier date. It was located on the east side of the "three notched road", near what is known as "Sandy Bottom", then in the lower part of the parish. When however, the bounds of the parish were curtailed in 1745, this little chapel fell within the limits of Saint Andrew's, and for further particulars of it, see the account of that parish.

In 1724, the Rev. Robert Scott, the then rector, reported to the Governor that the parish contained "two churches about twenty miles apart", a 'glebe with a small house on it'," two setts of communion service, two flaggons, cushions

---

1 Act, 1765, C. 5.
2 Records, All Faith Parish.

and valance for the pulpit " besides " 152 protestant and 52 popish families ".[1]

In May 1734, the Rev. Arthur Holt wrote the Bishop of London that " he had been inducted in the parish that year ", and that though in " most respects an agreeable position ", it was " such a laborious one ", that he was compelled to ask to be relieved from the charge. The parish, he stated " is but little short of 60 miles in length, and is very mountainous and hilly. One Lord's day I must ride (going and coming) about 14 miles, and the next about 34 miles. My congregations are much larger than my two churches can hold, so that the people are obliged to crowd at the outside of the doors and windows ".[2]

Than the last mentioned fact, it may be added, no other evidence is necessary to establish the position which Mr. Holt occupied in the parish as a pulpit orator, whatever may be the consensus of opinion upon his unwillingness to traverse the " gentle hills and beautiful valleys " of the lower Patuxent.[3]

The clergymen who officiated in All Faith from its organization as a parish to the Revolution, were Rev. Thomas Davis, 1694 ; William Dacres, (clerk of the vestry) 1695 ; Rev. Mr. Plats, (six sermons at 500 ℔s. of tobacco per sermon) 1698 ; Rev. Benjamine Nobbs, (minister for lower half of parish officiated occasionally at the Parish church) 1698, 1699 and

---

1 Perry's American Colonial Church.   2 Ibid.

3 In 1719, the vestry, through, Thomas T. Greenfield purchased in London, at a cost of £25, 15 s. " two silver Chalices, two silver Patens, two pewter bottle Flagons washed with gold or laquer ". In 1725 Robert Stourton bequeathed to the upper church of the parish a silver tankard weighing 35 ounces. In 1840 the vestry passed an order to have " the plate belonging to the church repaired or exchanged " the result of which order was that the old plate was exchanged for a new silver Chalice, Flagon and Paten, each piece being marked " All Faith Church 1840 ".—Record All Faith Parish.

1700; Rev. Joseph Holt, (six sermons) 1701; Rev. George Tubman, (four sermons) 1702; Rev. George Trotter, (one year) 1703; Rev. Mr. White, (six sermons on Saturdays) 1707; Rev. Henry Jennings, (at the chapel one year) 1708; Rev. Robert Scott, served from 1708 to time of his death, 1733, with Rev. Hugh Jones as assistant, at both churches from 1730 to 1733; Rev. Arthur Holt, (one year) 1734; Rev. John Urquhart, served from 1734 to time of his death, 1764; Rev. Mr. Lander, (eleven months, preaching every second Sunday only) 1764; Rev. John Stephens, Curate, from 1765 to 1769; Mr. Stephens was inducted Rector by Governor Eden in 1769, and served until 1777, when he resigned.[1]

In 1744, an Act of Assembly was passed directing the Justices, Sheriff, and Surveyor of Saint Mary's County, to lay out a new parish in the county, thus increasing the number to four. The Commissioners were to meet in Leonardtown on or before the 20th of August of that year, and to give twenty days notice of such meeting.[2] This Act not having been executed within the time prescribed, the following year a supplementary Act was passed, under which new commissioners were appointed, and the county laid out into four parishes.[3] The new parish thus formed, was called Saint Andrews, and was made up of parts of All Faith and William and Mary Parishes, the dividing line between it, All Faith and King and Queen, being Bretton's Bay and Run, and a line drawn from Major Barnes' mill on said Run to Coles' Creek on the Patuxent, and the one separating it from William and Mary, being a line drawn from Legrande's Creek, on the Patuxent, to a point on the Potomac, it is said, between Hampton and Tower Hill.

---

[1] Records of All Faith Parish.
[2] Act, 1744, C. 14.   [3] Act, 1745, C. 4.

THE EARLY CHURCHES

While the parish was thus formally laid out at that time, the division, it appears, did not actually take place until after the death of the then incumbents of the two parishes from which it was carved, the Rev. Mr. Urquhart, of All Faith, continuing to serve in that part severed from his parish, as did also the Rev. Mr. DeButts, of William and Mary. In 1753, the General Assembly authorized the parishioners "in that part of the parish made vacant by the death of the Rev. Lawrence DeButts, to elect a vestry church-wardens and inspectors for such vacant part".[1] In September of the same year this was done, the Rev. Moses Tabbs of William and Mary agreeing to officiate temporarily in such vacant part of the parish. He was succeeded there in 1757, by the Rev. Alexander Williamson, who in turn was followed, in 1761, by the Rev. Clement Brooke. The place of worship for that part of the parish was the Court House at Leonardtown, while that for the Patuxent side was the little chapel at Sandy Bottom, or the "Four Mile Run Church" as it was called, and which had hitherto been the Chapel of Ease of All Faith Parish.

Upon the death of the Rev. Mr. Urquhart of All Faith, in 1764, Saint Andrew's Parish was organized for the first time, by the election of a vestry, etc., for the entire parish, and the Rev. Francis Lauder, by appointment of Governor Sharpe, was inducted as its first minister. Steps were then taken, looking to the erection of a parish church, and in 1765,[2] the General Assembly authorized a levy of 200.000 ℔s. of tobacco, for the purpose. The site selected for the new church was "Waldrums Old Fields".[3] Two acres of this land was

---

1 Act, 1753, C. 19.   2 Act, 1765, C. 4.

3 A tradition prevails in the parish, that when the question of where the Parish Church should be located, was first before the congregation, some years before it was built, there was a strong sentiment, headed by

purchased of Samuel Bellwood, the then owner, the price paid being £5 currency. The architect was Mr. Richard Boulton; the contractors were Messrs. Samuel Abell, sr., Samuel Abell, jr. and Stourton Edwards; the contract price being 160,000 ℔s. of tobacco, and £100 sterling. The specifications called for a "brick building, fifty-five feet long in the clear, exclusive of the chancel, and forty feet wide in the clear, with a porch in front connecting two pyramids, or low towers, which ornamented each front corner of the church; the walls to be three bricks thick to the water table, and two bricks thick above; the aisles to be laid with flagstone, and the ceiling to be square on the sides and arched in the center". The unique and artistic alter-piece, containing the Lord's Prayer and Ten Commandments was carved by Mr. John F. Limner.[1]

The church was completed in 1767. It still stands, is well preserved, and is a pleasing specimen of early church architecture. After the completion of Saint Andrews Church, the little chapel at Sandy Bottom, having survived its usefulness, soon went to ruin. It appears for the last time upon the parish records, as having been the place of meeting of the vestry on September 6th, 1764, which met and determined upon the erection of the present parish church. No traces of it are now to be found, even in the recollection of the oldest inhabitants, except as imperfectly indicated by its old grave yard, which though neglected, and even plundered, it is said, of its once substantial brick enclosures, and left a barren and forsaken spot, it is still susceptible of identification, and

the Hon. George Plater, (father of Governor Plater) the most prominent man, perhaps, in the parish, in favor of building it on the site of the little Sandy Bottom Chapel. So pronounced were Mr. Plater's feelings in favor of that location, and so decided his convictions that his views would be carried out and his wishes gratified, that he requested to be buried in the chapel yard there, which was accordingly done.

1 Parish Records.

relatively points out the site once occupied by this early church—the first Chapel of Ease of All Faith, and the first place of Protestant worship in Saint Andrews Parish.

On April 13th, 1769, the vestry met at Saint Andrews Church to dispose of its pews. Thirty were taken, and the sum realized for them was £150, 5 s., the highest bidders being Hon. George Plater and Col. Abraham Barnes, who conjointly became the possessors of pew No. 1 for £16 sterling.

In 1755, 292 acres of land were purchased from Thomas Wheatty and Clement Norris, for a glebe for the parish, the price paid being 33,035 ℔s. of tobacco, and, in 1763, the vestry contracted with Samuel Abell, to erect a dwelling house thereon, for the sum of 26,000 ℔s. of tobacco. This glebe, it is said, was located on the road which leads from Leonardtown to Saint Andrews Church, and about three miles from the latter. After many years of service it was sold, and another, situated about half way between the church and the "Three Notched Road" was purchased in its stead.

In 1757 a silver Chalice and Salver were purchased for the parish, which are said to be the same now in use at Saint Andrews Church.[1]

The rectors of Saint Andrews Parish, in addition to those already mentioned were Rev. Robert Ranney, from 1765 to 1767; Rev. William West, from 1767 to 1772; Rev. Joseph Hindman, from 1772 to 1773; Rev. George Gowndril, curate, from 1773 to 1775; Rev. Joseph Messenger, from 1775 to 1787; (all inducted by appointment by the Governor), the

---

[1] While digging a grave in Saint Andrew's Grave yard in January, 1894, a memorial gold breast pin was found, of unique design with hair settings and bearing the following inscription: "Edmund Porteus ob March 28th, 1752. Aged 32". There was a Robert Porteus, from Baltimore City in the Continental Army in 1774, but the name in Maryland is a very uncommon one.

Rev. John Wilson, (first rector elected by the vestry, 1787) served 5 years; Rev. Francis Walker, from 1792 to 1818, when the Rev. John Brady was elected, who was succeeded in turn by the Rev. Clement F. Jones, Rev. John Claxton, Rev. James A. Buck, Rev. Mr. Scull, and Rev. George R. Warner.[1]

One of the most historical of the early parishes is Prince George, commonly known as Rock Creek Parish. It was erected in 1726, and embraced within its limits all the territory lying between the Potomac and Patuxent Rivers, and the eastern branch and a line drawn from thence to the Patuxent and extended westward to the westerly bounds of the Province; thus including not only a part of the District of Columbia, but Georgetown and all the Counties of Western Maryland and from it all the parishes now within that domain were originally carved, or are the result of subdivisions.[2]

---

[1] Records of Saint Andrews Parish.
The vestry men of the parish, during the same period were Col. Abraham Barnes, Robert Hammett, John Hammett, James Tarleton, John Newton, Samuel Abell, Matthew Wise, Enoch Abell, John Hall, Thomas James, Cyrus Vowles, John Black, George Plater, Hugh Hopewell, John Hammond, Michael Wellman, Stourton Edwards, Peter Urquhart, Philip Clarke, Charles King, William Martin, John Thompson, Cuthbert Abell, John Hatton Read, Timothy Bowers, Robert Watts, John DeButts, Archibald Campbell, William Somerville, Dr. Henry Reeder, William H. Brown, James Hopewell, John Abell, Edward Abell, Thomas Dillon, Peter Thompson, Charles Chilton, Joseph Hammett, Vincent Thornton, John B. Abell, Francis Abell, John S. Abell James A. Crane, John Rousby Plater, Matthew W. Simmonds, Dr. William Thomas, Richard Clark, Robert Hammett, George Clark, Joseph Harris, John Leigh, Adam Wise, G. N. Causeen, H. G. S. Key, George Plater, Bennett Hammett, John R. Plater, jr., George Dent, George Teal, James Forrest, Thomas Barbour, Hatch Turner, George S. Leigh, Chapman Billingsley, Thomas Hebb, J. M. Hammett, Dr. Walter H. S. Briscoe, Luke E. Barbour, William B. Scott, Benjamin G. Harris, Dr. Thomas J. Franklin, Enoch Hammett, John R. Thompson, Hezekiah Dent, Joseph H. Greenwell, Edward Plater, Henry Gough, and James R. Thompson.

[2] A detailed and interesting sketch of this parish may be found in Scharf's History of Western Maryland, vol. 2, p. 742.

THE EARLY CHURCHES 225

The first Rector of the parish was the Rev. George Murdock, who was commissioned by Gov. Charles Calvert, in December, 1726, and who officiated for thirty four years, and until his death, in 1761. He was followed by Rev. Alexander Williamson who served fourteen years, and was succeeded by the Rev. Thomas Read, who had previously been Curate of the parish, and also Rector of Saint Anne's, Annapolis. He was inducted in 1777, and continued to be Rector of the parish thirty-four years, when he resigned. During Mr. Read's pastorate of Rock Creek Parish, he kept a record of the marriages performed by him within the parish, and as well also a necrology covering the same period. A part of this record has been preserved—from 1796 to 1808, inclusive.[1] After the death of Mr. Read it came into the possesion of his son, the

---

1   MARRIAGES—MONTGOMERY COUNTY, 1796.

Jan. 12th,	John Buxton,	To	Eleanor Macoy,
Feb. 2d,	Theophilus Roby	"	Ann Willett
" 9th,	James Stewart,	"	Grace Clarke
" 11th,	Edw. Medcalf,	"	Cloe Butt
" 18th,	George Bowman,	"	Sarah Howse
" 22d,	Richd. Dorsey,	"	Anne Wayman
" 28th,	Wm. Welsh Cordingly,	"	Ann Moore
Mar. 3d,	Jno. Campbell,	"	Polly Craton
" 6th,	Rich. Thompson,	"	Eliz. Pelly
" 10th,	Jeremiah Nicholson,	"	Hester Nicholson
" 22d,	Jesse Wilcoxen,	"	Ruth Wilcoxen
" 24th,	Thomas Moody,	"	Mary Berry
" 28th,	Henry Jones' Geo.	"	Charles Jones' Polly, (Negroes)
Apr. 21st,	Wm. Wilson,	"	Anne White
" 21st,	Thomas Davis,	"	Catherine Worthington
May 15th,	Mr. Crabb's James and Clary (Negroes)		
" 15th,	Mrs Johns' Jerry and Mollie	"	
June 16th,	Rev. Nicholas Lane,	To	Esther Selby
" 17th,	Jonathan Sparrow,	"	Priscilla Smith
July 24th,	Wm. Groom,	"	Maryann Kelly
Aug. 2d,	Walter C. Williams,	"	Christiana Heugh
" 15th,	Richd. Downes,	"	Eliz. Rose
" 30th,	Benj. Nicholls,	"	Drusilla Culver

226   COLONIAL MARYLAND

late Robert Read, of Cumberland, after whose demise it was presented by his widow, Sarah Johns Read, through the author of this work, to the Maryland Historical Society. This old

Sept.	2?d,	William Lowry,	To	Rebecca Groome
"	18th,	Henry Lowe,	"	Ann Macbee
"	27th,	Caleb Windel,	"	Martha Parker
Nov.	17th,	Thomas Riggs,	"	Mary Riggs
"	24th,	Thomas Buxton,	"	Fanncy Macbeey
Dec.	1st,	Jno. Riddle,	"	Susanna Porter
"	8th,	James Ray,	"	Eliz. Warfield
"	15th,	Hezekiah Austin,	"	Eliz. Odle
"	22d,	Robert Fish,	"	Eliz. Jeans
"	25th,	John Leach,	"	Rachel Bowmen
"	29th,	Henry Hardey,	"	Frances West
1797.				
Jan.	17th,	Andrew Mudd,	To	Eleanor Green
"	17th,	William O. Lodge,	"	Frances Porter
"	24th,	Jno. Roberts,	"	Eliz. Heater
"	26th,	Lloyd Dorsey,	"	Anna Green
"	31st,	Erasmus Riggs,	"	Eleanor Wilcoxen
Feb.	5th,	Ely Denoon,	"	Henny Sanders
"	9th,	James McCoy,	"	Eliz. Brown
"	21st,	Clark Higgins,	"	Margaret Thomas
"	26th,	James Ridgeway,	"	Rebecca Hurdle
"	28th,	Nicholas Minstalled,	"	Mary Allison
"	28th,	Beale Warfield,	"	Amelia Ridgely
Apr.	17th,	Nicholas Feburiere,	"	Susan Tucker
"	18th,	Brice Warfield,	"	Sarah Collins
"	20th,	Jno. B. Allison,	"	Eliz. Higgins
May	4th,	Jno. Fields,	"	Mary Madden
"	21st,	Jno. Wight,	"	Cary Boyd
"	28th,	Jno. Hurley,	"	Eliz. Benton
June	1st,	Robt. Ricketts,	"	Kezia Ricketts
July	20th,	Zadoc Ricketts,	"	Ann Groome
Aug.	3d.	James Higgins,	"	Virlinda Wilcoxen
"	5th,	Sylvester Sullivan,	"	Rosanna Hawse
"	8th,	Samuel Lyon,	"	Linny Davis,
Sept.	14th,	Richd. Bean,	"	Prudence Kelly
Oct.	14th,	Benj. Reeder,	"	Anne Hungerford
"	26th,	William Benson,	"	Rachel Hensey
Nov.	23d,	Edw. Archey,	"	Eliz. Allison
Dec.	21st,	Nicholas Merriweather,	"	Eliz. Hood
"	26th,	John Gardner,	"	Cassandra Dowden

record is singularly valuable, not only because of the large area covered by the parish, embracing, even at that date, nearly the whole of Montgomery County, but more especially

1798.
Jan.	4th,	Jno. Higgins and Eliz Fisher		
"	9th,	Henry Culver,	To	Mary Patterson
"	11th,	Charles Bird,	"	Margaret Barton
"	16th,	Amasa Wellin,	"	Linney Trundle
"	25th,	Francis Hutchison and Sarah Ball		
"	25th,	Evan Trundle,	To	Anna Key
Feb.	6th,	Saml Love,	"	Sarah Jones
"	13th,	Richd. Snowden,	"	Eliza Warfield
"	24th,	Benj. Davis,	"	Eliz. Thrasher
Apr.	1st,	Christopher A Coal,	"	Sarah Claton
"	9th,	David Crafford's Edward and Linny (Negroes)		
May	3d,	Thos. H. Wilcoxon,	"	Sarah Prather
"	22d,	Ignatius Davis,	"	Margaret Wooten
Sept.	11th,	Amos Scott,	To	Annoe West
Oct.	7th,	Dawson Cash,	"	Jemima Beens
"	11th,	Benjamin Summers,	"	Virlinder Beckwith
"	15th,	David O'Neal,	"	Rebecca Lane
"	30th,	Robt. Willoson,	"	Eleanor Shekells
Nov.	15th,	Nathan Wells,	"	Sophia Duley
Dec.	8th,	Benjamin Crecraft,	"	Nelly Prather
"	18th,	Jno. M. Cox.	"	Eleanor Gray
"	20th,	Geo. Ward.	"	Ann Redman
"	23d,	Wm. Cox.	"	Liley Kelly
"	30th,	John Camobell,	"	Priscilla Oden.
1799.				
Jan.	3d,	Charles Davis,	To	Laurady Howse
"	3d,	Roby Penn,	"	Lucreta Howse
"	10th,	Richd. Turner,	"	Eliz. Beall
"	10th,	Daniel Carroll,	"	Ann Maccubbin
"	19th,	Jacob Swavaley,	"	Eleanor Fulks
"	22d,	John Adams,	"	Eleanor Collyer
"	22d,	Thomas Gratton,	"	Ruth Ray,
"	24th,	Charles Offutt Jones,	"	Rebecca Offutt
"	26th,	Benj. Thompson,	"	Eliz. Haney
"	27th,	Henry Parnnion,	"	Eliz. Sanders
		LICENSE GRANTED—ANNE ARUNDEL COUNTY.		
Feb.	5th,	James Groomes,	To	Sarah King
"	14th,	Thos· Garrott,	And	Elizabeth Fee
"	15th,	John Austin,	"	Cassandra Odle
"	26th,	Barak Ofutt,	"	Virlinder Offutt

by reason of the fact that the Montgomery records do not begin until 1798, and the necrology of the County being exceedingly meagre and limited. It is also worthy of note that this marriage record is somewhat more comprehensive than the

Mar.	14th,	James B. Crafford,	And	Ann Allison
"	19th,	Basil Waters,	"	Ann P. Magruder
Apr.	11th.	John Nicholson,	"	Tabitha Oden
"	18th,	Jesse Leatch,	"	Mary Letten
May	23d,	Edmund Riggs,	To	Jane Willson
Aug.	8th,	Solomon Pelly,	And	Massy Holland
"	29th,	Jacob Kirkman,	"	Susanna Hall
Nov.	5th.	Jno. Magruder,	"	Mary Linthicum
"	24th,	Jno Frey,	"	Turecia Lucas
Dec.	5th	Thos. Hood,	"	Rachel Wayman
"	10th,	James Magruder,	"	Eliz. Linthicum
Nov.	30th,	Jonas Parsley,	"	Eleanor Clayton
Dec.	12th,	Baruck Prather,	"	Casandra Swearingen
"	19th,	Jno. Perry,	"	Jane Alnutt
"	26th,	Richd. Stewart,	"	Eliz Renneton
1800.				
Jan.	2d,	William Ramsey,	And	Margaret Herren
"	14th,	Jno Lanham,	"	Lucy Ray
"	16th,	Camden Riley,	"	Anna Ray
"	21st,	Nathan Jones,	"	Anna Buxton
"	21st,	Edward Porter,	"	Mary Heiter
"	21st,	Nathan Orme,	"	Polly Beall
"	23d,	Solomon Holland,	"	Margaret Gatton
"	25th,	Jno. Redman,	"	Harriot Ward
"	30th,	Benedict Beckwith,	"	Eliz. White
Apr.	15th,	Edw. Harper,	"	Sarah Ann Boswell
"	15th,	Thos. Nicholls,	"	Priscilla Mackey
May	22d,	Michael Merrick,	"	Virlinder Bowman
"	22d,	Everrard Gary.	"	Ann Cloud
June	26th,	John H. Riggs,	"	Rebecca Howard
July	17th,	Thos. Odle Offutt.	"	Charity Benton
Nov.	18th,	Doct. Richd. J. Orme,	"	Ann Crabb
"	20th,	Elias M. Daniel,	"	Margaret Golden
"	27th,	Samuel Iulose,	"	Eliz. Stone
Dec.	4th,	Edw. O. Williams,	"	Eliz. Clagett
"	16th,	David Porter,	"	Mary Ray
"	20th,	Daniel Reintzel,	"	Ann Robertson
"	23d,	Arnold Lashley,	"	Eliz. Lee

THE EARLY CHURCHES

Montgomery records even after the latter were started, as it is not confined to marriages performed by license issued in that county, as are its records.

"	25th,	Notley Lanham,	And	Eliz. Hopkins
"	25th,	Benj. Kelley,	"	Eliz. Moore
"	28th,	William Wallace,	"	Margaret Brookes
"	30th,	Wm. Mullican,	"	Eliz, Dowden
1801.				
Feb.	1st,	Nathan Moore,	And	Eliz. Hantz
"	10th,	Leonard H. Johns,	"	Margaret Williams
"	17th.	David Clagett,	"	Salley Odle
"	24th,	Hatton Fish,	"	Sarah Benton
"	27th,	Levin Easton,	"	Druzilla Ricketts
Mar.	3d,	Leonard Young Davis,	"	Achsah Worthington
"	12th,	Samuel Magruder,	"	Eliz. Hawkins
"	31st,	Geo. Magruder,	"	Anna Turner
Apr.	5th,	Jno. Wiest,	"	Lydia Shuck
"	14th,	John Getty,	"	Eleanor Carey
May	24th,	Richd Langford,	"	Amelia Soper
July	9th,	Lewis Beall,	"	Eliza Wootton
Oct.	8th,	William Garrett,	"	Eleanor Higgins
"	8th,	Willson Walker,	"	Deborah Prather
"	8th,	Brice Selby,	"	Cathrine Marker
"	25th,	Josiah Bean,	"	Eleanor Wilson
"	27th,	Ezekiah Linthicum,	"	Mary Hickman
Nov.	19th,	Joseph Madden,	"	Susanna Sparrow
Dec.	1st,	Fredrick Linthicum,	"	Rachel Macklefresh
"	8th,	Nathan Dickerson,	"	Margaret Turnbull
"	10th,	Jesse Owings,	"	Hannah Hood
"	17th,	William Orr,	"	Eliz. Macklewain
"	22d,	Nathan Trail,	"	Susanna Buxton
"	22d,	George Heater,	"	Charlotte Porter
"	31st,	Wm. R. Jones,	"	Eliz. L. Richardson
"	31st,	Henry Fowler,	To	Lewis Beall's Mulatto Woman Nelly
1802.				
Jan.	7th,	Benj. W. Jones,	And	Margaret Willson
"	12th,	Lawrence O. Holt,	"	Sarah Oden
"	12th,	Thos. Clagett,	"	Rachel Offutt
"	21st,	Thos Davis,	"	Eliza Bowie
"	28th,	James Northcraft,	"	Rachel Fryer
"	30th,	James Cooke,	"	Patsey Beeding
Feb.	9th,	Barton Harriss,	"	Mary Griffith
Mar.	21st,	Wm. Sparrow,	"	Eliza Campbell

As much of the data contained in this old record is now otherwise inaccessible, it is of historic interest and value, and never having been published, it is here reproduced in full, except the necrology as well as the curious record of marriage and funeral fees, which were combined with it, are omitted.

Apr.	20th,	Andrew Offutt,	And	Eliz. Warfield
Aug.	3d,	Joseph Astlin,	"	Mary Beard
Sept.	2d,	Walter Madden,	"	Eliz. Mudd
"	12th,	James Groome,	"	Eleanor Fish
"	21st,	Joseph Cox,	"	Susanna Hogan
Nov.	9th,	Dr Jno. M. Read,	"	Maryann Clark
"	25th,	Saml. Bealmear,	"	Priscilla Williams
Dec.	7th,	George Buxton,	"	Maryann Trail
"	14th,	Azariah Kindle,	"	Amelia Nicholson
"	21st,	Wm. M. Elfresh,	"	Sarah Linthicum
"	30th,	Adam Klay,	"	Sabina Summers
1803.				
Jan.	18th,	Geo. W. Riggs,	And	Eliza Robertson
"	20th,	James Brown,	"	Ann Leek
Mar.	10th,	James Jarvis,	"	Eliz. Linch
"	31st,	Archibald Summers,	"	Margaret Pain
Apr.	10th,	Charles Porter,	"	Polly Fry
May	5th,	Jeremiah Browning,	"	Eliz. Summers
June	19th,	Isaac Forsythe,	"	Anna Letton
"	28th,	William Candler,	"	Rebecca Ray
Aug.	7th,	Edward Magruder,	"	Jane Ayton
"	28th,	Benjamine Lyon,	"	Rachel Davis
Sept.	11th,	Richd. Brooke Smith,	"	Sarah Letton
"	15th,	Nicholas Haney,	"	Sarah Golden
"	22d,	Brice Letton,	"	Hariot Moore
Oct.	20th,	Elias Elville,	"	Elizabeth Burress
"	27th,	Thos. Linsted,	"	Anna Maria Summers
Nov.	1st,	Zachariah Linthicum,	"	Anna Clagett
"	3d,	Warren Mugruder,	"	Harriot Holmes
"	17th,	Lloyd Hammon,	"	Elizabeth Merriweather
"	24th,	Thos. Hilleary,	"	Sarah Wheeler
Dec.	1st,	John Crown,	"	Eliz. Ball
"	29th,	Ashford Trail,	"	Anne Sanders
"	31st,	Hazil Butt,	"	Sarah Richards
1804				
Jan.	5th,	James Alex. Beall,	And	Eleanor Culver
Feb.	2d,	Benj. Perry,	"	Eliz. Magruder

The first Roman Catholic church in Maryland was at Saint Mary's City, the history of which has been given in the chapter entitled, "The First Capital". The next one in Saint Mary's County, of which there is a record, was at

Feb. 11th,	Joel Ketchen,	And	Sarah Hurst
" 12th,	Samuel Horner,	"	Mary McFarland
" 16th,	William Burditt,	"	Ruth Fitzgerald
Mar. 27th,	Joshua W. Dorsey,	"	Lucetta Plummer
Apr. 8th,	Peter Dent Moore,	"	Louisa Stanger
May 6th,	William O'Neal,	"	Anna Bell
June 9th,	Wm. Wheatley,	"	Mary Cashell
" 17th,	George Cashell,	"	Eliz. B. Edmonstone
" 19th,	James Rawlings,	"	Sarah Richardson
Sept. 6th,	Saml Golden,	"	Dollie Haney
" 6th,	Ninian Clagett,	"	Margret Burgess
" 8th,	Hezekiah Saffell,	"	Lydia Davis
" 25th,	Zachariah Muncaster,	"	Harriott Magruder
Nov. 29th,	Walter Bailey,	"	Sarah Ball
Dec. 7th,	Jesse Wade,	"	Mary Fleming
" 20th,	Aquila Gatton,	"	Mary Owen
" 23d,	Philip Garlon,	"	Sarah Willson,
1805.			
Jan. 8th,	Wm. Langville,	And	Naney Current
" 31st,	Thos. Sparrow,	"	Sarah Sparrow
Feb. 12th,	Reubin Riggs,	"	Mary Thomas
" 27th,	Charles Shook,	"	Priscilla Ball
Apr. 18th,	William Leemar,	"	Sarah Roberson
" 23d,	Archibald Mullican,	"	Anna Mathews
" 25th,	Walter Summers,	"	Sarah Swearingen
" 30th,	Abishai Gray,	"	Eleanor Miller
May 9th,	Robert Windsor,	"	Eliz. Thompson
June 6th,	Henry Rabbett,	"	Anne Wilburn
Oct. 15th,	Azel Waters,	"	Cassandra Williams
Dec. 29th,	James Beall,	"	Margaret Smith Benson
1806.			
Jan. 2d,	James Deselem,	And	Catherine Fulks
Feb. 4th,	Elbert Perry,	"	Rebecca Margruder
" 11th,	Daniel Robertson,	"	Sarah Greenfield
" 13th,	Jno. Heater,	"	Frances Shook
Mar. 4th,	Denton Porter,	"	Kitty Heater
Apr. 3d,	Thos. Gettings,	"	Christiana Perry
May 13th,	Dr. Peregrine Warfield,	"	Harriot Sappington
June 17th,	Dr. John Wootton,	"	Betsy Lynn Magruder

Newtown. On the 10th day of August, 1661, Mr. William Bretton, a prominent citizen of the Province, executed the following deed :

"AD. PERPETUAM MEMORIAM

"Forasmuch as divers good and zealous Roman Catholic inhabitants of Newton and Saint Clement's Bay, have unanimously agreed among themselves to erect and build a church or chapel * * * * and the most convenient place for that purpose, desired and pitched upon by them all, is a certain parcel of land belonging to William Bretton gentleman, Now know ye, that I William Bretton, of Little-Bretton, in ye conty of Saint Mary's in ye province of Md. Gentlemen,

Aug 28th,	Lawrence O'Neal,	"	Nany Galworth	
Sept. 18th,	John Dickerson,	"	Eliz. Turnbnll	
Dec. 4th,	Thos. S. Davis,	"	Creece Swearingen	
" 25th,	Jno. Williams,	"	Sarah Neritt	
1807.				
Jan. 1st,	Jacob Miller,	And	Naney Ricketts	
" 13th,	John Wesley Ward,	To	Eleanor Greentree	
Feb. 26th,	James Case,	And	Eliz. Bowman	
Mar. 5th,	George Ray,	"	Sarah Robertson	
" 8th,	Benj. Grymer,	"	Sarah Lowery	
" 26th,	Thos. W. Howard,	"	Elizabeth Crabb	
June 16th,	Henry Woodward Dorsey,	"	Rachel Cooke	
Oct. 13th,	Henry Gassaway,	"	Rachel Griffith	
" 20th,	Benj. Sedgwick,	"	Eleanor White	
Nov. 12th,	Wm. Elson Wilson,	"	Eleanor Swearingen	
Dec. 1st,	David Hammelton,	"	Ann Preston	
1808.				
Jan. 3d,	John Hurley,	To	Milly Offutt,	
Feb. 11th,	John Jenkins,	"	Charlotte Sparrow	
Apr. 18th,	Daniel Golding,	And	Eliz. Harris	
June 5th,	Hosea Edmonson,	"	Mary Orme	
Oct. 8th,	Allen Warfield,	"	Mary Dugan	
Dec. 27th,	Wm. Fish,	"	Hellen Joy	
1809.				
Jan. 12th,	Walter Stewart,	And	Eleanor Gray	
Feb. 12th,	Joseph Gittings,	"	Tabitha Beans	

with the hearty good-liking of my dearly beloved wife Temperance Bretton, * * * * have given, and do hereby freely forever give, to the behoof of the said Roman Catholic inhabitants, and their posterity or successors, Roman Catholics, so much land as they shall build ye said church or chapel on * * with such other land adjoining to ye said church or chapel, convenient likewise for a church-yard wherein to bury their dead, containing about one acre and a half of ground, situated and lying on a dividend of land called Bretton's Outlet, and on the east side of ye said dividend, near to ye head of the creek called Saint Williams creek, which falleth into Saint Nicholas creek, and near unto the narrowest place of ye freehold of Little-Bretton, commonly called The Straits".[1] Upon this ground was erected Saint Ignatius Chapel, the first Roman Catholic church at Newton, It was apparently a frame building, though a few scattered brick may still be seen around its site, and which are the only traces of it, that are to-day visible. But the old graveyard, surrounding the spot where once it stood, has been used as a place of Roman Catholic burial for nearly two hundred and forty years.[2] It is recorded that upon at least two occassions, the little chapel of Saint Ignatius was the recipient of legacies, one in 1670 and another the following year.[3]

The manor of Newtown or Little Bretton, patented to William Bretton in 1640,[4] passed out of the family, and was purchased by the Jesuit missionaries. In their hands the house and handsome chapel Saint Francis, since erected near by, have long been a centre of Catholicity. The house, said to have been built by Mr. William Bretton, of English brick,

1 Lib, S. 1658 to 1662, p. 1026 ; Day Star, p. 227.
2 Shea, pp. 78 & 349.
3 Wills, Wm. Tattershall & Col. Jarboe, Annapolis.
4 Kilty, p. 73.

is still standing, its original story-and-a-half having had another added, making it an imposing and stately looking mansion.[1] It occupies a commanding position, over-looking Bretton's Bay, Saint Clements Bay and the Potomac River.[2]

In 1698, the Sheriff's return of Saint Mary's County, upon the requisition of Governor Nicholson, states, that there were then in the county four places of Roman Catholic worship; a brick church at Saint Mary's City, a frame chapel at Saint Clement's town, a frame chapel at Mr. Gulick's, and a frame chapel near Mr. Heywood's, beyond the Patuxent road. There were at the same time two priests, Rev. Nicholas Gulick, and Rev. John Hall, and one lay brother in the County.[3]

When the first church at Saint Inigoes was built is not definitely known. While it became a Jesuit Mission at a very early period, owing to its proximity to Saint Mary's City, where there was a Roman Catholic church, it is not probable

---

1 Shea, p. 78.

2 William Bretton, the Lord of the manor of "Little Bretton, came to Maryland in 1637, with his wife Mary, the daughter of Thomas Tabbs, and our child. He was a member of the Assembly in 1648 and 1649; was clerk of the Assembly in 1650, and was clerk of the Lower House from 1661 to 1666 inclusive. The last official notice of him appears to have been his appointment as a Justice of the County Court of Saint Mary's in 1667. In 1651, he married 2d Mrs. Temperance Jay. His latter life is veiled in obscurity, and, though at one time possessed of a large and productive estate, he is supposed to have died in poverty. His children, a son and daughter, became objects of charity, being reported in "extremity of want", and from this fact, it has been suggested, arose the euphonius name which that beautiful neck of land that constituted the Manor of Little Bretton, to-day bears—" Beggar's Neck ".—See Liber I, p. 69; Arch., Ass. Pro. 1648 to 1650, and 1661 to 1666, inclusive; Ibid, Cl. Pro., 1667, p. 33; Day Star, p. 226; Old Brick Churches. p. 59.

In August, 1670, the Sheriffs of the several counties, were ordered by the Governor, to meet at the house of Thomas Cosden, at Newtown, to "make up their accounts with Mr. Thomas Notley, Receiver General", and to "bring a list of taxables within their respective counties".—Archives, (Cl. Pro. 1670) p. 70.

3 Cl. Pro. H. D. p. 539.

that Saint Inigoes had a church for many years after the settlement of the Colony. The site of the first chapel there is still pointed out. The present Saint Inigoes church, close by, is said to be the third in order.[1] The Manor of Saint Inigoes was patented to Mr. Thomas Copley, a Jesuit priest, known officially as Father Phillip Fisher,[2] the Superior of the Maryland Mission.[3] He died in 1653, leaving the Rev. Lawrence Starkey his successor.[4] It contained two thousand acres, and is still retained by the Jesuits, almost in its entirety. It is divided into small farms, which are rented for the support of the church. The manor-house, a quaint building, is beautifully located at the juncture of Saint Inigoes Creek and the Saint Mary's River. It was built in 1705, under the auspices of Father Ashbey, of the bricks, it is said, from the old Catholic church at Saint Mary's; and about the same time a small church was erected in the chapel-field, and a grave-yard was laid out and attached to it.[5] This was, in all probability, the first church on Saint Inigoes Manor.[6] In 1778 the British

---

1 Bryant, History United States, p. 513.
2 That Thomas Copley and Father Philip Fisher were one and the same person there can be no doubt. Both are represented as born at Madrid at the close of the 16th century; each came to Maryland in 1637, (August, 8) with Father Knowles; each was carried off, and each died in 1652. Neither recognizes the existence of the other. Copley took up lands for all the Jesuit Fathers, but no lands for Fisher, and Fisher as Superior alludes in his account of the mission to no Father Copley—Shea, p. 47, note; Foley records, 7, 1146; Woodstock letters, 11, pp. 18, 24.

The Statutes of Mortmain prohibited the taking of land to pious uses, and hence a necessity for this separate identity. The second tract taked up in Maryland by Copley for the use of the church, was Saint Thomas and Cedar Point Neck in Charles County, and which, with Saint Inigoes Manor, has gone far toward supporting Roman Catholic worship in their respective counties, for more than two centuries and a half.—
" Foundation of Maryland ". For further particulars as to the Statutes of Mortmain in Maryland, see chapter on "The Land Tenure of Colonial Maryland ".

3 " The Foundation of Maryland ", p. 200; Shea, p. 47.
4 Shea, p. 75.   5 Archives (Cl. Pro.) p. 418,
6 Fenwick, Brief Account. Settlement of Maryland; Shea, p. 370.

sloop of war, General Monks, threw a shot through the walls of the house, the Rev. Father Lewis having just left a bed over which it passed. In October, 1814, this house and chapel were robbed and pillaged by the crew of the British sloop Saracen, who not only took all that was valuable of the household furniture, plate and clothing, but even invaded the sacred precincts of the church—desecrated some of its most holy vessels, and carried many of them away. Complaint having been made to the Commander of the vessel, some of the property was returned, but the loss on this, and a former like occassion, was estimated at about twelve hundred dollars.[1]

On the Manor was located Fort Saint Inigoes, erected in 1637. It stood on the Point still known as "Fort Point", and about half a mile from the mouth of the Saint Mary's River, which it was intended to guard. By the Act of 1650, all ships trading within the Saint Mary's River, were required to pay a half pound of powder and two pounds of shot, as a port duty to Fort Saint Inigoes, and also to ride at anchor for two whole tides, both coming and going, within command of the said Fort.[2] Many of the early proclamations were dated at, and issued from this Fort, and the General Assembly of 1646 met there.[3] It was also, by order of Governor Calvert, made the place of general refuge, in times of threatened attack, for the women, children and helpless men living between Saint Inigoes Creek and Trinity Creek.[4] Captain John Price was the first Commander of the Fort, and he held the position for many years. The early records furnish repeated instances in which corn and cattle, by order of the Governor, were "pressed" for the use of the garrison at Fort Saint Inigoes,

---

[1] Schart, 3. p. 127.
[2] Archives (Ass. Pro.) 1650, p. 293.
[3] Ibid (Ass. Pro.) p. 209.   [4] Ibid (1st Cl. Pro.) p. 108.

THE EARLY CHURCHES

which occured in time of peace, would to-day be regarded as a somewhat remarkable exercise of executive power.

How the Fort was built and mounted the records do not show. Some of the cannon from there, however, are still to be seen. In 1824, the Rev. Joseph Carberry drew out of the river several of them, which, either from the washing of the Point, or the force of the current, were two hundred yards from the shore.[1] One of these early muniments of war and fortification, is now on the State House grounds, at Annapolis ; two of them are at Georgetown College, and at least one of them, it is said, is still on Saint Inigoe's Manor, where it now performs the function, painful to relate, of an ordinary boundary post.[2]

In speaking of this Fort and its situation, Bryant says : "at the lower end of the bay of Saint Ignatius (of whose name saint Inigoe's was an old, and once common corruption), was a bluff much like that at Saint Mary's, though lower and less picturesque. From it, looking to the north, across the bay, could be seen the point of the first landing, and to the south, the view extended to the mouth of the Saint Mary's River. It was a commanding site, and on it Governor Calvert erected a Fort, which effectually guarded the approach to the town above. Near, or in the Fort, stood a mill, and above it a few scattered buildings. No ruins of either Fort or houses remain, save a few scattered bricks and hewn stone ".[3]

---

[1] Scharf, I. p. 76.

[2] To the Saint Inigoes Mission is due the credit of having collected and preserved almost the only relics now to be seen, which was associated with the early history and first Capital of the Province. Among these may be mentioned the "Council Table", "the old bell", and Governor Calvert's "Cut Lass and leather scabbard" as well as some of the early muniments of war and fortification. The most of these, as well as the records of the order, are now at Georgetown College.

[3] Bryant, United States, p. 312.

Of the Roman Catholic churches in Saint Mary's County belonging to the Colonial period, around which the greatest local interest centres, by reason of the fact that its graveyard, from an early date, became the place of interment for many of the more prominent Roman Catholic families in the county, was perhaps, "old Saint Josephs". It was erected, it is said, about 1740, but the earliest recorded notice of its existence, which has been found, is the fact, that Father Joseph Mosley was officiating there in 1759.[1] It was a brick building, about 25x45 feet, with steep roof and square windows, and though unpretentious in design, it was a substantial and church-like edifice. About three hundred yards north of where it stood, a large and handsome church has been erected in recent years, after which the old building was allowed to crumble, though its site can yet be identified. It stood near the centre of the old grave yard, still used as a place of Roman Catholic burial.

When Saint John's, Sacred Heart and Saint Aloysius churches (the latter situated near Leonardtown, and long since disappeared) were built, has not ascertained. A legacy[2] however, to "Saint John's Chapel" in 1786, a tombstone in the graveyard of Sacred Heart, to the memory of Mrs. Susanah Margan, dated 1795, and one in the graveyard of Saint Aloysius, to the memory of Ignatius Benedict Denry, dated 1803, prove them all to belong to an early period. Owing to the stingent laws passed, the intollerant spirit, and the ungenerous policy pursued against Roman Catholics in Maryland, from 1698, to the Revolution, it is not probable they were built within that time, though they appear to have been erected soon after the latter date.

---

1 Old Catholic Maryland, Tracey, p. 134.
2 Will of Mary Henrietta Taney, Saint Mary's County.

CHAPTER X.

The Great Seal of Maryland and Her Flag.

IT has been aptly noted, that Maryland is unique in her Great Seal and presents a marked contrast to those of the other States of the American Union, in that it consists of armorial bearings of a strictly heraldic character, the Great Seal of most of the States bearing "emblems indicative of agriculture and commerce, plenty and prosperity, or kindred subjects, represented in a more or less pictorial or allegorical manner".[1]

The first Great Seal of Maryland, brought over by Governor Leonard Calvert, in 1643, was in the language of Baltimore, "treacherously and violently taken away by Richard Ingle or his accomplices, in or about February, Anno Domini 1644, and hath been ever since so disposed of it cannot be recovered".[2]

No impression of this seal appears to be extant, owing perperhaps, partly to the destruction of the records of the times, and partly to the fact that its use was more limited at first than at a

---

1 A thorough and interesting treatise on the Great seal of Maryland was read before the Maryland Historical Society by Major Clayton C. Hall, and published by the Society in 1886 as "Fund Publication No. 23, to which the author is indebted for much of the material of this chapter.

2 Archives (Cl. Pro.) 1648, p. 214.

later date, it not having been attached to land grants until 1644,[1] the same year it was lost. In 1648, Baltimore sent to the Province through Governor William Stone, a second Great Seal which in the minute description accompanying it is represented as "cut in silver" like its predecessor, and very similar to it in size and design. The escutcheon of this Seal bore the Calvert and Crossland arms quartered. The first and forth quarters consisted of "six pales" or vertical bars alternately gold and black, with a "bend dexter counter charged"—that is a diagonal stripe on which colors are reversed—being the Calvert arms; the second and third quarters consisted of a quartered field of red and white charged with a greek, or equal, limbed cross, classified as "botonny"—its arms terminating in trefoils — and also counter charged, that is with the colorings reversed, red being on the white ground and white on the red—the latter quarterings being from the Crossland, Baltimore's maternal arms — Alicia Crossland having been the mother of the first Baron of Baltimore. These quarterings were surmounted by an earl's coronet and full-faced helmet, which indicated his rank in America as that of a Count Palatine—his rank in England being that of a Baron only—a distinction which no other American colonial charter conferred. On the helmet rested the Calvert crest—a ducal crown with two half bannerets, one gold and one black. The escutcheon was supported on one side by the figure of a farmer, and the other by that of a fisherman—symbolical of his two estates, Maryland and Avalon. Below them was a scroll bearing the Calvert motto : "Fatti Maschii Parole Femine"—manly deeds, womanly words, or more strictly deeds are males, words females. Behind the escutcheons and coronets was engraved

---

[1] Bland, Maryland Report, 1. p. 308.

GREAT SEAL OF MARYLAND:
(DIAMETER 3¾ INCHES)
UNDER THE PROPRIETARY GOVERNMENT.

an ermine lined mantel, and surrounding all, on a border encircling the seal, was the legand : "Scuto Bona Voluntatics Tue Coronasti" With favor will thou compass him as with a shield.[1]

The heraldic terms used in describing the colors in the Calvert arms are *or*[2] and *sable*, which mean *gold* and *black*,[3] and *not* orange and black, as it has so frequently been misinterpreted.[4]

On the obverse side was a representation of Baltimore on horseback, with drawn sword, helmet decorated with feathers and in full armour, adorned with his paternal coat of arms, below which was engraved a seashore, grass and flowers, and around the whole an inscription containing his name and titles : Cecilius Absolutus Dominus Terrae Mariae et Avaloniae Baro de Baltimore.[5]

In the accompanying illustrations of the Great Seal under the Proprietary government, it should be noted, that on the obverse side of the word "Carlos" appears on the marginal circle instead of "Cecilius". Charles Calvert, became, on the death of his father, Cecilius, Baron of Baltimore in 1675, and through him and his grandson Charles, the fifth Lord Baltimore (except from February 20th, to April 5th, 1715, the length of time which Benedict Leonard survived his father) the title to the Province was in a Charles, Lord Baltimore until 1751, when the last of that name died. It was therefore but natural that the Great Seal of the Province should have borne the word Carlos during that period. When

---

1 Archives, (Cl. Pro,) 1648, pp. 214, 215 ; Hall, pp. 17, 23.

2 Ibid.   3 Clark's Heraldry, p. 16.

4 Most prominently of all by the State itself, in the handsome painting of the Great Seal which now decorate the Senate Chamber of the State House at Annapolis.

5 Archives (Cl. Pro. 1648) pp. 214, 215.

 the change was made, the records do not disclose, but a careful examination of the old Seal now in the Land Office, at Annapolis, clearly shows that it was accomplished by simply substituting on the original Seal, the one name for the other. The small illustration shown here, corresponds exactly with the description which accompanied the Great Seal in 1648, except that it is reduced in size, and represents it as it appeared when used during the administration of Cecilius himself.

This Great Seal passed, with the government, into the hands of Cromwell's commissioners in 1652, where they remained until 1657, when the government was restored to the Proprietary. The conditions of surrender provided also for the return of the Great Seal, but the records do not distinctly show that this was done.[1] Fearing that the Great Seal may have been lost, Baltimore had a third one made while the negotiations of surrender were pending, but it was to be used only in the event of its predecessor not being recovered.[2] As no description accompanied this Seal, and as no impression appears to be extant of the Great Seal between 1648 and 1657, it is impossible to definitely determine which of the two was subsequently used. Bacon however, in his preface to "The Laws of Maryland", published in 1765, says the one of 1648, is the "same which is in use at present", and the fact that the impressions of the Great Seal used after the Baltimore government was re-established, many of which still exist, correspond literally with the description which accompanied the Great Seal of 1648, would seem not only to justify the con-

---

[1] Archives (Cl. Pro. 1657) pp. 333, 340. [2] Ibid, pp. 322, 329.

THE GREAT SEAL AND FLAG

clusion reached by Bacon, as also, that the one of 1657 was never used at all, since it was only to be done in the event that the former Seal was not restored.

While the Province was under the jurisdiction of the Crown, the seal known as the "Broad Seal", adopted in 1692, and another in 1706, were used,[1] and the Baltimore Great Seal was limited in use, during that period, to land grants, Baltimore's territorial rights not having been disturbed. But upon the restoration of the Province in 1715, the old Great Seal again came into use, and continued to be the Great Seal of Maryland until after the revolution.

It has been stated that a new Great Seal was adopted in 1765,[2] but no authority for the statement is given, and none has been found. There is no doubt that there were other Seals in the Province, intended and used for different and various purposes, but not as the Great Seal. A wood cut of one, modelled somewhat after the Great Seal, but with the motto "Crescite et multiplicamini", was printed on the title-page of Bacon's "Laws of Maryland"—1765—but Bacon, in the preface to the work, says the Great Seal of the Province then in use, was the old seal of 1648.

There were also in use in the Province, Seals known as Lesser Seals. One of these appears on a copy of the Laws of Maryland between 1642 and 1678. Another, called the Lesser Seal at Arms, of which a representation is here given, was used in connection with the Land Office. There is now in that office, a warrant attested with this seal, to lay out land in Somerset County, for George Gale, and which concludes as

---

[1] Hall, p. 25.   [2] Scharf, 1, p. 198—Note.

follows : "given under his Lordship's Lesser Seal at Arms, this 14th day of May, An. Dom. 1740.

But the most interesting perhaps, certainly the one less commonly known, of the smaller Seals, is the one which formed a part of the plate used in printing the paper money of the Province. It contained the escutcheon of the Great Seal as well as all of its other heraldic devices, but bore the motto, "Crescite et multiplicamini"—a motto first introduced into Maryland, as far as the records disclose, in 1659, it having appeared on the coin struck for Maryland at that time. The accompanying impression of this little Seal, it may be interesting to note, is not made from a copy of it, as would be necessarily the case with printed impressions of other Seals of the Province, but, through the courtesy of its owner, is here reproduced from the original  itself, just as it was blocked and used for stamping its impression on the money of its time. As bearing upon the later history of this valuable relic, see note below.[1]

When the Revolution[2] swept away Proprietary rights in Maryland, and the state government was established, it was

---

[1] This interesting relic is now in the possession of Mr. John E. McCuske, of Annapolis. It was found, he informed the author, under the following curious circumstances : by direction of the State Treasurer, about fifteen years ago, he was having a window placed in the end of the rear wing of the old Treasury Building, at Annapolis, and after cutting through the outer wall, he encountered an inside wall, about three feet distant. In the space between these two brick walls, he found the quaint old iron chest, still preserved in that building, and in it, among other things, was this seal, which was then presented to him by the Treasurer, together with other parts of the plate, the most of them have since unfortunately been lost.

[2] THE GREAT SEAL OF THE UNITED STATES.
Shortly after the Declaration of Independence, Congress appointed a committee to prepare a seal for the infant republic ; and Franklin, Adams and Jefferson employed a swiss artist, DuSimitiere, to furnish

decided to retain this beautiful relic of Maryland's Colonial days,[1] and it continued to be used as the Great Seal of the State until 1794, when a new one was adopted.[2] It bore on the one side, a figure of Justice, with the scales in one hand

---

designs and to illustrate such suggestions as were made by the committee. The artist produced a device consisting of a shield supported on one side by the Goddess of Liberty, and on the other by a rifleman in hunting costume. The shield bore the armorial ensigns of the countries from which America had mainly drawn her population.

Franklin proposed for the device ; Moses lifting his wand and dividing the Red Sea with the water destroying Pharaoh's host, borrowing the motto from Cromwell, "Rebellion to tyrants is obedience to God".

Adams proposed the choice of Hercules; the hero leaning on his club, with Virtue pointing to her rugged mountains on one hand and Sloth trying to persuade him to follow her flowery path on to the other.

Jefferson suggested the Children of Israel in the Wilderness, led by a cloud by day and a piller of fire by night. On the reverse he proposed to place representations of Hengist and Horsa, the Saxons from whom we are descended, and whose political principles are the foundation upon which our government is built.

As a sort of compromise, Franklin and Adams asked Jefferson to combine their ideas in a compact description of the proposed seal, which he did in a paper now in the office of the Secretary of State at Washington.

This composite design is a shield with six quarterings, which display the rose, the thistle and the harp, emblematic of England, Scotland and Ireland ; the lillies of France, the imperial eagle of Germay and the crowned red lion of Holland. This was DuSimitiere's idea.

The shield was bordered with a red ground, displaying thirteen gold stars linked by a chain bearing the initials of the States. The supporters were the Goddess of Liberty in a corselet of armor, in allusion to the then state of war, and the Goddess of Justice with sword and balance. The crest was the eye in a radiant triangle, and the motto *E Pluribus Unum*. Around the whole were the words, "Seal of the United States, MDCCLXXVI" ; reverse : Pharaoh passing through the Red Sea in his chariot in pursuit of the Israelites ; Moses standing on a shore illumined by rays from a pillar of fire in a cloud. Motto, " Rebellion to tyrants is obedience to God ".

It seems that no part of Adam's classic allegory was embodied in this device.

The committee reported to the Contiuental Congress on the tenth of August, 1776, but for some reason the affair was not placed on record.

---

1 Cl. Pro. 1777, 1779.   2 Cl. Pro. 1794, 1799.

and an olive branch in the other. The figure was surmounted by rays of light, and at its feet lay the fasces, with the cap of Liberty, and crossed olive branches. The inscription was simply "Great Seal of Maryland". On the opposite side was a tobacco hogshead, with bundles of leaf tobacco lying on top, two sheaves of wheat standing by the side and the the cornucopio of plenty lying in front. In the background was a ship

---

On March 24, 1779, Mr. Lovell of Massachusetts, Mr. Scott of Virginia and Mr. Houston of Georgia were appointed to make another design. Early in May these gentlemen reported in favor of a seal four inches in diameter; a shield with thirteen diagonal red and white stripes with, for supporters, Peace with an olive branch and a warrior with a drawn sword. Motto: *Bello vel pace,*—For war or peace. The reverse side was to represent Liberty seated in a chair holding cap and staff. Motto, *Semper*—Forever; and underneath, the date.

The report was submitted, and resubmitted with slight modifications, but was not accepted; and so the matter rested until April, 1782, when Middleton, Boudinot and Rutledge were appointed a third committee to prepare a seal. But their work seems to have resulted in a failure to satisfy Congress, and on June thirteenth of the same year, the whole matter was finally referred by that body to Charles Thomson, its secretary.

He procured several devices, among them an elaborate one by William Barton of Philadelphia, but none of them met with congressional approval until John Adams, then in London, sent him a design suggested by Sir John Prestwich, an Englishman who was a warm friend of America and an accomplished antiquarian.

It consisted of an escutcheon bearing thirteen stripes, white and red on a blue field, displayed on the breast of an eagle holding in his right talon an olive branch, and in his left a bundle of thirteen arrows; in his beak a scroll inscribed, *E Pluribus Unum.* For a crest it had over the head of the eagle a golden glory breaking through a cloud, surrounding thirteen white stars on a blue field. Reverse: An unfinished pyramid; in the zenith, an eye in a triangle; over the eye the words: *Annuit cœptis*—God favors the undertaking. On the base of the pyramid are the Roman numerals MDCCLXXVI, and underneath the motto, *Novus ordo seclorum*—which may be translated freely, A new era.

This design was accepted; and thus, after six years of fruitless effort on the part of our own countrymen, we became indebted for our national arms to a titled aristocrat of the kingdom with which we were then at war.   Francis Zuri Stone—"The Companion".

approaching the shore, and surrounding all, the motto: "Industry the means and plenty the result".[1]

In 1817, this seal was superseded by one fashioned after the Great Seal of the United States, containing only an eagle, a semicircle of thirteen stars, and the words, "Great Seal of Maryland".[2] This seal, in 1854, was ordered to be changed for one showing the original arms of the State, and containing the motto, "Crescite et Multiplicamini", and the inscription, "1632. The Great Seal of Maryland. 1854", but in making this seal, the eagle was retained in place of the coronet and other emblems.[3]

In 1874, it was decided to discard this, and to restore the ancient seal, the arms of which were to conform to the arms of Lord Baltimore, as represented in Bacon's Laws of Maryland (1765). Investigation, however, proved that Bacon's representation of the Baltimore arms did not correspond with that given by Lord Baltimore himself in his commission to Governor Stone, which accompanied the Great Seal, in 1648. This resulted in the adoption, in 1876, of the present Great Seal of Maryland,[4] which is designed after the original, and bearing the same arms, emblems, motto, and inscriptions; and thus Maryland to-day enjoys the distinction of having this historic seal, emblematic alike of the "nature of her foundation and the lineage of her founder" as the symbol of her honor, and as the signet by which her official acts are authenticated and accredited.

In executing the order for the present Great Seal, the date of the Maryland charter—1632—which did not appear on the old seal, was inserted at the base of the marginal circle. The pennons, or bannerets, were also changed, being made to

---

1 Hall, p. 31.   2 Cl. Pro. 1813, 1817.
3 Hall, p. 35.   4 Ibid, p. 37.

flow towards the dexter (right), instead of the sinister (left) side, as they appeared on the old seal. The latter change, unauthorized by the resolution, and of doubtful propriety, was made, presumably, in order that the seal would conform in that respect, to the Baltimore family arms, on which they are represented as flowing toward the dexter side, which latter may have been the result either of an error of the engraver, or Baltimore's fancy, as, in heraldry, they are almost universally represented as flying toward the left side, as if being carried toward the right.[1]

The obverse of the old seal was not included in the order adopting the present Great Seal. The representations upon that side were wholly personal to Baltimore, apart from the fact that it possesses no practical value under the existing method of using the Great Seal, the old pendant seal of wax, and impressed on both sides having been superseded by the impression of the seal being made on the document itself.

The Maryland flag, like the Great Seal, is unique, in that it is strictly of heraldic design. It is composed of the armorial bearings and colors of the Calvert and Crossland arms, quartered as displayed on the escutcheon of the Great Seal.[2]

It has been stated, and is generally believed, that no design was ever formally adopted for the official flag of Maryland, and that it was simply accepted by common consent. This would appear to be true as to the State, but not so with respect to the Proprietary government. The Maryland flag, like the Great Seal, was evidently designed and adopted

---

[1] In 1884, while searching for historic relics in the vault of the old Treasury Building, at Annapolis, the old seal, of 1648, was found, as well as one of the lesser seals and the Great Seal, adopted in 1694, all of which are now preserved in the Land Office, at Annapolis.

[2] For a minute description of these see pages 240, 241.

THE PRESENT GREAT SEAL OF MARYLAND,
ADOPTED 1876.

by Cecilius, Lord Baltimore, and sent out by him with the colony, as it was unfurled and officially used a few days only after taking formal possession of the Province, when Governor Calvert, to more forcibly impress the natives, ordered the "colors to be brought on shore", and a military parade.[1]

In honor of Sir John Harvey, Governor of Virginia, who visited Governor Calvert shortly after his arrival, the flag was also used. On that occasion, says the Relation, of 1634, "wee kept the solemnitie of carrying our colors on shore". The next recorded instance in which the Maryland flag was used, was in 1638, when Governor Calvert made his expedition to Kent Island for the purpose of reducing the Claiborne force to subjection, when he and his followers "marched with Baltimore's banner displayed". In the famous battle, also, upon the Severn, in 1655, between the Baltimore forces and the Parliamentary party, the former marched under the Maryland flag, the latter setting up the standard of the commonwealth of England.[2]

[1] British Empire in America, 1, p. 184.   [2] Bozman, pp. 525, 697.

ORIGIN AND HISTORY OF THE STARS AND STRIPES.

In 1775, Congress appointed a committee of three gentlemen-- Benj. Franklin and Messrs. Harrison and Lynch--to consider and devise a national flag. The result was the adoption of the "King's Colors" as a union (or corner square), combined with thirteen stripes, alternate red and white, showing "that although the colonies united for defense against England's tyranny, they still acknowledged her sovereignty".

The first public acceptance, recognition, and salute of this flag occured January 2, 1776, at Washington's headquarters, Cambridge, Mass. It was named "The Flag of the Union", and sometimes called the "Cambridge Flag".

In the spring of 1777 Congress appointed another committee, "authorized to design a suitable flag for the nation". This committee consisted of General George Washington and Robert Morris. They called upon Mrs. Elizabeth Ross, who was a dressmaker, milliner, and upholstress, and who had the reputation of being the finest needle worker in America, and from the pencil drawing made by General Washington, engaged her to make a flag.

It is stated that a Maryland flag was borne by the Maryland troops that accompanied Braddock, in 1756, in his expedition against Fort Duquesne, and also that one was carried throughout the entire civil war by the Frederick volunteers, which became part of the First Maryland Regiment, Confederate States of America.[1]

Apart from its historic interest, the Maryland flag, as may be seen from the accompanying illustration, possesses marked symmetry and beauty. The parallel and diagonal lines of the Calvert quarterings being in singular harmony with the crosses and transposed colors of those of the Crossland arms. The combination, too, of the colors of the former—gold and black —while in brilliant contrast with those of the latter quarterings—silver and red—is both effective and pleasing.

This flag was the first legally established emblem, and was adopted by Congress, June 14, 1777, under the following act:

" Resolved, That the flag of the United States be thirteen stripes, alternate red and white ; that the Union be thirteen stars, white in a blue field, representing a new constellation ".

The first American flag was first unfurled by Captain John Paul Jones, on the *Ranger*, when it became the standard of the new American Republic.

In May, 1777, Congress made an order on the Treasurer to pay Mrs. Ross £14, 12s, 2d, for flags for the fleet in the Delaware River, and gave her a contract to make all government flags.—Historical Publishing Company, Chicago, 1893.

The first American flag unfurled in Maryland, was the one sent from Philadelphia, November, 1776, by Commodore Hopkins to Commodore Joshua Barney, for use on the *Hornet*. "The next morning at sunrise, Barney had the enviable honor of unfurling it to the music of drums and fifes, and hoisting it on a staff, planted with his own hands, at the door of his rendezvous. The heart-stirring sounds of the musical instrument, then a novel incident in Baltimore, and the still more novel sight of the *rebel colors* gracefully waving in the breeze, attracted crowds of all ranks and sizes to the gay scene of the rendezvous, and before the setting of the same day's sun, the young recruiting officer had enlisted a full crew of jolly rebels for the *Hornet*".—Memoirs of Commodore Barney, p. 30.

1 Hollander, Political Institutions.

CHAPTER XI.

Chronicles of Saint Mary's County.

AS the oldest County organization in the State ; as the place of first landing of the Maryland Colony ; as the seat of Maryland's first provincial capital ; as the theatre of her infant struggles, and the cradle of her civil and religious liberty, the colonial history of Saint Mary's County is invested with peculiar interest and special inspiration.

That the colonists landed there amid enthusiastic admiration of that section of the country, may well be understood, for it presented to them a profile of forest and plain, of hill and dale, traversed by bold, deep and picturesque rivers, bays and tide water tributaries, with high rugged banks and gently sloping shores, combining a variety and richness of scenery, probably the finest in Maryland, and perhaps nowhere surpassed.

It was not, however, the fact alone that Saint Mary's was thus "graced by the natural beauties of God's own handiwork", which gave it the distinction of having been selected as the seat of the Maryland settlement but it was due also to its superior commercial position, connected as it is by the noble Chesapeake, the broad Potomac and the majestic Patuxent with so large an area of inland country, and by the same waters with the world which lay beyond the ocean.

The Chesapeake bay and its tributaries gave to the people of tide-water Maryland, it has been well said by an eminent historian,[1] "a facility of communication with one another and with the outside world not possessed by any other colony on the continent * * The bay was to the early colonists of Maryland, much more than the railroad is to the present settler in the western wilderness ; and from the first they regarded it as the most valuable private possession of the Province. They traded and travelled on it, fought and frolicked on it, and its inlets and estuaries were so numerous and so accommodating, that nearly every planter had navigable salt water within a rifle's shot of his front door * * * * In the colonial times, the planter had the still further advantage that the ships that brought out his supplies from Bristol and London, and took his tobacco in exchange, anchored, so to speak, within sight of his tobacco-houses, and the same barges and lighters which carried his tobacco hogsheads to the ship, returned freighted with his groceries and osnaburgs, with the things which were needed to supply his cellar and pantry, and his wife's kitchen and work basket. * * * * It was this free, open, safe and pleasant navigation of the Chesapeake and its many inlets, which not only gave to the people a freedom and facility of intercourse not enjoyed by any other agricultural community, but shaped their manners and regulated their customs to an extent which it is difficult to exaggerate ".

They furnished too the means of a luxurious and independent living, and one, which to all was "as free as grace ", for they were alive with innumerable water-fowl and shell fish. "Every point that jutted out was an oyster bar, where the most delicious bivalves known to the epicure might be had for the taking. Every cove and every mat of seaweed in all the channels abounded in crabs, which shedding five months in every year, yielded the delicate soft crab, and at any point on

---

[1] Scharf, 2, pp. 2, 3, 4.

salt water, it was only necessary to dig along shore in order to bring forth as many soft shell clams, as one needed. They abounded also "in an almost incalculable number and variety of water foul, from the lordly swan and the heavy goose to the wee fat dipper". While there is "no evidence earlier than the begining of the present century that the diamond-back terrapin was appreciated, the more famous canvas-back duck certainly was known, and its qualities appreciated at a much earlier date". They were filled too with the finny denizens " and these, as was the case with both the flora and farma of the State generally, embraced northern and southern species at once. The bass and the blue fish did not exclude the pompano and the bonito; the shad and the sturgeon on their journey to fresh water, met the cat-fish and the perch; and the cost of a weir, or the trouble of staking out a net, was repaid to planters all the year round in a full supply of the most delicate sorts of table fish".[1]

It was this land of rich topography, delightful streams, and hospitable estuaries, that the Maryland colony selected, as the place of "peace and hope", where "conscience might find breathing room", and where the foundations of a commonwealth might be securely laid.

The name first bestowed upon the territory which Governor Calvert purchased of the Yaocomico Indians, (for the details of which see chapter on The Landing), and which, for several years constituted the whole district settled by the Maryland Colonists, was called "Augusta Carolina"[2]—a name presumably given in honor of King Charles.[3]

---

[1] Ibid.   [2] Relatio Itineris.

[3] It was Baltimore's desire to call Maryland Carolina, but was prevented by the fact, that the territory lying south of Virginia, had in 1629, been patented to Sir Robert Heath under that name.

The district was thirty miles[1] long, and was embraced within the present limits of Saint Mary's County. It did not however, long retain that name, though just when, or by what authority it was changed, the records do not show. As late as September, 1635, it was still called "Augusta Carolina",[2] but in January, 1637, the same territory was officially denominated "Saint Maries County",[3] the name it, with additional domain, has ever since retained.

For sixteen years after the colonization of Maryland, there were but two civil divisions in the Province—Kent and Saint Mary's—the former embracing the entire settlement on the Eastern, and the latter, the entire settlement on the Western Shore. These limits were not curtailed until April, 1650, when Anne Arundel County—"all that part of the Province over against the Isle of Kent"—was enacted.[4]

In November of the same year, another County was formed out of Saint Mary's, with the following bounds: "beginning at Susquehannah Point (near the mouth of the Patuxent) and extending from thence southward into the middle of the woods towards Saint Mary's (City); thence westward along the middle of the woods, between the Patuxent and Potomac Rivers, (near the Three Notched Road), as far up as Matapania (creek) toward the head of the Patuxent, and from thence eastward along the river side to said Susquehannah Point". It was called Charles County, and Robert Brooke, Esq., of "De La Brooke", was made its commander.[5]

In September 1653, however, Robert Brooke, having actively associated himself with the Cromwell Party in Maryland, as against the Proprietary, serving in the capacity of

---

1 Ibid. 2 Will of Wm. Smith, 1635.
3 Archives (Pro. Cl. 1637) 61. 4 McMahon 80; old Kent, Act, 1650.
5 Archives (Pro. Cl. 1650) 260.

SAINT MARY'S COUNTY

President of its Council of State, and thus, as acting Governor of the Province, was deposed by Baltimore as Commander of this County,[1] and soon thereafter, the order under which the County had been erected, was also annuled. The latter Act, was by order of Governor Stone and the Council, dated July, 1654, and, while making void the order under which Charles County had been formed, provided also that a new County should be erected in its stead, embracing all of the former County with additional territory.

It was called Calvert County, and lay on both sides of the Patuxent, that part on the north side of the river being separated from Anne Arundel by a line from " Herring Creek " to the " head of the Patuxent ", and the part on the south side of the river being separated from Saint Mary's by " Pyne Hill River or Creek to the head thereof, and from thence through the woods to the head of the Patuxent ", which says the order constitute the northerly bound of Saint Mary's County.[2]

" Pyne Hill River or Creek ", which thus partly separated Saint Mary's and Calvert, and which continued such dividing line for nearly half a century, empties into the Chesapeake Bay about three miles below " Cedar Point ", its source or head being westerly, and near Jarboesville on the Three Notched Road. It is no longer navigable, and though it retained for many years its original name, it has long since lost its identity as a river, and is now known as " Mill Run " except at its mouth, when it bears the name of " Piney Creek ".[3]

The question of the location of this stream has been one upon which historians have bestowed no little labor and in-

---

1 Bozman, pp. 442, 499.   2 Archives (Pro. Cl. 1654) p. 308.
3 See Patents for "Smith's Discovery" to Richard Smith, March 9, 1705 This tract of land borders on the stream referred to in the text (Mill Run), and which is designated in the patent, as "the main branch of Pine Hill River or Creek ".

dulged in much speculation, among them the careful and painstaking Bozman, who, owing to the change in its name as well as in its character, was unable to locate it, and suggested that the "Pyne Hill River" referred to in the order of July, 1654, was Piney Creek which empties into the Eastern Branch of the Potomac, near Washington City—a physical impossibility, apart from the fact that the records clearly indicate that the Eastern Branch had not at that early day been explored, and hence that its tributaries had not been named.

In October, 1654, the name of Calvert was changed by Cromwell's Commissioners to Patuxent County, which it continued to bear until 1658, when Baltimore's government was re-established, and its former name restored.[1]

In October, 1658, another County was carved out of Saint Mary's. It was called Charles (still so known), and was embraced within the following indefinite bounds: "the river Wicomico to its head, and from the mouth of that river up the Potomac as high as the settlements extends, and thence to the the head of Wicomico".[2]

This limited Saint Mary's County to the territory lying between the Chesapeake Bay and the Calvert line on the one side, and the Potomac and Wicomico Rivers on the other, and extending from Point Lookout up the country indefinitely, except that which was embraced within the limits of Charles, Calvert and Anne Arundel. And thus its boundaries continued, until 1695, when the territory lying above Matawoman Creek and Swanson Creek was erected into a new County, called Prince George; that part of Calvert lying on the south side of the Patuxent River, as far up as Indian Creek, was

---

[1] McMahon, p. 86.

[2] Liber, P. C. R. pp. 52, 54, Maryland Historical Society. Scharf, 2, p. 271; McMahon, 87.

returned to Saint Mary's, and that part of Saint Mary's and Calvert lying north westerly of Buds Creek and Indian Creek, was given to Charles.[1]

By this Act, the present boundaries of Saint Mary's County were thus specifically defined : "Saint Mary's County shall begin at point Lookout and extend up the Potomac River (and Wicomico) to the lower side of Bud's Creek, and so over by a straight line drawn from the head of the main branch of the said Bud's Creek to the head of Indian Creek in the Patuxent River, including all that land lying between the Patuxent and Potomac Rivers, from the lower side of said two creeks and branches by the line aforesaid, and by Point Lookout".[2]

The first civil divisions of Saint Mary's County were denominated hundreds. These were erected from time to time, as the increase of population and the development of the different section of the County demanded. In 1637, there were two hundreds in the County. Saint Mary's, which included the town and vicinity of Saint Mary's, and Saint Georges,[3] which embraced the settlement on the opposite side of the river—a district of country still bearing the same name. Mattapany, the settlement on the lower Patuxent, was not sufficiently numerous at that time for an hundred, and yet was recognized as a distinct legal division.[4] In 1638, however, it became an hundred, and the same year, Saint Michaels hundred, extending from Saint Inigoes Creek to Point Lookout, was also erected. In 1639, Saint Clements hundred, embracing the neck lying between Saint Clement's Bay and the Wicomico River, was formed. Newtown hundred, lying between Saint Clement's Bay and Bretton's Bay, was referred to, apparently for the first time, in 1646 ; Saint

---

1 Act, 1695, C. 13.   2 Act, 1695, C. 13 ; McMahon, p. 81.
3 Archives (Pro. Cl. 1637) p, 59.   4 Ibid (Pro. Ass. 1637) p. 2.

Inigoes hundred, carved out of Saint Michael's, and lying between Saint Inigoe's Creek and Trinity (Smith's) Creek, in 1649; Chaptico hundred, embracing the north western extremity of the County in 1688; Resurrection and Harvey hundreds, and the Patuxent settlement, were in Calvert County until 1695, when they were annexed to Saint Mary's.[1]

In 1777, the County contained the following hundreds: Saint Michael's, Saint Inigoe's, Saint Mary's, Poplar Hill, Saint George's, New Town, Saint Clements, Chaptico, Harvey, Lower Resurrection and Upper Resurrection.[2] These early political divisions each had a Conservator of the Peace and high Constable, and until 1659, every hundred was entitled to representation in the General Assembly.[3] In many respects they bore close analogy to the system of civil divisions now known as Election Districts, by which they were superseded. The latter system had its origin under the Act of 1798.[4] The Commissioners appointed to execute it for Saint Mary's County were Messrs. George Plater, Henry Gardiner, Charles Chilton, Richard Watts and Benjamine Williams,[5] who in July, 1799, divided the County into three districts, Chaptico, Leonard-Town and Saint Inigoe's.[6]

The first levy for Saint Mary's County was made in June, 1648.[7] It was made by a general meeting of the freemen of the County, and is the first instance on record in which County charges were levied in Maryland separately and distinctly from the general or provincial charges. The record

---

[1] Archives (Ass. Pro. 1st) pp. 28, 259; Ibid (Pro. Cl. 1st) pp. 89, 177; Ibid, (Pro. Cl. 3rd) p. 50; Act, 1795, C. 13.

[2] Journal House Representatives, 1777.   [3] McMahon, p. 465.

[4] Act, 1798, C. 115.   [5] Act, 1799, C. 50.   [6] Ibid.

[7] In 1694, the Council ordered colors for horse foot and dragoon in the several counties as follows: Saint Mary's, red; Kent, blue; Anne Arundel, white; Calvert, yellow; Charles, bronze; Baltimore, green; Talbot, purple; Somerset, jack flag; Dorchester, buff; Cecil, crimson.

of this meeting is as follows : "This day the ffreemen of the County of Saint Marie's mett together at the Gov^rs to advise touching the levy of the charges incurred this pr^t yeare and determined by the Govr and Councill on the 9th Octob^r last to be levyed out of the County. The whole charges amounting to 7752 ℔s, Tob and Cask. The ffreemen allege th^t the charges for impresonment of the Indians is unduly laid upon the County ; but alleged not anything material for it. Whereuppon the Govr found noe reason to alter his former order sett downe by the Govr and Councill as above. As concerning the manner of leveying the s^d charges the ffreemen unanimously agreed and concluded th^t it should be leveyed upon all tytheable p^sons inhab^ts of St. Marie's County equally pr head th^t were residing in the County from the 10th day of June last, wch resultieth in 55^l Tob. June 14th, 1648 ".[1]

This appears to be the only instance in the history of the Province in which a County levy was made by a general meeting of the freemen. In 1650, delegates were elected from the several hundreds of the County for that purpose—a system which continued until 1704, when the duty of "laying the County levy" devolved upon the Justices of the County Court,[2] and subsequently, upon the tribunal known as the "Levy Court".

The average value of land in Saint Mary's County in 1785, as established by General Assembly for purposes of assessment, was 24 shillings and 9 pence per acre, the fourth highest valuation in the State.[3]

The first County Seat of Saint Mary's, was Saint Mary's, and in 1695, it was provided that the County Courts and records should be held and kept "forever hereafter in the State House in the City of Saint Mary's".[4]

1 Archives (Ass. Pro. 1648) 231. 2 Act, 1704, C. 34.
3 Act, 1785 ,C. 53. 4 Act, 1695, C. 13.

In 1708, however, the Legislature ordered a town to be laid out at "Sheppards Old Fields", near the head of Bretton's Bay, a Court House to be erected, and the County Court of Saint Mary's County thereafter to be held there.[1] "Sheppard's Old Fields" then belonged to Philip Lynes. Commissioners were appointed and directed to purchase fifty acres of it for the use of said town, and to lay the same out into one hundred lots. It was first called "Seymour Town"—a compliment, presumably, to the then Governor, John Seymour.

In 1728, the Legislature, after reciting the fact, that the laying out of the town, as provided by the former Act, had not been completed, appointed new commissioners to do so. They were directed "to purchase, by agreement, or valuation of a jury, fifty acres of land adjacent to the place where Saint Mary's County Court House now stands, and to cause the same to be surveyed and laid out for a town, into eighty lots, with convenient streets, lanes, etc.," without prejudice to the lots already there, or to the buildings and improvements of the heirs at law of Thomas Cooper. They were also directed to expose the lots for sale, giving the owner of the land his choice for two lots, and limiting the sale of the rest to one lot to each individual, and restricting, also, for the first four months, the sales to inhabitants of Saint Mary's County. The purchaser of every lot was to consent to erect thereon, within twelve months, a house covering at least four hundred square feet, with brick or stone chimneys. The proceeds of the sales were to go to "the public use and benefit of the town"; every lot was to be sold subject to a quit rent to Lord Baltimore of one penny per annum, and the lots remaining unsold at the end of seven years were to revert to the owner of the land.[2] By this Act also, all writs issued by the Court were to be made

---

1 Act, 1708, C. 3.   2 Act, 1728, C. 16.

SAINT MARY'S COUNTY

returnable there, and the name was changed to *Leonard-Town*[1]—the name it still retains—in honor of Benedict Leonard Calvert, the then Governor of Maryland.

In 1730, Mr. Thomas Spalding, who is referred to as the then owner of the land, was granted permission by Act of Assembly, to use the lots not taken up, but not to remove any of the boundary posts. It appearing also, that the deed for "the part of one acre of land" known as the "Court House Lot", and which had been given to the County by Mr. Philip Lynes, had not, through neglect of the clerk, been placed upon record, "though three of the bound posts are still standing and the place of the other well known", special provision was made by this Act for curing the defect and vesting "the title to the said lot in the Justices of Saint Mary's County to the use of said County forever".[2]

The County Surveyor was by the same Act directed to "make a fair plat of Leonard-Town" to be subscribed by the Commissioners and recorded among the land records of the County. The records have perished, but the map has been preserved,[3] of which the annexed illustration is a copy. This is believed to be one of the oldest maps extant of any existing town in Maryland the first map of Annapolis having been lost, it is said, and the first one of Baltimore City being of about the same date (1730) as that of Leonard-Town. On the back of this map, and inscribed by its maker, is the list of persons who had purchased lots in the town, presumably between 1728, when it was laid out, and 1730, when the map was made.

This indicates, that, while a number of lots had been purchased, there was in the town at that time, besides the

---

1 Ibid.   2 Act, 1730, C. 5.
3 It is now in the possession of Mr. Francis V. King.

Court House, and the houses of Col. Greenfield and Mr. Brice, but one other building—the storehouse of Mr. Nicholas Lowe, standing on lots Nos. 41 and 42, though it likewise indicates, that all the other lots which had been taken up were then being built upon, except lot No. 39, property of Jno. Stewart.

The first Court House at Leonard-Town was built between 1708 and 1710. It was completed by the latter date, and was referred to by the General Assembly of that year, as the "new Court House built at Seymour Town, otherwise Sheppards Old Fields".[1]

In 1736, it was pulled down and a new brick building was erected on the same site.[2] This building, well remembered by many persons still living, and said to have been a capacious, well proportioned and stately structure, stood until March, 1831, when it was destroyed by fire, and was replaced by the present Court House.

---

[1] Act, 1710, C. 6.   [2] Act, 1636, C. 14.

The first County Jail in Leonard-Town was built under the Act of 1737,[1] which authorized the Justices of the county to purchase the necessary ground for the same.

In 1799, the Jail was reported in a "ruinous condition, and unfit for use", and it was ordered to either to be repaired or pulled down and rebuilt, the cost not to exceed two thousand dollars.[2] The latter course, it appears was adopted.

An ancient land-mark of the original town, and still well remembered, was the quaint little building known as the "Old Brick Office", which, before the present Court House was built, was, it is said, the County Clerk's Office, and the Office of the Register of Wills. In recent years, when the main avenue of the town was widened, the "Old Brick Office" was left standing in the middle of the street, thus making its removal apparently necessary. It was shortly afterward pulled down, and the material used, it is said, in the construction of the present County Jail. It stood in front of "Moore's Hotel", on a site now partly covered with locust trees and still perfectly discernable.

The Saint Mary's County "Alms House" was erected under the Act of 1773. A levy, not exceeding 15 ℔s. of tobacco per poll, for three years, was ordered to be made for the purpose, and Messrs. George Plater, Abraham Barnes, Zachary Bond, John Reeder, and James Jordan, the incorporators, were directed to purchase one hundred acres of land as near Leonard-Town as it could be advantageously obtained, have the necessary buildings erected and furnished, and to appoint an overseer; the general management of the institution to remain under their supervision.[3] Having purchased the land (located about three miles below Leonard-Town), the

---

[1] Act, 1737, C. 6.　　　　　　[2] Act, 1799, C. 51.
[3] Act, 1773, C. 18.

trustees advertised to meet on September 22d, 1774, at Francis Smith's, in Leonard-Town, to receive bids for putting up the building.[1]

The other places associated with the early annals of Saint Mary's County, and which were denominated "Towns", were: "Harvey Town", on the Patuxent, at Town Creek ; "Saint Joseph's Town", on the Patuxent, at Abbington Creek ; "Saint Jerome's Town", on Saint Jerome's Creek ; "New Town", between Saint Clement's Bay and Bretton's Bay ; "Saint Clement's Town", at the head of Saint Clement's Bay, and "Wicomico Town", on the Wicomico River, between White Point (Island) and Bluff Point.[2]

These towns were named and ordered to be erected by the Legislature, which also provided for the purchase of one hundred acres of land for each of them and the appointment of Commissioners to lay them out, etc. The situation of each of them was eligible, but like most of the "paper towns" of Maryland of that day, they never exceeded a small aggregation of houses, and have so far perished and passed away, that, with a few exceptions, even the site of their location is not to-day susceptible of identification.

"Lowentown" was the name of a section of country rather than a town, and was that which lay between Trinity Creek and Point Lookout, including the village known as "Tall Pine". It is said that Saint Mary's City was expected to develop into a town of "magnificent proportions", and to extend down to the lower part of the county ; hence the name —a corruption of lower end of the town.[3]

---

1 Maryland Gazette, September, 1774.

2 Acts, 1683, C. 2 ; 1684, C. 2 ; 1688, C. 6 ; 1706, C. 14 ; Report of Sheriff, 1698.

3 Allen Papers, in Whittingham Library.

Chaptico, or Choptico as it was first called, enjoys the distinction of being the oldest "village", except Saint Mary's City, in the County. Reference to it is found as early as 1652.[1] Chaptico had the honor of a visit from Governor Calvert in 1663,[2] and is otherwise noted in the early annals of Maryland, as the place at which the soldiers were mustered in, and the army organized for the "Protestant Revolution" in Maryland, and which, in July, 1689,[3] resulted in the capture of the provincial capital, the overthrow of the Proprietary and the establishment of a royal government in the Province.[4]

The "Queen Tree", situated on the Patuxent River, near Forrest's wharf was also a Colonial village of very early date, and of no inconsiderable importance. It has long since disappeared, except in name, but the estate on which it stood is still called the "Queen Tree Farm". As late as 1774, it was still a "trading post", and the place where public sales of property in the neighborhood were usually conducted.[5] A few miles below, on the Three Notched Road, was the old

---

1 Archives (Cl. Pro. 1652) p. 293.

2 Ibid, Ass. Pro. 1663, p. 474.   3 Ibid, Cl. Pro. 1689, p. 121.

4 In 1660, the King of Chaptico was indicted by the Court Leet of Saint Clement's Manor for stealing hogs. Deeming it however, inconsistant with his official standing to try the case in a Court Leet, it was referred to "ye Hon[ble] ye Gov[r]", (Saint Clement's Court Records). In 1688, complaint was made to Lord Baltimore by the King of Chaptico against Francis Knott and others, for "destroying the corn and beans of the Indians" and for "bringing strong drink into said Chaptico town". (Archives, Cl. Pro. 53.) The Chapticons was one of the six tribes of Indians that Lord Baltimore proposed to settle on Calverton Manor containing about 10,000 acres, but his plan of colonization appears to have proven entirely impracticable, as in 1692, a formal treaty was entered into between Governor Copley and "Tom Calvert, King of Chaptico", defining the rights and privileges of the latter over his ancient domain. Bozman, 676; Archives (Pro. Cl. 321.) As to this Manor, see chapters on The Land Tenure.

5 Maryland Gazette.

"wayside inn", known as "Floyd's". It was standing in 1813,[1] and the place of its location still bears the name.

The following are the ports or places of entry in Saint Mary's County, established from time to time, by Act of Assembly, and where all *imported* goods and wares coming to the County, were required to be unloaded, and all tobacco and other commodities to be *exported* had to be taken for inspection and payment of export duty: Saint Mary's City; Saint Inigoes, on Stephen Milburn's land; Saint George's, on Gilbert Mackey's land; Leonard-Town, on Abraham Barnes' land; New Town, on William Bretton's land; Bretton's Bay, on John Bailey's land; Wicomico River, on John Llewellin's land; Indian Town, on his Lordships Manor; Chaptico, on Philip Keys land; Westwood, on Thomas Gerrards land; Piles Fresh, on Joseph Piles land; (the two latter in Saint Mary's County until 1695) Hamburg, on Philip Key's land; Cole's Creek, on the Patuxent, Mr. Cole's land; Harvey Town, on Town Creek, on Hugh Hopewell's land, and Saint Joseph's, at Abbington Creek, on the Patuxent.[2]

The old brick "ware houses", which were erected at these ports, and which stood as monuments to the shipping trade of the past, for many years after they ceased to be used for the purpose of their construction, have all yielded to the ravages of time and have passed away. Several of them, however, were still standing within the recollection of persons still living, among them, the one at Brambly on the Wicomico, at the warehouse farm in Saint Georges and at Town Creek on the Patuxent.

The first public road in Saint Mary's County of which there is any record, is the one leading from Saint Mary's City to the Patuxent. It was called the "Mattapany Path", and

---

1 Griffith's Map of Maryland.   2 Bacon; Hanson.

was referred to as early as 1639.[1] In 1643 it was stated by Father Philip Fisher, the priest in charge at Saint Mary's, in a letter to his Provincial, that "a road by land through the forest has just been opened from Maryland to Virginia."[2] This is interesting as showing the existence of a road however impossible to identify it from so scant a reference. In 1674, an Act was passed "for amending the ways out of Charles County into the City of Saint Mary's", and which, after reciting the fact that the crossing at the head of the Wicomico River had been rendered dangerous "since the building of the mill there", provided that the Counties of Charles and Saint Mary's should construct a highway "passable for horse and foote over such place of Zachiah swamp within two miles of said mill upward as shall seem most convenient".[3] The road thus referred to was probably the one which still leads from Charles County to Saint Mary's by way Allen's Fresh, Chaptico and Leonard-Town. An early reference is also made to a road leading from Saint Clement's Manor, by way of the "Wolf's Trap" and "Ironstone Hill" to Chaptico. It was called the "Chaptico Indian Path".[4] The road leading from Point Lookout to the northern extremity of the county was in use as early as 1692, and was then called the "Patuxent main road".[5] In 1704, this, in common with certain other roads in the Province, was by order of the General Assembly[6] marked by having notches cut in the trees at stated intervals along the road. The number of notches for this road, it being the one that led "to the Port of Annapolis", was three,[7] and

---

1 Patent to Mary Throughton, 1639, Liber, 1, p. 67.
2 Neill's Maryland, p. 49. 3 Archives (Ass. Pro. 1674) p. 408.
4 Will, Luke Gardiner, 1703, Saint Mary's County.
5 Archives (Cl. Pro. 1692) p. 475.
6 Act, 1704, C. 21.   7 Ibid.

from these primitive guide marks, some of which may still be seen—it was called the "Three Notched Road " the name it bears to-day.

The first mail route established in Maryland was in 1695. It started at "Newton's Point upon Wicomico River" and extended by way of "Allen's Mill", Benedict, Annapolis and Newcastle to Philadelphia. The post rider was John Perry, who received £50 per annum, and was required to make the round trip eight times a year.[1] It is stated that the system did not pay, and after the death of the first postman, in 1698, ceased to be carried on, and was not afterwards revived.[2] But that it was revived is proven by the fact that in 1773, Charles Lansdale had the contract for the mail route between Leonard- Town and Annapolis, and advertised to receive orders at the various stopping places for purchases on commission.[3] These places in Saint Mary's were James Jordan's, Wicomico and Chaptico.[4]

Prior to 1661, letters were sent in Maryland by private hand or special messenger, or were left at the nearest tavern or public house to be sent by the first conveyance which the landlord found available, but by Act of Assembly, of that year,[5] all "letters touching the public affairs" of the Province, were, "without delay, to be sent from house to house by the direct way, until they be safely delivered as directed". Each householder was required to start it to the next house, within half an hour after receiving it, under penalty of 100 lbs. of tobacco.

In 1713, this curious system was abolished, and the duty devolved upon the Sheriffs of the several counties, who were

---

1 Journal U. H. 1695, p. 809 ; Scharf 1, p. 361.
2 McMahon, p. 266.   3 Maryland Gazette, April 14, 1773.
4 Ibid.   5 Archives (Ass. Pro. 1661) p. 415.

required to "take care of all public letters and packets, and to expeditiously convey them, according to their respective directions, to the Sheriff or Under Sheriff of the next adjacent county",[1] for which the Sheriff of Saint Mary's County received as compensation, 800 ℔s. of tobacco.[2]

These Acts of Assembly, however, only applied to letters of a public character. For the conveyance of private letters, no provision was made until 1695, when the mail route before mentioned, was established; and, in 1713,[3] it was made, for the first time, a penal offence in Maryland, to open a letter without authority.

Among the older land-marks in the county, are its "ancient mill seats". Recognized as a public necessity, water mills, from an early date, were made in Maryland, the subject of special legislation, granting to the owner unusual privileges, and, at the same time, imposing wholesome restrictions upon them, among others the right to obtain through a Court of Chancery, ten acres of land on each side of the stream where the mill was to be located, and making it a misdemeanor to charge more *toll* than *one-sixth* for corn and *one-eighth* for wheat.[4]

Of the mills erected in Saint Mary's at an early date, the exact location of many of them is still perfectly discernable. Among them may be mentioned the mill on "Mill Creek", at Saint Mary's City, and which was there as early as 1634; Dandy's mill, at Newtown, there before 1657; Lord Baltimore's mill, on "Gardiner's Creek", at Mattapany, there before 1690; the mill on "Tomakokin Creek", on Saint Clement's Manor, there before 1701; the mill at head of Saint Mary's River, at "Great Mills", there before 1728; Major Barnes' mill on

---
1 Act, 1713, C. 2.   2 Ibid.
3 Ibid.   4 Act, 1704, C 16.

"Bretton's Bay Run", above the "Plank Bridge", there before 1748; Keys mill on "Saint Clement's Bay Run", there before 1764; Bond's mill on "Chaptico Run" there before 1774; the "over shot water mill", at "Charlotte Hall", there before 1775; Tubman's mill, at the head of "Trinity (Smith's) Creek", there before 1813.[1] Wind mills also, were not uncommon in early Maryland. Several of these old relics, in appearance like watch towers, zealously guarding the past, were to be seen in Saint Mary's up to a very recent date. The last of them standing were at "New Town", "Saint Clement's Manor", and "Corn Field Harbor", but they, like their companions, have at last yielded to that ruthless plunderer — time.[2]

---

[1] Relation of Maryland, 1635; Archives (Test. Pro. 1657) pp. 535, 543; Archives (Pro. Cl. 1690) 182; Will, John Coode; Will, Philip Key; Will, Zack Bond; Act, 1748, C. 4; Maryland Gazette, September 15th, 1774; Map, Maryland, 1813, Griffith.

[2] On the road leading from Leonard-Town to Chaptico and about fifty yards above the "plank bridge" over the fresh of Bretton's Bay, was the old ford, or crossing place. A few rods west of the ford, and about the same distance from the bridge, on the east side of the road, stands a small house on a little hill, and which is known as "Gibbet Hill". It is said that the last execution there was of a negro man, for the murder of a lady and her two daughters. The scence of the tragedy was the residence———, which stood on the Saint Joseph's branch of the same road, a short distance above Shanks' Mill, and about a quarter of a mile north of the "Maryland Spring". As the story is recorded, during the absence of his master, a negro man, Peter, believing that by the death of the family his freedom would be obtained, murdered his mistress and her two daughters, and when caught was lying in wait for his master, who was at Shanks' mill, and his two sons who were at school, near by. After his trial and conviction, Peter was taken to "Gibbet Hill" for execution. Tradition says that he was hung up in an iron cage, in front of the public road, and there left to die from starvation. It is also said that the screams of this starving criminal were so distressing, that many persons refused to travel the road. The good sense of the community revolted at the inhumanity of such a method of punishment, and Peter, it is said, was the last criminal in Saint Mary's County who died on the Gibbet.—Saint Mary's, Beacon, February, 24th, 1853. There

The first will probated in Saint Mary's County, was dated September 22nd, 1635. The caption is as follows: "The last will and Testament of Mr. William Smith, made at *Augusta Carolina*, at Saint Mary's City, in Maryland, anno dmi 1635". The document indicates careful preparation, and strongly marks the religous faith of the testator, at that day not an uncommon custom. The clause making reference to this is as follows:

"And further I profess that I die a member of the Catholic Roman Church, out of wch there is noe salvation". As a counterpart to this, the will of Thomas Allen, made soon thereafter, indicates very different religious convictions. It provides that the overseers of his will are not to allow his children "to live with a papist". In making further provision for his children, he directed, that, if his estate proved insufficient to maintain them, and it should be necessary to put them out to work, they "should not be put to the morter", or made "morter boys", thus showing the hard labor attending the then common process of converting corn into meal and hominy. On the back of his will and of even date, he curiously requests that, should he "die suddenly, and the cause be not directly known, speedy inquiry be made, and that Nick and Marks, Irishmen, at Piny Neck, be questioned as suspicious persons to me best known". This singular feature of his will seems to

---

are many traditions in old Saint Mary's connected with the early settlement of the State, and with times of a later date, which if collected and published, would be of great interest. Hardly a neighborhood but has its old story to be recounted by some old dame of a past generation. The old people are passing away, and these old legends with them. It would be well, while yet time, for some lover of legendary lore to gather these old legends and preserve them from irretrievable loss. An Irving would have found in them rich material; and but for some humble chronicler that great "Wizard of the North" could not have given to the world his immortal master-pieces.—J F. Morgan, in "St. Mary's Beacon".

have been the result of well founded apprehension, rather than a mere excentricity, since shortly afterward he was "found dead upon the sands by Point Lookout in Saint Nicholas Manor, badly shot and mutilated".[1]

As reflecting upon the interesting question of Colonial life, business persuits, dress, furniture, etc., the early wills and inventories of Saint Mary's—an unbroken record from 1680 to to the present time—are among the richest repositories of "historic lore" to be found in Maryland, and are of inestimaable value.

In the matter of dress—then a decided badge of rank and station in life—they furnished a ready key. The "cloth suit", "dimity suit", "mohair suit", "leathern suit", "hair skin suit", "plush coats", silk and satin "waiscoats", dimity and velvet "waiscoats", silk "socks", Irish, Dutch and Holland "socks"; silver, gold, cloth and leather "belts"; silver and gold "knee" and "shoe buckles"; silver, gold and leather "hat bands"; hat "feathers" and "plumes"; silk and worsted "hoods", "head cloths" and "scharfs"; "spangled peticoats"; tufted Holland peticoats; "taffeta suits"; "surge suits"; "silk gloves"; "buckskin gloves"; "signet rings" and "finger rings", are among the articles of wearing apparel used by men and women during the first fifty years of Colonial life in Saint Mary's. Later reference to "watches", and still later to "wigs", is to be found.

In the matter of furniture, table appointments, etc., may be mentioned, the "parlor bed"; "trundle bed"; the "dresser"; the "chest of drawers"; the "looking glass"; later the "peir glass" and still later the "chimney glass"; silk and worsted "bed curtains"; beds, pillows and boulsters with "conuise ticking" and filled with "feathers", "flock"

---

[1] Archives (Pro. Ct. 1637) 403.

or "cat tail"; Dutch linen "sheets" and "napkins"; "Holland Blankets"; "dimity coverlets"; "quilted coverlets"; "Turkish rugs"; "forms"; "crickets"; "stools" and "chairs" (the latter not common); the "harpsicord" and "spinnet", the "joined dining table"; brass and iron "andirons"; silver, brass and iron "candlesticks"; "silver salvers"; "iron knives"; "silver knives"; wooden "dishes"; and "platters"; the "silver sack cup"; "sugar tankard"; "tea tankard"; "pewter plates"; "pewter dishes"; "pewter cups and saucers"; "pewter salt sellers"; "pewter spoons", and pewter household vessels of almost every description. It is worthy of note, that the reign of pewter in early Maryland was practically unbroken for the first forty years, when the silver service made its appearance, and still later, with the introduction of tea and coffee, came china cups and saucers, and soon full sets of porcelain table ware. Occasional references are to be found to the "sedan chair", the "bladen" and the "horse chair", but it curiously appears that neither the table fork or the plow are mentioned in the testamentory proceedings of Saint Mary's County during the first eighty years of its history.

On the 3rd of December 1773, the Maryland Gazette proposed and published a plan for consolidating into one institution the free schools of Southern Maryland, of which each County had one.[1]

---

[1] The first general school system in Maryland was inaugurated under the Act of 1723, which provided for one school in each County; each school to be governed by a board of seven visitors, who were to purchase 100 acres of land as near the centre of their respective Counties as practicable, and with due regard to the boarding of children, and were to have the necessary buildings erected and employ a competant teacher of "grammar, good writing and arithmetic" who was to have the use of the farm and to receive the sum of £20 sterling per annum. The visitors appointed under the Act of Saint Mary's County, were Rev. Leigh Massey

The following year, a similar plan, but embracing only the Counties of Saint Mary's, Charles and Prince George, was urged upon the General Assembly of Maryland and passed[1]—the origin of Charlotte Hall. The Act provided for the sale of the lands and houses of the free schools in the three Counties, the proceeds to be added to the "sums of money which sundry persons have subscribed to further the commendable purpose", as well as the money then in the hands of the visitors of the free schools for said counties, and that with said several sums of money, "one school be erected at the place commonly called the *Cool Springs*, in Saint Mary's County, to be called *Charlotte Hall*". The institution was to be governed by a president and twenty-one trustees, who were created a body politic, with right of succession, of whom fifteen were to constitute a quorum, reduced in 1777[2] to seven, and in 1783 to five.[3]

In 1798, the school fund of Calvert was united to Charlotte Hall. This County thus acquired the right to participate in its management, and became entitled to a representation of

---

and Messrs. James Bowles, Nicholas Lowe, Samuel Wilkinson, Thomas Waughop, Thomas Trueman Greenfield and Justinian Jordan. (Act, 1723, C. 19) As early as 1671, an effort was made to establish through the Legislature, a "public educational institution" in Maryland, but it was not successful. In 1694, however, an act was passed "for the maintainance of free schools" and the following year another was passed "for the encouragement of learning", both of which provided a "school fund", to be raised by an export duty on furs, etc. In 1704 and again in 1717, this duty was extended to other articles, and in 1719 an Act was passed giving to the public "school fund" the estates of persons who died in the Province intestate and without known legal representatives. In addition, certain fines and forfeitures went to the "school fund". From these various sources a fund had been accumulated by 1723, sufficiently large to purchase a farm of 100 acres and erect a school in each of the twelve Counties in the Province.

1 Act, 1774, C. 14.   2 Act, 1777, C. 3.
3 Act, 1783, C. 19.

seven in its Board of Trustees,[1] subsequently however, the funds which belonged both to Calvert and Prince George were withdrawn from Charlotte Hall for the exclusive use of those Counties, thus leaving the control of the institution to Charles and Saint Mary's.

One of the first official acts of the Trustees, was an effort to get a water mill built there, as will appear from the following advertisement: "To let, to the lowest bidder, at the Cool Springs in Charlotte Hall, on Tuesday, the fourth day of October, 1774. The building of an overshot water mill at said place. A full meeting of the Trustees for Charlotte Hall, is earnestly requested". Henry Tubman, Clerk.[2] The actual operation of the school commenced in 1796.[3]

Few institutions have established a higher record for honor and usefulness, than Charlotte Hall; none has contributed more in moulding the character and shaping the destiny of the youth of Maryland, and the splendid results which it has achieved in its labors of more than a century, may well be a source of pride and gratification to the people of the State.[4]

---

1 Act, 1798, C. 92.   2 Maryland Gazette, September 22, 1774.
3 School Records.

4 The first Board of Trustees of Charlotte Hall, was composed of Governor Robert Eden, president; Hon. George Plater, Rev. George Gowndrill, John Reeder, Thomas Bond, Richard Barnes, Philip Key, and Henry Greenfield Sotheron, for Saint Mary's; Rev. Isaac Campbell, Richard Lee, William Smallwood, Francis Ware, Josias Hawkins, George Dent and Dr. James Craig, for Charles; Hon. Benedict Calvert, Rev. Henry Addison, Josiah Beall, Robert Tyler, Joseph Sim, Thomas Contee, and Dr. Richard Brooke, for Prince George. (Act, 1774, C. 14.) The following is a list of the Principals of Charlotte Hall from the begining of its operations to the present time: Rev. Hatch Dent, elected 1796; Rev. George Ralph, 1799; Hugh Maguire, 1809; Dennis Don Levy, 1810; Rev. William Duke, 1812; Rev. John Ireland, 1813; Nathaniel K. G. Oliver, 1815; John Wade, 1816; Philip Briscoe, 1817; John Miltimore, 1826; Philip Briscoe, 1837; Dr. Charles Kraitsir, 1840; Rev. George Claxton, 1842; Rev. Samuel Callahan, 1846; N. F. D.

In 1798, the General Assembly made Charlotte Hall the subject of a perpetual endowment. The Act provides that the Treasurer of Maryland, " shall be forever hereafter, authorized and required to pay annually, on or before the first day of June, to the president and trustees of Charlotte Hall, the sum of eight hundred dollars ".[1]

It may be interesting to note, that the " Cool Springs ", at which this early and successful seat of Academic learning is located, are the oldest known medicinal springs in Maryland, and became historic in the very early annals of the Province.

As early as 1698, Governor Francis Nicholson, "having received an account of some extraordinary cures wrought at ye Cool Springs ", in order that their beneficial properties might be availed of by all persons, the legislature appointed trustees " to purchase the land adjoining to ye Fountains of Healing waters, called ye Cool Spring, in Saint Mary's County, for houses to be build on for ye entertainment of such poor, impotent persons as should resort hither for cure ".[2]

Brown, 1852; Herbert Thompson, 1875; William T. Briscoe, chairman, 1877; R. W. Silvester, 1887; George M. Thomas, 1892. The following is also a list of the President's of the Board of Trustees within the same period: Right Rev. Thomas John Claggett, 1796; Dr. Parnam, 1799; Major William Thomas, 1812; John Campbell, 1813; Luke W. Barber, 1826; George Thomas, 1837; Gen. William Matthews, 1852; Gen. Walter Mitchell, 1857; Col. Chapman Billingsley, 1871; Col. John Henry Sotheron, 1875, and Col. John F. Dent.

The "Washington Society", organized February 22nd, 1797, whose membership is composed of students elected from Charlotte Hall, enjoys the proud distinction, it is said, of being the oldest surviving literary and debating society in Maryland. On its list of members may be found the names of many of Maryland's most distinguished sons. Motto: "*Palmam qui meruit ferat*". On October 24th, 1871, the "Stonewall Society" was united with it, and since then it has been known as the "Washington and Stonewall Society". The Society library contains about two thousand volumes, and among them, are some rare and valuable works.

[1] Act, 1798, C. 107.   [2] Act, 1698, C. 16.

An appropriation of £100 s. was made,[1] a building was erected, bibles and prayer-books were furnished and a lay-reader appointed, who was to read prayers twice a week, for which he was to receive twelve pence per day. " His Excellency is also pleased to allow to the said people, every Sunday, a mutton, and as much corn as will amount to thirteen shillings a week ".[2] It was also " ordered, that, the person who reads prayers take an account of what persons come thither, who are cured, and of what distempers ".[3]

Governor Nathaniel Blackistone subsequently alluded to the subject in an address to the General Assembly, in which, after enumerating the many blessings for which the people should be thankful, he added, "and for restoring health to us

---

[1] Scharf, I. p. 364.

[2] Allen's MSS. in Whittingham Library.

[3] The following is the record of the first proceedings of the Commissioners appointed to execute this Act.

"NOVEMBER ye 24th 1698

"At a meeting at ye coole Springs by Col: John Coarts Esqr. Captn: Philip: Hoskins: Captn: James: Keech: Captn: John: Beane: Capt: Jacob: Mooreland. and Captn: Ben. Halle. appointed trustees by act of Assembly for ye purchasing of fifty Acres of Land of Captn: John: Dent: or anny other person interrested in ye Sd: Land whereon ye Sd: Springs or fountains of healing waters doth lye. for the settleing and building of a house uppon ye Sd: Land ; wherein ye sd: fountains should be included according to ye sd: act to them directed they ye sd. trustees in pursuance with ye sd. act. did at ye sd. meeting treat with ye sd: Captn: John: Dent: & ye sd. Captn: John: Dent: did make appear before them that ye interest lay in him; whereuppon ye sade trustees did buy and purchase of him ye sd: Dent fifty Acres of the sade Land wherein ye sd: Springs or fountains of healing waters weere included in compliance with the sd: Act of Assembly to them ye sd: trustees directed for which sd: fifty Acres of Land, they ye sd: trustees weere to pay him the sd: John: Dent: twenty five pounds sterling. And it was likewise ordered by the sd: trustees, that Capt: James Keech, was to send for ye Surveyor of St. marys County to have ye sd: fifty Acres of Land laid out by the last tuesday in march next, and to have a conveyance drawne by the sd survey that ye sd Land may be made over by ye sd Captn John Dent according as ye lawe prescribes ".— Vestry Records of All Faith Parish.

and blessing us with several beneficial and healing springs of water, called the Cool Springs, which by His blessing, have wrought many wonderful and signal cures ".[1]

In this connection it should be noted, that "ye Fountain of Healing Water" still flows, and doubtless possesses the same virtue and efficacy which gave to them their early renown.

The delegates from Saint Mary's County to the several Provincial Conventions of Maryland, which sounded the keynote of the American Revolution, signed the famous articles of "Association of the Freemen of Maryland" and established the "Council of Safety" as the Provincial Government of the State, were Abraham Barnes, Henry Greenfield Sotheron and Jeremiah Jordan, June 1774; John Allan Thomas, Richard Barnes, Jeremiah Jordan and John DeButts, December, 1774; same in July 1775, with John Reeder, Jr., in place of John Allan Thomas; same in December 1775, with John Allen Thomas, in place of John Reeder, Jr.; George Plater, Richard Barnes, John Reeder, Jr., and Athanasius Ford, May 1776; same in June 1776, with Jeremiah Jordan in addition; same in August 1776, with Ignatius Fenwick, in place of Mr. Ford.[2]

Saint Mary's was quick to respond to the suggestion to elect a "Committee of Safety" and "Correspondence" for the County, and the following is the record of the meeting for that purpose, held December 23rd, 1775:

"SAINT MARY'S COUNTY.

"On public notice being given for the gentlemen, freeholders and others, of the said County to meet at the Court House, at Leonard-Town, on Friday, the twenty-third day of December last. Met agreeable to said notification a considerable number

---

[1] Scharf, Vol. I, p. 364.   [2] Journal of Conventions.

of the most respectable inhabitants, when it being proposed that, for the more orderly and effectually carrying on the present business, it would be necessary to make choice of a chairman, as also to appoint a clerk to officiate for the day, Mr. Jeremiah Jordan was thereupon unanimously elected to the chair, and Timothy Bowes appointed clerk to the said meeting,

" MR. JEREMIAH JORDAN in the chair.
" MR. TIMOTHY BOWES, clerk.

" Several of the proceedings of the continental congress being read, as well as the late resolves of the provincial convention, which were unanimously approved of. The chairman, addressing himself to those assembled, informed them, that the intent and design of the present convention, among many other things, was principally to make choice of a general committee for the country—a committee of correspondence—as also a committee, to meet, if necessary, the provincial committee, to be held at Annapolis on Monday, the 24th day of April next, in order to carry into execution the association agreed on by the continental congress, as well as the resolves of the late provincial convention. Upon which the following gentlemen were chosen as a general committee for the county, to wit: Mr. William Thomas, Mr. Cornelius Barber, major Zachariah Bond, Mr. William Hammersly, Mr. John Llewellin, Mr. James Eden, Mr. Gerard Bond, Mr. John Shanks, Jun., Mr. John Eden, Jun., Mr. Wilfred Neale, Mr. William Bond, Mr. Meveril Lock, Mr. Richard Bond, Dr. John Ireland, Mr. Cyrus Vowles, Mr. Athanasius Ford Col. Abraham Barnes, Dr. Henry Reeder, Mr. John Barnes, Mr. Richard Barnes, Mr. Timothy Bowes, Mr. William Williams, Mr. John Fenwick, Mr. John Greenwell (of Ignatius) Mr.

Vernon Hebb, Mr. William Watts, Mr. George Guyther, Mr. Ignatius Combs, Mr. John McLean, Mr. John McCall, Mr. John Black, Mr. John DeButts, Mr. William Taylor, Mr. Maffey Leigh, Mr. George Cook, Mr. James Adderton, Mr. Robert Armstrong, Mr. Bennet Biscoe, Mr. Richard Clark, Mr. Edward Fenwick, Mr. Thomas Griffin, Mr. William Jenkins, Jun., Mr. Nicholas Sewall, Mr. Nicholas L. Sewall, Mr. Willian Cavenaugh, Mr. Jenifer Taylor, Mr. Ignatius Taylor, Mr. Robert Watts, Mr. Henry Carroll, Mr. Hugh Hopewell, Mr. Hugh Hopewell, Jun., Mr. John Abel, younger, Mr. Samuel Jenifer, Mr. John Abell, sen., Mr. Edward Abell, jun., Mr. Peter Urquhart, Mr. John H. Read, Mr. Thomas Forrest, sen., Mr. Ignatius Fenwick, (Coles) Mr. John Smith, (Patuxent) Mr. Enoch Fenwich, Mr. John Reeder, Jun., Mr. Thomas A. Reeder, Mr. William Killgour, Mr. John H. Broome, Mr. William Bruce, Mr. Henry Tulman, Mr. Henry G. Sotheron, Mr. Robert Hammit, Mr. Herbert Blackiston, Mr. John A. Thomas. Mr. Jeremiah Jordan, Mr. William Bayard, Mr. Joseph Williams, Mr. Samuel Abell, sen., Mr. Samuel Abell, Jun.

"A general committee for the county elected, the next step taken was making choice of a committee of correspondence when the following gentlemen were chosen, with power for any three or more of them to act as occasion should require, to wit: Col. Abraham Barnes, Mr. Richard Barnes, Timothy Bowes, Mr. Athanasius Ford, Dr. Henry Reeder, Mr. John DeButts, Mr. Jeremiah Jordan, Mr. John A. Thomas, Mr. John Black.

"This business completed, a committee was choosen to meet the provincial committee, to be held at Annapolis, on Monday the 24th day of April next, if necessary, when the following gentlemen were elected for that purpose, to wit:

Mr. Jeremiah Jordan, Mr. Richard Barnes, Mr. John Reeder, Jun., Mr. John Barnes, Mr. John A. Thomas, Mr. John DeButts, Mr. Henry G. Sothoron,

"Signed per

"Timothy Bowes, clerk".[1]

In the "*Council of Safety*" and in the "*Continental Congress*". Saint Mary's was represented by the Hon. George Plater, elected to the former in 1776,[2] and the latter in 1778.[3]

In addittion to its regular quoto of men in service, under requisition, Saint Mary's furnished to the revolution a large independent company, under command of Captain John Allen Thomas.[4] This Company became identified with the regular army, and for it valor and efficiency, was honorably mentioned by Major General Wm. Smallwood, in his report of October 1776, to the Maryland Convention.[5]

On the reorganization of the "Maryland Line" in 1794, in compliance with the Act of Congress, the following officers from Saint Mary's County were elected : Brigadier General John Hanson Briscoe ; Lieut. Cols. George Plater and Henry Neale ; Majors William Thomas, John Armstrong, William Somerville and Francis Hamersley.[6] While the first attempted infringement of the "non importation agreement", of the Maryland Convention was in the arrival in the Saint Mary's River in August, 1774, of the brig, *Mary and Tom*, from London, with tea, consigned to Robert Findlay and others (but which, was not unloaded, and was returned),[7] Saint Mary's County was the scene of but one actual engagement during the Revolution. In July 1776, Lord Dunmore, with ut 30abooemn in armed galleys, took possession of Saint

---

[1] Maryland Gazette, January 5th, 1775. [2] McMahon, 419.
[3] Scharf, 3, p. 753. [4] Journal of Convention.
[5] Annals of Annapolis. [6] Maryland Gazette, June 12, 1794.
[7] Scharf, 2, p. 159.

R

George's Island. In an engagement with Captain Beall's Company of Militia he was wounded and a mid-shipman on the "Roebuck" was killed, Dunmore's fleet, amounting to about forty sail, was anchored at the mouth of Saint Mary's River. On the 26th of July, Captain Nicholson of the "Defence", and Major Price, attempted to recapture the Island, but were unsuccessful. Price, however, stationed a battery on "Cherry Field Point" and drove the sloop of war "Fowey" out of the river. Early in August the enemy abandoned the Island, leaving several galleys and some military stores behind them.[1]

The members of the committee from Saint Mary's County appointed by the General Assembly, to draft the famous Resolutions declarative of the constitutional rights and priviledges of the people, and also, the instructions for the government of the members from Maryland of the Stamp Act Congress of 1765, and which passed the "Remonstrance to Parliament", were the Hon. Edmund Key and the Hon. Daniel Wolstenholme [2]

In 1774, Saint Mary's County raised by private subscription, for the Maryland "Revolutionary Fund", the sum of £600 sterling, the fifth largest contribution made by any county in the State.[3] In 1776, an additional sum of £224, 1 s. and 3 p. in gold was raised, which, while not a gratuity from the county, was an advance, to be redeemed only in paper money of the Continental Congress.

In this connection it should be noted, that in 1780, when the State was without means or credit, and the army without supplies and in danger of dissolution, the Hon. Philip Key, a patriotic son of Saint Mary's, and then a representative in the

---

1 Scharf, 2, pp. 268, 269.
2 Old Kent, p. 253; Scharf, 1, p. 538.   3 Scharf, 2, p. 168.

SAINT MARY'S COUNTY

Legislature of Maryland, furnished to the cause, out of his own private means, the sum of £1500 in money, and 10 hogsheads of tobacco, the third largest subscription made by any single individual in the State.[1]

The representatives[2] from Saint Mary's, in the first General Assembly held after the Declaration of Independence,

---

[1] Ibid, 2, p. 375.

[2] The earliest local officers of Saint Mary's County were, Thomas Cornwaleys, "Commander"; James Baldridge "High Sheriff", and John Lewger, "Conservator of the Peace". The judicial powers of the latter, were analogous to those vested in the "County Court" as subsequently established. The first Justices of the County Court, were Wm. Evans, John Abbington, Thos. Matthews, Thos. Dent, Richard Willan, John Lawson, Thos. Turner and Luke Gardiner. The first Clerk was Walter Hall, who was in turn; succeeded (during the period preceeding the establishment of the Royal Government in Maryland) by Nicholas Painter, John Skipwith, John Llewellin and Henry Denton. Vacancies on this bench, during the same period, were filled by the appointment from time to time, of the following Justices: Robert Slye, John Nuthall, Nicholas Young, John Jarboe, Wm. Bretton, John Vanhockman, Randall Hanson, Wm. Rosewell, Wm. Barton, Wm. Boarman, Richard Lloyd, James Martin, John Warren, Richard Gardiner, Kenelm Cheseldine, Joshua Doyne, Wm. Langworth, Robert Mason, Wm. Hatton and Robert Carville.

The office of Judge of the Orphans Court was one of responsibility and dignity, and was filled by the leading men in the County. They were appointed by the Governor. Those who served in Saint Mary's during the half century succeeding the Revolution, were: John Hatton Read, from 1778 to 1780; Thomas Bond, 1778 to 1783, and 1784 to 1787; William Kilgour, 1778 to 1783, and 1784 to 1797; John DeButts, 1779 to 1783, and 1784 to 1797; Ignatius Taylor, 1782 to 1783; Vernon Hebb, 1782 to 1783; Ignatuis Fenwick, 1782 to 1786; Hanson Briscoe, 1782 to 1791; John Shanks, 1782 to 1784; John Ireland, 1783 to 1784; Zachary Forrest, 1786 to 1791; William Somerville, 1787 to 1803; Edmund Plowden, 1791 to 1805; Maj. William Thomas, 1797 to 1802; Henry Gardiner, 1802 to 1803; Raphael Neale, 1802 to 1806; Philip Key, 1803 to 1804, and 1808 to 1812; James Egerton, 1804 to 1810; Philip Ford, 1804 to 1805; Thomas Barber, 1804 to 1815; Athanatius Fenwick, 1806 to 1807, and 1820 to 1821; Dr. Henry Ashton, 1810 to 1811; Gen. James Thomas, 1811 to 1813, and 1819 to 1822; Dr. Joseph Stone, 1812 to 1813, and 1819 to 1835; Zachary Forrest, 1812 to 1813; Henry Gardiner, 1812 to 1814; Luke W. Barber,

and which formally established, in 1777, the first State Government in Maryland, were the Hons. William Thomas, James Jordan, Athanasius Ford, and John Hatton Read.[1] The Senator was the Hon. George Plater. The election—the first in Maryland as a State—was held in Leonardtown, on November 25th, for Senate electors and on December 18th, (1776) for members of the House of Delegates, the Judges of election being Major, Henry Tubman, Abraham Barnes, and Hugh Hopewell.[2] The representatives from Saint Mary's in the convention which framed the first constitution of the State, were, Hon. George Plater, Ignatius Fenwick, Richard Barnes

1813 to 1820; Col. John Rousby Plater, 1815 to 1816; Henry Neale, 1815 to 1816; John Leigh, 1815 to 1817; James Hopewell, 1816 to 1817; Henry G. S. Key, 1816 to 1819; William B. Scott, 1817 to 1819; George Thomas, 1822 to 1832; John Hanson Briscoe 1830 to 1831; Stephen Gough, 1831 to 1835; Cornelius Combs, 1834 to 1835.

The Registers of Wills during the same period were, Jeremiah Jordan, 1777 to 1804; James Forrest, 1804 to 1826; E. J. Millard, 1826 to 1834; George Combs, 1834 to 1856. The duties of this office were performed, prior to the organization of the State Government, by a Deputy Commissary General. Those who filled the office from the beginning of the last century to the above date, were: James Keech, 1700 to 1706; William Aisquith, 1706 to 1718; John Baker, 1718 to 1723; Thomas Aisquith, 1723 to 1762; Stanton Edwards, 1762 to 1766; Samuel Abell, jr. 1766 to 1770; John Allen Thomas, 1770 to 1777. It is regretted that, owing to the destruction of the records, a complete list of the names of the "High Sheriffs" of the County, prior to the Revolution, (when the office lost much of its importance and the name was changed to that of Sheriff only) can not here be furnished, but among them, were: James Baldridge, 1637, (first High Sheriff); C. Thorougood, 1641; Edward Parker, 1642; Philip Land, 1649; Nicholas Guyther, 1659; Daniel Clocker, 1660; Richard Willan, 1662; Wm. Evans, 1663; Thos. Dent, 1664; John Lawson, 1665; Nicholas Young, 1666; John Jarboe, 1667; Walter Hall, 1668; Wm. Boarman, 1679; Joshua Doyne, 1684; John Baker, 1686; Garrett VanSweringin, 1687; Robert Carse, 1690; Robert Mason, 1692; John Coade, 1694; Thos. Hatton, 1700; Jas. Hay, 1702; John Coade, 1706; Thos. T. Greenfield, 1720; John Cartright, 1739; Wm. Cartright, 1743; Gilbert Ireland, 1745; Robert Chesley, 1748; M. Lock,

1 House Journal, 1777. 2 Ibid.

and Jeremiah Jorden.[1] The representatives in the Convention for the ratification of the Constitution of the United States and of which George Plater was president, were the Hons. George Plater, Richard Barnes, Nicholas L. Sewall, and Charles Chilton.[2]

The first local officers for Saint Mary's County, under the State Government, were, County Lieut. Richard Barnes;[3] Justices of the County Court, Jeremiah Jordan, John Reeder, Jr., Henry Greenfield Sothoron, Richard Barnes, Henry Reeder, Vernon Hebb, Ignatius Taylor, Henry Tubman, Bennet Biscoe, John Shanks, John Hanson Briscoe, John Ireland, Ignatius Fenwick, Robert Watts, Nickolas L. Sewall, and Robert Armstrong. The Judges of the Orphans Court were, Henry Greenfield Sothoron, Richard Barnes, Henry Reeder, Vernon Hebb, and John Reeder, Jr.; Sheriff, Jenifer Taylor; Clerk, Daniel Wolstenholme; Register of Wills, Jeremiah Jordan; Surveyor, Jesse Lock; Coroners, James Mills, Thomas Greenfield, Stephen Tarlton, John Attaway Clark, and Mackelery Hammett.[4]

At the first constitutional convention for Presidental Electors, 1788, Saint Mary's had two candidates, the Hon. George Plater on the Federalist, and the Hon. Wm. Thomas, Jr., on the Anti-Federalist ticket. The former ticket was triumphantly elected throughout the State.

1754; Philip Key, 1755; John Eden, 1760; Jeremiah Jordan, 1766; —— Watts, 1770; Jenifer Taylor, 1772, and Samuel Abell, 1776.

Among the County clerks during the period embraced between the establishment of the Royal Government in Maryland and the Revolution, and for the succeeding century, were: John Skipwith, John Llewellin, Henry Denton, Richard Ward Key, Benj. Young, Daniel Wolstenholme, Timothy Bowes, James Kilgour, Joseph Harris, Wm. T. Maddox, Jas. T. Blackistone, John A. Comalier.

1 Journal of Convention.   2 Ibid.
3 Scharf, 2, p. 453.   4 Scharf, 3, Appendix.

The representatives in Congress from Saint Mary's have been the Hons. Philip Key in the 2nd ; Raphael Neale in the 16th, 17th, and 18th ; Clement Dorsey in the 19th, 20th, and 21st ; J. M. S. Causin in the 28th, and Benjamin G. Harris in the 38th, and 39th.

Saint Mary's has had the honor of two Governors of Maryland under State Government, the Hon. George Plater, elected in 1792, and the Hon. James Thomas, elected in 1832, and reelected the two succeeding terms.[1]

---

[1] Scharf, 2, p. 549.

CHAPTER XII.

Chronicles of Saint Mary's County.

IN the absence of skilled labor, variety of material and effective mechanical tools and wood working machinery, the houses in Saint Mary's, in early colonial times, were necessarily small and unpretentious. They had outside brick chimneys, and many of them brick gables up to the line of the roof plates, above which the ends, like the sides, were usually of frame, constructed of heavy and roughly squared timbers, put together with mortise and tenon, and boarded up with thick plank, sometimes covered with clapboards or shingles. They were generally one and one-half stories high, with steep roof, covered with lapped shingles, which, with the weather boarding, were put on with wrought iron nails. A little later, the gambril roof and the hipped roof, with deeply sunken mullion and dormer windows became prominent features, and with them came more capacious buildings. A few were constructed with double roof, with porch running the whole length of the house, and the porch roof being extended up and joined on to the comb of the main roof. The effect of this curious design is exceedingly odd and quaint, what ever may be said in favor of the protection and comfort which it afforded. By the early part of 1700, however, many handsome and stately buildings had been erected, some of which still stand and are models of ease and liberality, as well as of the higher order of architecture of that day, and which in their impression of graceful design and handsome finish, are scarcely surpassed by the more costly country dwellings of modern times.

The whole of Saint Mary's county lying south of Smith's Creek was originally comprised in three large Manors; Saint Michael's, which extended from Point Lookout to a line drawn from Oyster Creek to Deep Creek; Saint Gabriel's, which extended from the north side of Saint Michael's Manor to a line drawn from Saint Jerome's Creek to Broad Creek; Trinity Manor, which extended from the north side of Saint Gabriel's to a line drawn from Trinity (Smith's Creek) to Saint Jerome's Creek.

These Manors were granted to Governor Leonard Calvert in 1639,[1] with the right of Court Baron and Court Leet, a right which appears to have been exercised at least once, as shown by the following record : "At a Court Baron held at the Manor at Saint Gabriel, on the 7th of March, 1656, by the Steward of the Manor, one Martin Kirke took of the lady of the Manor in full court, by delivery of the said Stewart, by the rod, according to the custom of said Manor, one message lying in the said Manor, by the yearly rent of and etc., and the said Kirke, having done his fealty was thereof admitted tenant".[2]

The mansion house of these manors was located at "Piney Neck", near what is now known as the "Pine", and is referred to as a large frame building with brick foundations and chimneys.[3] The first tenants on these manors, of which there is any record, were Thomas Butler on Saint Michaels, Henry James and Martin Kirke on Saint Gabriel, and John Langford and Robert Smith on Trinity.[4] In 1707, these Manors, the

---

[1] Liber, 1, pp. 121, 122.
[3] Archives (Pro. Ct.) pp. 189, 321.
[2] Bozman, 581.
[4] Kilty, p. 103.

Piney Neck estate excepted,[1] were owned by the children of George Parker, by inheritance from their mother, the daughter of Gabriel Parrot.[2] They are now divided into numerous farms among which may be mentioned "Calvert's Rest", and the beautiful estate called "Cornfield Harbor".

On the opposite side of Smith's Creek from Trinity Manor was Saint Elizabeth's Manor, which contained two thousand acres and within the limits of which the "Jutland" estate is located. It was granted to Thomas Cornwaleys in 1639, but was subsequently owned by the Hon. Wm. Bladen.[3] Adjoining this on the northeast, was Saint Inigoe's Manor (for an account of which see Saint Inigoe's Church), while bordering on it, and Saint Inigoe's Creek, was the estate called "Cross Manor". It contained two thousand acres, and was the home of the Hon. Thomas Cornwaleys, one of the wealthiest, as well as one of the most distinguished men in early Maryland, to whom it was granted in 1639. There is evidence that the

---

1 This estate was purchased from the Hon. Wm. Calvert, the only son of Governor Leonard Calvert, by Charles Egerton, Esq., who in 1698 devised it to his eldest son Charles Egerton, who had married Mary, the only daughter of James Neale by his first wife, Elizabeth Calvert, the only daughter of William, and grand-daughter of Governor Leonard Calvert. Their grandson, James Egerton, in 1765; devised it to his only son, Charles Calvert Egerton, in the possession of whose descendants it remained for many years.

2 Rent Rolls, Saint Mary's County.

3 This was the early home in Maryland of the Hon. William Bladen, member of the House, Clerk of the Council and the first "public printer" of the Province. He was the father of Governor Thomas Bladen, who married Barbara, daughter of Sir Thomas Janssen, and also of Ann, the wife of Col. Benjamine Tasker, Commissary General, Commissioner of the Land Office, member of the Council, and, by virtue of his position as "first in the Council", became Governor of the Province upon the death of Governor Samuel Ogle. He was the son of Col. Thomas Tasker, member of the House and Treasurer of Maryland, and was the father of Rebecca Tasker, the wife of Daniel Dulaney, and of Elizabeth Tasker, the wife of Christopher Lowndes.

the old Cornwaleys' house (long occupied by the family of Captain Randolph Jones) was built at a very early date,[1] and it is probably the oldest brick house to-day in Maryland. Whilst so materially modified, that an accurate description of its original architecture cannot be obtained, the lines separating the old walls from the new, are distinctly marked, and show it to have been a substantial and capacious building.

Mattapany, beautifully located near the mouth of the Patuxent, is historic by reason of having been the residence of Charles, Lord Baltimore, and the place from which many of the Proprietary orders and proclamations were issued, and where one session of the General Assembly, and several meetings of the Council were held.[2] On it was originally located the Indian Village of the Mattapients. Shortly after the landing of the Maryland Colonists, King Pantheon presented this plantation to the Jesuits, who established a store-house and missionary station there.[3] As a result, however, of the conflict between Baltimore and the Jesuits in 1641, a formal release was executed to the former, for Mattapany, in common with all other lands in Maryland held by the society, or by other persons for its use.[4]

In 1663, a special warrant was issued for Mattapany containing 1,000 acres, with addition of 200 acres, by the Proprietary to Hon. Henry Sewall, Secretary of the Province and member of the Council from August, 1661, to the time of his death, April 1665. On April 20th, 1665, the patent for Mattapany and addition, was granted to his widow,[5] Jane Sewall, who, in 1666, married Governor Charles Calvert, after-

---

[1] Archives (Pro. Ct. 1642) p. 182 ; Ibid, 1650, p. 306 ; Scharf 1, p. 149.
[2] McMahon, p. 237 ; Scharf, 1, p. 316 ; Pro. Cl. 1778.
[3] McSherry, p. 47 ; Johnson, p. 56.
[4] Brown, p. 55 ; Johnson, p. 86.   [5] See Patent in Land Office.

wards Lord Baltimore.[1] Governor Calvert erected at Mattapany, a large brick mansion, which was for many years his private residence. The house, says an early writer, was built "for convenience rather than magnificence".[2] A fort and magazine were also erected there,[3] and "Brick Hill Point" on the estate, was the place of general rendezvous for the militia, by order of the Council.[4] In 1682, an Act was passed making provision for a "sufficient guard to be kept at Mattapany, for the defense of the Right Hon. the Lord Proprietary, and with him the magazine and military supplies there".[5]

When the Maryland Deputies were driven from Saint Mary's City during the Protestant Revolution, they took refuge in the garrison at Mattapany, and it was there that the formal articles of surrender were executed in August, 1689.[6] In 1690, the Proprietary petitioned the Maryland authorities

---

1 Lady Baltimore, (widow of Hon. Henry Sewall, was the daughter of Vincent Lowe and Anne Cavendish of London, and a sister of Col. Vincent Lowe, of Maryland. She had by her first marriage, children— Nicholas, who married Susannah, daughter of Col. William Burgess; Mary, married Col. William Chandler; Anne, married, 1st, Col. Benjamin Rozier, and 2nd, Col. Edward Pye; Jane, married Hon. Philip Calvert, and Elizabeth, married, 1st, Dr. Jesse Wharton, and, 2nd, Col. William Digges, a member of the Maryland Council and son of Governor Edward Digges, of Virginia. Colonel Digges was in command at Saint Mary's at the time of its evacuation, in 1689. After that, he located on "Warburton Manor", in Prince George's County, Maryland, nearly opposite Mount Vernon. He left a son, William, a daughter, Jane (who married Col. John Fitzgerald, of Virginia), and grandchildren, Charles, George, and Thomas. Through the Sewalls and Digges, there are still many descendents of Lady Jane Baltimore living in the Counties of Southern Maryland.

It may be interesting to note that old "Fort Warburton" stood on a part of Warburton Manor. The land for it was purchased by the United States in 1794, for $3,000. When rebuilt, after it was blown up in 1814, it was called "Fort Washington".

2 Old Mixon. 3 Scharf, 1, p. 316.
4 Archives (Cl. Pro. 1676) p. 31.
5 Ibid, Ass. Pro. 1682, p. 338. 6 McMahon, p. 237.

to deliver to him the Mattapany house, plantation and stock, and to render an account of the operation of his Lordship's mill there, located on Gardiner's Creek. This was denied, except as to the stock, upon the ground that, the whole plantation and all of its appurtenances, had with the garrison, been "surrendered" under articles to His Majesty's use ".[1] Two years later, however, by order of Council, the estate was given up aud formally placed into the possession of Col. Henry Darnall, the agent of the Proprietary.[2]

The last notice of the old Calvert house was in 1773, when it was reported to be in a state of dilapidation and decay. It has long since disappeared, though its foundation and cemented celler may still be seen. The building was about 60 x 30 feet, with a capacious wing, and stood about 250 yards southward of the present commodious dwelling house of Mattapany. The garrison, the site of which is still discernible, stood about 100 yards nearer the river, and on the river bank in the rear of the present dwelling house, are the remains of an old earthen fortification—probably a remnant of the ancient bulwark of defense for Mattapany.

"Mattapany", or "Mattapany Sewall", as it was called, came back into the possession of the Sewalls in 1722, by grant from the 2nd Charles Lord Baltimore to Nicholas Sewall, son of the original proprietor, and it remained in the family until early in the present century.

Susquehannah, adjoining Mattapany on the east, and situated on the Patuxent, is noted as having been the home of Christopher Rousby, the King's Collector General, who was fatally stabbed in an altercation with Col. George Talbot, a member of the Council and Surveyor General of the Province.[3]

---

1 Archives (Cl. Pro. 1690) p. 182.   2 Ibid, 1692, p. 311.

3 Talbot was at once arrested, and in spite of the efforts of the Council to have him tried in Maryland, he was carried off to Virginia and

The tombstone, a massive marble slab, covering the grave of Colonel Rousby, on this estate, bears the following inscription:

"Here lyeth the Body of Xpher Rousbie esquire, who was taken out of this World by a violent Death received on Board his majesty's ship 'The Quaker Ketch', Capt. Thomas Allen command'r the last day of Oct'r 1684. And alsoe of Mr. John Rousbie, his Brother, who departed this natural Life on board the Ship Baltimore. Being arrived in Patuxent river the first day of February 1685, memento mori".

Susquehannah is otherwise noted as the place at which the Council held its meeting July 1st 1661, and determined upon the famous expedition against the Dutch on the Deleware.[1]

---

delivered up to the rapacious Governor, Lord Howard of Effingham, who treated all the remonstrances of the Marylanders with contempt. Baltimore, anxious that his kinsmen should have, at least, the chance of a fair trial, obtained an order from the Privy Council to have him sent to England. But when the order, dated January 1685, reached Virginia, the bird had flown. In the dead of winter, Talbot's devoted wife, and two brave and faithful retainers, sailed down the bay in a little skiff, and up the Rappahannock to a point near Gloucester, where he was imprisoned. Here they contrived by some devise to effect the release of the prisoner, and carried him off in safety to his distant Manor, Susquehannah, in Cecil County. The hue and cry was proclaimed, and so hot was the pursuit, according to local tradition, that Talbot was forced to secret himself in a cave, where he was fed by two trained hawks which brought him wild fowl from the river. However, this may have been, he soon surrendered himself to the authorities, who delivered him to Effingham. The order of the Privy Council being disregarded, he was, in April, 1685, tried and convicted. The Proprietary was, however, not idle in his kinsman's behalf, and obtained from the King a pardon, in time to save his life—Brown, History of Maryland, 146.

1 On the Calvert side of the Patuxent, and nearly opposite Susquehanna, is the estate known as Rousby Hall—one of the handsomest, and until the dwelling house was destroyed in the war of 1812, one of the most highly improved places in Southern Maryland. It was the home of Col. John Rousby (possibly a descendant of John Rousby who is buried at Susquehannah) who was the father of Ann, wife of Hon. Edward Lloyd and of the Hon. John Rousby of Rousby Hall, the father of Ann,

After the death of Colonel Rousby, Susquehannah reverted to the Proprietary, and, in 1700 it was granted to Richard Smith. This patent was executed by Mary Darnall,[1] the wife of Colonel Henry Darnall, the agent of the Proprietary, and is one of the very few instances in which such authority was exercised by a woman in Maryland. Shortly afterward it

---

wife of Gov. George Plater. Col. John Rousby's wife was Barbara, the daughter of Henry and Francis Morgan of Kent County, and the author of the famous narative of the troubles in Maryland consequent upon the Protestant Revolution. She married secondly Richard Smith of Saint Leonards, Captain of Militia, of Calvert County, Surveyor General 1693, died 1714, son of Richard (and Eleanor) Smith of Calvert County, who came to Maryland in 1649, Attorney General in 1655, and member of the House from 1660 to 1667. Richard and Barbara Smith had sons, Richard, Charles, Somerset and Walter, who have representatives still living in Calvert and Saint Mary's, and daughters Anne, Elizabeth and Barbara, progenitors of the Parker's, Hellens'. and Dawkins' of Calvert County. Hon. John Rousby, only son of Col. John Rousby, and the father of Mrs. Plater, died in 1750 at the early age of twenty-three, and is buried at Rousby Hall, where his tomb may still be seen.

The following romantic incident in the life of Mrs. Plater is handed down by those who vouch for its truth. Mrs. Rousby her mother, noted alike for her beauty, dignity, position and wealth, became a widow at the age of twenty, her only child being then an infant. Among her many suitors was Col. William Fitzhugh of Virginia. His position and fortune were good, but the fair widow of Rousby Hall was inflexible. Colonel Fitzhugh, however, who had served under Admiral Vernon at Carthegena, was not to be subdued and continued to press his suit. On one occasion having paid a visit to Mrs Rousby, and on leaving the house to take his boat, the nurse appeared, bearing in her arms the infant heiress of Rousby Hall. Snatching the child from the nurse's arms, and unheeding the cries of the baby, the desperate soldier-lover sprang into his boat and ordered his men to push from the shore. When some distance out in the Patuxent, he held the child over the water, threatening to drown it if its mother did not relent and agree to become his wife. The mother half frantic, stood upon the river bank while her mad lover held her innocent child between sky and water. Believing that the threat would be executed she yielded and sealed her fate, by becoming shortly afterwards Mrs. Col. William Fitzhugh, and the baby that was not drowned became the wife of Gov. George Plater.

1 See Patent in Land Office.

became the property of a branch of the Maryland, Carroll family, and for many generations continued to be their attractive homestead.

Cedar Point, at the mouth of the Patuxent, and adjoining susquehannah, was the Sewall estate. It was granted by Lord Baltimore, in 1676 to Nicholas Sewall, his step-son, in whose family it remained until a very recent date.[1]

These three estates, Mattapany, Susquehannah, and Cedar Point, originally occupied nearly the whole of that fertile and beautiful plateau bordering on the mouth of the Patuxent.

Above Mattapany, and near Town Creek on the Patuxent was Saint Joseph's Manor, containing 1350 acres. It belonged to the Edloes,[2] and subsequently to the Platers.[3] On Abbington Creek, on this Manor, the port of Saint Joseph's was erected in 1688.

---

[1] Major Nicholas Sewall, Secretary of Maryland in 1683, member of Council from 1684 to 1689, and son of Hon. Henry Sewall, of "Mattapany", married Susannah, daughter of Hon. William Burgess, of Anne Arundel County. They left sons Charles and Henry. The latter's widow, Elizabeth, in 1728, married Hon. Wm. Lee of the Council, father of Thomas, the father of Governor Thomas Sim Lee. Nicholas, son of Henry and Elizabeth Sewall, married Miss Darnall of "Poplar Hill" Prince George County. Among the more prominent of the Sewalls of later times, were Hon. Nicholas Lewis Sewall of "Cedar Point", member of convention for ratification of the constitution of the United States, and Robert Darnall Sewall of "Poplar Hill". The last named estate is a part of the once famous and beautiful plantation in Prince George's County, known as the "Woodyard", and the home of Col. Henry Darnall, who came to Maryland in 1665, his brother John Darnall, having located at Portland Manor, Anne Arundel County. Eleanor, daughter of Col. Henry Darnall, married Clement Hill. Archbishop Carroll's mother, Eleanor Brooke Darnall was of the "Woodyard", as was also Mary, the wife of Charles Carroll of Carrollton. Robert Darnall, grandson of Col. Henry Darnall, lost all of this magnificent estate except "Poplar Hill"—about 800 acres—and which came into possession of the Sewall's through the marriage above mentioned.

[2] Patent in Land Office.   [3] Will, George Plater, 1751.

Between Town Creek and Cuckolds Creek was "Resurrection Manor". It was patented, in 1650, to Thomas Cornwaleys.[1] Shortly afterwards it came into possession of the Plowden family, where it remained for several generations.[2] On this Manor, two sessions of the Privy Council were held, the one on December 12th, 1659, the other, June 27th, 1662.[3]

"Satterly", now called Sotterly, on the Patuxent, opposite Saint Leonards Creek, was the Plater homestead. It is beautifully located and highly improved. The house, built about 1730, is a handsome model of antique architecture. It is in the shape of the letter "Z", is one and a half stories high with steep gambrall roof, surmounted by a cupola and penetrated by triangular capped dormer windows. It is a frame building with brick foundations, brick gables, brick porches and flagstone colonade. A secret brick arch-way leads from the cellar to the foot of the hill below the house. The rooms are capacious, with ceilings of medium height on the lower floor, and hipped and low on the upper floor. The main hall, library, and original dining room, are furnished in handsomely panneled wood from the ceiling to the floor. The parlor is finished entirely in wood, both ceiling and side walls, artistically paneled and elaborately carved. The shell carvings forming the ceilings of the parlor alcoves are especially unique and handsome. The window frames are of walnut and the door solid mahogany, swung on solid brass strap hinges extending about two feet across the door. This room presents one of the finest specimens of colonial interior finish and decoration to be found in Maryland. The stairway is also of mahogany, with grooved rail, and balustrade and newel

---

1 Patent in Land Office.
2 Will of George, Edmund and Henrietta Plowden.
3 Archives (Cl. Pro.) p. 381, 460.

post of an ingenious device of filigree work. A tradition in the Plater family is that the work on the parlor and stair-way was done by a mechanic named Bowen, who was one of the "King's seven year convicts", transported to Maryland, purchased by the Hon. George Plater and liberated in consideration of his masterly workmanship at Sotterly. In the front yard formerly stood two small square buildings, with cone shaped roofs. The one stood at the garden gate and was used as a wine and smoking room; the other stood immediately opposite, and was used as the office of the Collector and Naval Officer of the Patuxent District. The former of these is now at the foot of the yard, opposite the old "Gate Lodge"; the other is in the barn yard, flanked by a series of sheds and used as a granary. Near the centre of the garden, and about thirty yards from the house, still stands in good preservation, a relic of the olden times—the Sotterly sun dial. A capacious brick stable and carriage house bears the date of its erection—1734, carved in the brick.

Sotterly was originally a part of "Fenwicks Manor". It was purchased from it by the Hon. James Bowles, contained 2000 acres and was for many years known as "Bowles' Separation". Its present name, after the Plater homestead in England, as well as many of its architectural beauties, it owes to its subsequent owners—the Platers—in whose possession it came by intermarriage with the widow of Mr. Bowles.[1]

---

[1] Of the marriage of the Hon. George Plater, father of Governor Plater, in the Maryland Gazette of June 16th, 1729, the following notice appeared: "On Thursday last the Hon. George Plater was married to Mrs. Rebecca Bowles, relict of James Bowles, Esq., a gentlewoman of considerable fortune".

Mrs. Rebecca Bowles was the daughter of Col. Thomas Addison and Elizabeth, his wife, the daughter of Thomas Tasker, treasurer of Maryland. James Bowles, her first husband, who died January, 1727, was a member of the Council of Maryland, and son of Tobias Bowles, of London.

For more than a century, Sotterly was conspicuous as the homestead of this family—than which none other, perhaps, was more closely identified with the history of Maryland, both as a colony and as a State. The Hon. George Plater was a member of the Assembly and Attorney General of Maryland as early as 1691, and from 1692 to 1720, was the Collector of Customs for the Patuxent. His son, George Plater, was for many years a member of the Council, and was Naval Officer of the Patuxent, and, from 1746 to 1755, was Secretary of the Province. His son, George Plater, was a member of the

Their children were Eleanor, who married, 1st, William, son of Governor Sir William Gooch, and married, 2nd, Warner Lewis, both of Virginia; Mary and Jane Bowles, one of whom married William, son of Henry and Martha (Burwell) Armistead of Virginia.

Hon. George Plater died June 17th, 1755, his wife having died before 1751. They left children—Governor George, Ann, Elizabeth, and Rebecca Plater, who married, in 1744, Col. John Taylor, of Mount Airy, Virginia, and who died in 1787, leaving children: Elizabeth, married, in 1767, Edward Lloyd, father of Governor Edward Lloyd, of Maryland; Rebecca married, in 1769, Francis Lightfoot Lee, "the signer"; Eleanor married, in 1772, Ralph Wormly; Ann, married, in 1773, Thomas Lomax; Mary, married, in 1776, Mann Page; Catherine, married, in 1780, Landon Carter; Jane, married, in 1791, Robert Beverly; Sarah, married, in 1799, Col. William Augustine Washington (all of Virginia); John, born 1771, married 1792, Anne, daughter of Governor Benjamin Ogle, of Maryland, died 1828, leaving many children, among them Henry Tayloe, of Alabama, and Benjamin Ogle Tayloe, of Washington. D. C.

Governor George Plater, only son of Hon. George Plater, and heir of Sotterly, was born in 1736, and was educated at William and Mary's College. In 1760 he visited England, where he was introduced by letters from Governor Horatio Sharpe. He seems to have made an agreeable impression while there upon Lord Baltimore, who shortly after indicated to Governor Sharpe his desire to have him associated "in the affairs of the Province", and with which he soon became so prominently connected. He married Ann Rousby, the only child of Colonel John Rousby, of the once famous and beautiful estate on the Calvert side of the Patuxent, known as " Rousby Hall ". Mrs. Plater enjoys the reputation of having been a woman possessed of rare personal beauty and stately elegance. Her rich patrimony, added to the already large estate of her husband, enabled the occupants of Sotterly to live in courtly style,

House of Delegates in 1758; Naval Officer of the Patuxent, from 1767 to 1774; Judge of the Provincial Court, from 1771 to 1773; Member of the Council, in 1773 and 1774; Member of the Council of Safety of Maryland, in 1776; Member of the Constitutional Convention of Maryland, in 1776; Member of the Senate of Maryland and President of that body, in 1784; Delegate to the Continental Congress, from 1788 to 1791; Member of the Convention for the ratification of the Constitution of the United States, and President of that body in 1788; Presidential Elector, in 1789; and Governor of Maryland, in 1792.

Besides being so closely identified with Maryland in her struggle for independence and in laying the foundations of free government, his name conspicuously appears upon the pages of his country's history, during a period of half a century, in nearly every important move made by her people. He died

and in full keeping with their distinguished position, as is clearly attested by the will of Governor Plater and the inventory of his estate. Governor George and Ann Rousby Plater left two daughters, Ann and Rebecca (whose fame for beauty and accomplishments have lived to the present day), and three sons, George, Thomas, and John Rousby Plater. Ann Plater married the distinguished jurist and statesman, Philip Barton Key, and Rebecca married General Uriah Forrest, of the Maryland line; George, eldest son of Governor George Plater and heir of Sotterly, married, 1st, March 9th, 1795, Cecelia B. Bond. of "Southampton", and 2d, March 22d, 1798, Elizabeth Somerville. He died in 1802, leaving by his first marriage, George, who inherited Sotterly and lost it, and by his second, Ann Elizabeth Plater, who married her cousin, John Rousby Plater. Judge John Rousby, second son of Governor George Plater, married Elizabeth Tuttle, of Annapolis, Maryland. He died in 1832, leaving children—1, Elizabeth, who married May 5th, 1818, Stephen Gough, and left issue, Elizabeth A., Stephen, Sophia, Mary, Louise, Georgiana, and John Rousby Gough; 2, Dr. William, who married, 1st, Mrs. McEldeny, by whom he had one son, William, and 2d, Louise Hobbie, by whom he had children, John Rousby, Mayhew, married Alice Bland, and Louisa Plater; 3, Sophia, married William G. Ridgely, nephew of Hon. Charles Ridgely, of Hampton, and had issue, Elizabeth, Thomas, Louise, Emily, William, Ann Key, and Sophia Matilda Ridgely;

at Annapolis, February 10th, 1792. His remains "attended by the Council and State officials, were taken the next day, by way of South River, to Sotterly", where he is buried in what is now an open field, and without even a simple slab to mark the last resting place of a son of Maryland, whose statemanship and zeal are so closely interwoven with her government, and whose whole life, from the dawn of early manhood to the grave, was conspicuous for disinterested devotion and distinguished service to the State and to the Nation. Oh! Spirit of Liberty, where sleeps your thunder!

His sons were—George, a colonel in the Maryland line, Thomas, a member of Congress from Maryland, from 1801 to 1805; and Judge John Rousby Plater, who was Presidential Elector in 1797; in 1812, and for several terms thereafter, he was a member of the House of Delegates of Maryland, and from 1823 to the time of his death, 1832, filled with distinction and honor, the position of Associate Judge of the First Judicial District of Maryland.

Below De La Brooke, and separated from it by Cat Creek, was "Fenwick's Manor", granted in 1651, to Mr. Cuthbert Fenwick, prominent in the early councils of the Province, and the progenitor of a long line of descendants, distinguished

4, John Rousby, married, 1st, November 3d, 1816, his cousin, Ann E. Plater, who died without issue, and 2d, Matilda Edmonson, by whom he had issue, John Rousby and Charlotte Plater, the latter being the wife of General E. Law Rodgers, of Baltimore.

Thomas, the third son of Governor George Plater, inherited the famous estate, "Rouseby Hall", and sold it. His daughter, Ann Plater, was another noted beauty of the family, and of whom many reminiscences still survive. She became the wife of Major George Peter, of Montgomery County, distinguished in the military service in 1812—a belle and a hero of ye olden time.

Early in the present century, Sotterly passed out of the Plater family, and since then, the mansion house and a small portion (about 400 acres) of the once vast domain of Sotterly, has been in the possession of the family of Dr. Walter Hanson Stone Briscoe.

both in Church and State. The manor extended down the Patuxent as far as Saint Cuthbert's (Cuckold's) Creek, and that part of it bordering on this creek still retains its original name—Saint Cuthbert's.

The manor house, it is said, stood on the site occupied by the residence of the late Joseph Forrest. This house was referred to as early as 1659, in the famous proceedings against Edward Prescott, for "hanging a witch", in which Colonel John Washington, of Virginia, the great-grandfather of General George Washington, was the principal witness. "He will be called", says the summons of Washington, "uppon his tryal the 4th or 5th of Octob^r next, at the Court to bee held then att the Patuxent, near Mr. Fenwick's house". In this connection it may be interesting to note that Colonel Washington, in reply to this summons, wrote that he would be unable to attend court on the days named "because then, God willing, I intend to gette my yowng sonne baptized. All the Company & Gossips being allready invited". The proceedings also show that at the trial of the case, no witnesses appearing, the prisoner was acquitted.[1]

Near the manor house of Fenwick's Manor, stood "Fenwick's Mill", long since disappeared, though the outlines of the old mill dam were plainly visible within the recollection of many persons still living, and near the mouth of Cole's Creek stood one of the public warehouses of the Province, known as "Cole's Inspection". There was on the manor, also, "Fenwick's Tavern", a part of which is still standing and constitutes a portion of the dwelling house on the estate of Mr. James T. King.[2]

---

[1] Record of this case is printed in full in Brown's History, pp. 84-86.

[2] On the north side of, and close to the road leading from Oakville to Forrest Wharf (presumably on that part of Fenwick's Manor which was the estate of Henry Lowe), may still be found an old tombstone

De-la Brooke, on the Patuxent, was settled in 1650, by Robert Brooke, a member of the Council, and, during the ascendency of the Cromwell party in Maryland, was President of the Council and, as such, Governor of the Province.[1] In the written memorandum which he left of his family, he says: "Robert Brooke, Esq., arrived out of England on the 29th day of June, 1650, in the 48th year of his age, with his wife and ten children". "He was the first that did seat the

---

bearing the following inscription: "Here Lyeth interred the Body of Susannah Maria Lowe, Late wife of Henry Lowe, of the family of the Bennetts, who departed this life the 28th day of July 1714 In the 48th year of her Age". Mrs. Susannah Maria Lowe was no less a personage than the daughter of Richard Bennett and his wife, Henrietta Maria Neale, the daughter of Captain James Neale. She married, 1st, John Darnall, and had a daughter, Henrietta Maria Darnall. She married, 2d, Colonel Henry Lowe, who died in 1717. They left children—Elizabeth, who married Henry Darnall, of Portland Manor; Bennett, Thomas, Dorothy, who married Francis Hall; Mary, who married Edward Neale; Nicholas, Ann, Susannah, and Henry Lowe. Susannah Lowe married Charles Digges, and their daughter married Governor Thomas Sim Lee, the grandfather of Mary Digges Lee, mother of Governor John Lee Carroll.

1 Robert Brooke was the son of Thomas Brooke, of Whitechurch, England, and Susan Foster, his wife, the daughter of Sir Thomas Foster, and sister of Sir Thomas Foster, Jr., Lord Chief Justice of England. He married, 1st, Mary, daughter of Thomas Baker, of London, and 2d, Mary, daughter of Roger Mainwaring, Dean of Worcester, and Bishop of Saint David's. Robert Brooke was commissioned, by Lord Baltimore, Commander of Charles County, and a member of the Privy Council, before he left England, in 1650. Why he subsequently united with Cromwell's Commissioners for the reduction of Maryland, is a question upon which but little light has been thrown. It has been suggested that he was actuated by the belief that by accepting a position in the Cromwell Council he could the better serve and protect Baltimore's interests in the Province, but the latter did not so understand it, for he was quick in retribution, deposing him both as Councilor and Commander. The facts rather point to the conclusion that his religious sympathies were with the Cromwell party, and hence his attitude. Historians, generally, have assumed that he was a Roman Catholic, though Bozman says he was a "Puritan", and Allen, that he was a "High Church Protestant". Certain it is, that he stood very high in the confidence of the Cromwell

Patuxent, about twenty miles up the river, at De-la Brooke".[1] Besides his own family, he brought at his own cost and charge, twenty-eight other persons.

The settlement was erected into a county, called Charles, and Mr. Brooke made its Commander. De-la Brooke, containing two thousand acres, which formed the chief seat of the Brooke colony, was erected into a manor, with the right of Court Baron and Court Leet, and his oldest son, Baker Brooke, made lord of the manor.[2]

The house at De-la Brooke stood about a mile from the river, on the brow of the hill, and about fifty yards north of the road leading from the present De-la Brooke House to the Three-Notched Road. It was a commanding situation—the broad plains below; the river, with its curves, creeks, coves, and islands, giving it a land and water view most imposing and picturesque. It was a brick building, about thirty by forty feet, one and one-half stories high, with steep roof and dormer windows. The rooms on the lower floor were handsomely wainscotted, and the parlor was also embellished with massive wooden cornice and frieze, on which were carved in relief, roses and other floral designs. The house was destroyed about sixty years ago, but it still stands in the recollection of many persons familiar with its quaint architecture and handsome finish. A mass of moss-covered bricks and an excavation still mark the spot where, for nearly two hundred years, stood the first manor house on the Patuxent. De-la Brooke is otherwise noted as the place at which the Council, with Governor Charles Calvert, met on July 19th, 1662.

---

party, in fact, as President of its Council, was practically made its leader; and his son, Thomas Brooke, was a member of the Council under the Royal Government in Maryland, as well as one of the first Vestrymen of Saint Paul's Parish, Calvert County.

[1] Memoirs of R. B. Taney, p. 25. [2] See Patent in Land Office.

The lower part of De-la Brooke manor, subsequently came into the possession of Henry Queen, John Ford, and John Francis Taney ; the mansion house and the upper part of the manor in Richard Boarman,[1] and later in his daughter, Catherine Brooke Boarman, wife of Major William Thomas, and a descendant of Baker Brooke, the first lord of the manor, and his wife Ann, the daughter of Governor Leonard Calvert.

Adjoining De-la Brooke, is Cremona, and, while a more modern estate, perhaps, than those embraced in the period under consideration, it should be mentioned because of its singular beauty, both in its picturesque location, and in the imposing and hospitable appearance of its attractive mansion.

Higher up the river, is the fine estate known as "Trent Hall".[2] It was granted, in 1658, to Major Thomas Truman, a member of the Privy Council.[3] When first granted it was

[1] Rent Rolls.

[2] On this old estate is the Truman and Greenfield grave yard, noted as containing probably the oldest tombstones in Maryland. The earliest of them are to the memory of General James Truman, "who died the 7th day of August, 1672, being aged fifty years"; "Nathaniel Truman, Gent", who "died the 4th of March, 1678"; Thomas Truman, "who died the 6th of December, Anno. 1685 Aged sixty years The memory of the just is Blessed. Prov. ye 10 ch & ye 7 vrse"; Mary, "wife and relict of Thomas Truman, Esq., who died the 6th of July, Anno. 1686, Aged fifty-two years"; Thomas Truman Greenfield, "who departed this life December 10th, 1733, in the fifty-first year of his age"; Walter Greenfield, "son of Colonel Thomas Truman Greenfield, and Anne his wife, who departed this life on the 28th of May, 1739, in the fourteenth year of his age. A Dutiful Son : the Glory of his Mother"; Captain Thomas Truman Greenfield "son of Colonel Thomas Truman Greenfield and Susanna, daughter of Kenelm Cheseldyne and granddaughter of Thomas Gerrard, Esq., of Bromley in Lancashire, who died 29th of November, in the 23d year of his age, A. D. 1744".

[3] Major Thomas Truman commanded the Maryland militia in the joint attack made by Maryland and Virginia, in 1763, upon the Indians on account of a number of murders alleged to have been committed by t hem, the Virginia forces being led by Colonel John Washington, Colonel

called "Trent Neck", and contained six hundred acres, but in 1705, under a re-survey for his nephew, Thomas Truman Greenfield, it was enlarged to two thousand, three hundred and fifty-four acres.[1]

Mason, and Major Alderton. On reaching the fort of the Susquehannoughs, Major Truman summoned their chiefs to a parley, and after receiving assurances that it was not they, but the Senecas, who had committed the outrages, expressed himself as satisfied with the truth of that statement. Thus reassured, the chiefs returned to the colonial camp the next day, by which time the Virginia militia had arrived. They were again interrogated as to the affair, with the result that Colonel Washington, and a large number of soldiers in both companies, became convinced, it would seem, that at least five of the Indians then before them, were guilty, and urged that they be at once killed. Truman protested, but, it appears, ultimately yielded, and the five were taken out and tomahawked. For this offense, Major Truman was arraigned before the Lower House, where articles of impeachment were brought against him, and the General Assembly convicted him of violating his instructions and commission. The two houses, however, being unable to agree upon the penalty —the Upper House insisting upon the death penalty, and the Lower House, upon a pecuniary fine only—he escaped punishment altogether, but the Proprietary dismissed him from the Council.

Many historians have done Major Truman the—perhaps unintentional—injustice of simply recording the fact of his attainder and conviction. But it is due to him that it be said, that the proceedings in his case indicate that he was largely the victim of policy, growing out of a desire to pacify the Indians, as well as a narrow construction of the terms of his commission. The testimony shows that Major Truman, at first, warmly protested against the act, and only yielded when he found the Virginia Commanders, as well as the soldiers, keen for what they believed to be a summary act of justice, and when he thought further opposition useless, or, in the language of the reply of the Lower to the Upper House, when it was the result of "the unanimous consent of the Virginians, and the general impetuosity of the whole field, as well Marylanders as Virginians, upon the sight of the christians murdered", * * * and the "very Indians that were there killed being proved to be murderers, both of them and several others", and further, when the act became a necessity to prevent a mutiny of the whole army. But the Upper House thought differently, and insisted that if Truman escaped lightly it would "not give any satisfaction to the heathens, with whom the public faith had been broke, and until such actions are in a more

[1] 1st H. & J., Maryland Reports, p. 316.

The "Plains", at first called "Orphans' Gift", situated on the Patuxent, above "Trent Hall", is an old estate of exceptional attractiveness.[1] It was, in its earlier history, the home of the Jowles family—a family which, though now extinct in name, at least in Southern Maryland, was one of great distinction in the colonial annals of the State—but it subsequently, through intermarriage, came into the possession of

public manner disowned the Indians may take notice thereof". * * * "It is not to be expected that any faith or credit will be given to any treaties we shall have with them, which in this dangerous juncture of affairs, the country will stand in need of".—(Archives (Ass. Pro. 1676) pp. 475-481, 485-493, 500-504.) That the Susquehannoughs held the Virginia, and not the Maryland forces responsible for the occurence, is fully attested by the fact that when they attempted to seek revenge, their whole aim was directed at Virginia, and resulted in the famous Bacon's rebellion.

1 The "Plains" formerly embraced within its domain, the estates of "Chesley's Hill" and "Orphans' Gift", and in the old family graveyard there, may be found tombstones bearing the following early inscriptions:

"Here lies Interred the body of Colonel Henry Peregrine Jowles, who departed this life the 31st day of March, 1720, in the 49th year of his age".

"Here lies Interred the body of Mr. John Forbes, who departed this life the 26th day of January, 1737, in the 37th year of his age".

"Here is interred the body of Mary Sothoron, wife of Henry Greenfield Sothoron, only child of Major Zachariah Bond. Born the 14th day of January, 1736, and died the 11th of October, 1763, Aged 26 years".

"Under this tomb is deposited the remains of John Forbes, who was born on the 19th day of March, 1757. He departed this life on the 31st day of Dec. 1804, in the 48th year of his age. He was a good man".

"Maria Forbes, born 1803, died 1805".

At "Chesley's Hill" is a stone bearing the following: "This monument is erected to the memory of John Chesley of Saint Mary's County, who died December the 5th, 1767, in the 64th year of his age. He was magistrate of said County upwards of 30 years, during several of which he presided as judge of the Court, and always distinguished himself for ability and uprightness.

"Beneath this stone the cold remains are laid,
Of one who has the debt of nature paid,
Truth as she passes drops the silent tear,
Laments the Husband, Parent, Friend,
Duty and love have thus inscribed his name,
But virtue ranks it in the Book of Fame".

the Sothorons, and for many generations has been their interesting homestead. The dwelling house—a capacious brick building, and erected, it is said, prior to the Revolution, by the Hon. Henry Greenfield Sothoron—is a unique and imposing specimen of colonial architecture. This old mansion still bears the scars of war, inflicted upon it in 1812, in a conflict between the British fleet and the Maryland militia stationed there, in the attempt on the part of the latter to prevent the fleet from going further up the river.

On the opposite side of the Patuxent, and forming an interesting historical, as well as a picturesque feature of the landscape, and which can be seen from the Saint Mary's side of the river, may be mentioned Point Patience, once under consideration as the site of Maryland's Capital ; the house of Richard Preston, the seat of government under the Puritan reign in Maryland ; Saint Leonard's Creek, famous as the scene of the heroism and exploits of Commodore Barney ; Brome's Island, near Saint Leonard's, noted as the place selected for the execution of the first capital punishment in Maryland ; Calverton, but shortly afterward called "Battle Town", on Battle Creek, laid out as the first county seat of Calvert County, and which it continued to be until 1725, when the county seat was removed to William's Old Fields, called Prince Frederic after 1728. Near Battle Town is the handsome Taney homestead, the seat of that distinguished family for many generations, and the birth-place of the illustrious Chief Justice Roger Brooke Taney, while separated from it by Battle Creek, is Brooke Place Manor, in latter life the home of Governor Robert Brooke.[1]

---

[1] Archives (Ass. Pro. 1662) p. 435 ; Bozman, 2, p. 205 ; Annals of Annapolis, p. 46 ; Memoirs Com- Barney, pp. 256, 257 ; Archives (Test. Pro. 1657) p. 545 ; Ibid, Cl. Pro. 1669, p. 47 ; Ibid, Ass. Pro. 1682, p. 280 ; Act, 1725, C. 11 ; Act, 1728, C. 17 ; Memoirs R. B. Taney, p. 20.

Among the places of interest lying between the Patuxent and Wicomico rivers, should be noted "Forrest Hall", "Hilly Lee", 'Indian Town", "Hamburg", and "Luckland", the latter, formerly a large estate, embracing among others, the beautiful homestead of Mr. John A. Barber.[1]

"Deep Falls", the Thomas homestead, is situated near village of Chaptico. In the Proprietary grant, dated March 26th, 1680, it was called "Wales", but when the improvement, known as "the falls", was completed, the name was changed to the one it bears to-day. The present mansion was erected by Major William Thomas, about 1745. It is, in appearance, an English country dwelling house, and, while its builder aimed at massive simplicity, rather than architectural display, it is of graceful and pleasing design and finish. It is a large, double, two-story frame building, with brick foundations and brick gables to the upper line of the first story, when the brick work branches into two large outside chimneys at each gable end of the house. It is sixty feet long and forty feet deep, with wide piazzas, front and back, running the whole length of the house, and supported by handsome, massive pillars.

On a line with the front of the house, is a long corridor, with a capacious wing, one and a-half stories high, and which constitutes the culinary department. The hall, as

---

[1] Dr. Luke Barber, the progenitor of the Barber family in Southern Maryland, came to Maryland in 1654, distinguished himself in the battle of the Severn, and for his bravery on that occasion, and his fidelity to the Proprietary throughout the Puritan rule in Maryland, he, together with Major Thomas Truman, William Barton and others, was made the subject of a special donation, each receiving one thousand acres of land, by order of Baltimore. In 1656, he was appointed a member of the Privy Council, and the following year, was promoted to the office of Deputy Governor of the Province, acting in the absence of Governor Fendall. He died before 1671. His widow married John Bloomfield, or Saint Mary's City.

distinguished from a mere passage, is a feature that does not exist, it is believed, in any other colonial house in Saint Mary's. It is a large, well finished, square room, and is flanked on one side by a parlor, on the other by a dining-room, separated from it by a partition consisting of a series of folding doors, and in the rear by a long passage, running at right angles, into which it opens, and through which entrance is obtained to the back porch, by a door immediately opposite the front door, and the archway between the hall and the passage. The stairway is in the passage. Its sides are carved, with maple newel posts and rosewood top, surmounted with an ivory knob, rosewood rail, and bird's-eye maple balustrade, the two latter extending around the corridors above.

In front, is the entrance to the house, through a gently ascending avenue, about forty yards wide and three hundred yards long, lined on each side with a row of ornamental trees, with a background of cone-shaped cedars. In the rear, are five falls, or terraces, each one hundred feet long and ten feet deep, which lead to a plateau below. About two and a-half acres of this plateau is the garden. It is Queen Anne in design, is artistically laid off, and, at one time, was highly ornamented with fine specimens of shrubbery and flowers. On the right and left of the house, is a broad lawn of about three acres, made picturesque by its gentle undulations, and its rich and varied foliage. "Deep Falls" is one of the few places in Saint Mary's, which is still in the family of its original proprietor, and the old graveyard there, dedicated to family burial more than a century and a half ago, contains within its sacred limits, the successive generations that have lived and passed away.

"Basford Manor", or "Bashford", as now called, situated near Chaptico, was granted to Dr. Thomas Gerrard, in

March, 1650.[1] It was bounded as follows: "On the south with the Manor of Saint Clement's, on the west with the Wiccocomoco River, on the north with a bay called Chapticon Bay, on the east with a line drawn southeast from a marked oak standing in a marsh, near the said bay, called Tapster's Marsh, unto the first fountain of Tommahkockin, or the fresh creek running into Saint Clement's Bay", and was laid out for fifteen hundred acres, but by a re-survey it was found to contain a much larger area. The annual quit-rent was fifteen bushels of corn. This manor was sold by Dr. Gerrard to Governor Thomas Notley, who, in 1678, laid off 300 acres of it as the "Manor Lodge", named it "Bachelor's Hope", and placed it in the possession of Colonel Benjamin Rozer,[2] a member of his Council when Governor of the Province, and who married Ann Sewall, step-daughter of Lord Baltimore. Governor Notley sold "Bashford Manor" to Lord Baltimore, who conveyed "Bachelor's Hope" to Joshua Doyne, the remainder of the manor being subsequently divided up and sold as follows: 100 acres to James Mills, 100 to Notley Goldsmith, 100 to Michael Goldsmith, 100 to John Goldsmith, 100 to John Reeves, 104 to Nathaniel Truman Greenfield, 200 to Benjamin Moulton, 200 to Edward Turner, 200 to John Smith, 69 to Samuel Maddox, 150 to John Maddox, and 277 to John Eden[3]

The manor house, a frame building with brick gables and chimneys, one and a-half stories high, and steep gambrel roof, while unpretentious in exterior design, contained a great deal of handsome interior decoration, consisting of elaborate wood-carving. It occupied a commanding position on the Wicomico

---

1 See Patent, Liber A. B. L. H. p. 166, Land Office.
2 Rent Rolls, Saint Mary's and Charles County, 1, p. 41.
3 Rent Rolls, Saint Mary's County, 1, Manors, p. 29.

River. This old monument of colonial times, stood almost unchanged until a few years ago, when it was destroyed by fire. The road passing through "Bachelor's Hope" is still known as the manor road. In 1773, the manor house at Bashford, and about three hundred acres of the manor, came into the possession of Major William Thomas, Sr.,[1] and it continued to be owned by his descendants until late in the present century, when it was disposed of, and that part of the manor known as "Bachelor's Hope", purchased in its stead.

"Notley Hall", on the Wicomico, and adjoining "Bashford Manor", was the home of Governor Thomas Notley. He sold it to Lord Baltimore, who owned it for many years. Baltimore was deprived of the use of it after the Protestant Revolution, in Maryland, but it was restored to him in 1692, by order of the Council.[2] Nothing remains, it is to be regretted, of the old Notley house, save a few broken yellow bricks, and a brick under-ground passage-way, which led from the cellar to the river, about fifty yards below, to mark the spot on which it stood.

"Notley Hall" is frequently mentioned in the early provincial records, and is a place of historic interest, as well as of rare and exceptional beauty. It may be interesting to note that among the references which the early records make to this old estate, is one of a visit to Lady Baltimore, at "Notley Hall", in 1683, by Mrs. Doyne, of "Bachelor's Hope".[3]

"Saint Clement's Manor" was granted, in November, 1639, to "Thomas Gerrard, Gent", for many years a member of the Council, and one of the most prominent men in the Province. It contained, at first, Saint Clement's Island and

---

[1] Deed, John Goldsmith to William Thomas, Land Office; will, William Thomas, Saint Mary's County.

[2] Archives (Cl. Pro. 1692) p. 311.   [3] Ibid, 1683, p. 183.

the neck of land lying between the Potomac River, Saint Clement's Bay, and a line drawn from Saint Patrick's to Saint Katherine's Creek, in all about 1030 acres. In June, 1642, a second patent was obtained for the manor, by which it was extended over to the Wicomico River, and was made to embrace all the land which lay between the "Potomack River", the "Wicocomoco River", "Saint Clement's Bay", "Gerrard's Creek", and "Tomaquoakin Creek", and a line drawn from the head of "Gerrard's Creek", 460 perches, to a Spanish oak, "marked with twelve notches, standing on the head of Tomaquoakin run, or fresh creek", as well, also, as the islands of "Saint Clement's, Saint Katherine's, and Saint Margaret's",[1] containing, as was supposed, 6,000 acres, but in reality embracing 11,400 acres.[2]

Saint Clement's was erected into a manor, Mr. Gerrard made lord of the manor, and vested with all the royalties and privileges usually belonging to manors in England, among them the right of Court Baron and Court Leet. It is worthy of note, that Saint Clement's has passed into history as the only one of the old Maryland manors whose records, to any material extent, have survived the ravages of time. The records, written in quaint old English, of the Courts Baron and Courts Leet, held on Saint Clement's, between 1659 and 1672, have been preserved. They are in the Maryland

---

1 See Patents in Land Office.

2 The Proprietary "quittrent" for Saint Clement's, was at the rate of one shilling per annum for every fifty acres. The following interesting receipt has been preserved by the Maryland Historical Society:

"March 8th 1659. Received then of Thomas Gerrard of St. Clement's manor, the full summe of sixty pounds in full discharge of ten years rent ended at Christmas 1659 [for St. Clement's manor], the said being paid in Tob., at two pence per pound.

"I say received by me, Phillip Calvert, Trer.
"Witness William Ffuller, Ri. Even".

Historical Society, and may be found herein printed in full in Chapter VI, "The Judicial System of Colonial Maryland".

Among the older estates carved out of Saint Clement's Manor, may be mentioned "Longworth Point", the Blackiston homestead, and the residence of Nehemiah Blackiston when President of the Council, in 1690; "Saint John", the Gardiner homestead; "Little Hackley", the Shanks homestead; "Bluff Point", the Coade homestead; "Mattapany", the Cheseldine homestead,[1] and "Bushwood", the Slye homestead. At the latter place, then the home of Robert Slye,

---

[1] Kenelm Cheseldine and John Coade were, perhaps, the most prominent leaders in the Protestant Revolution of 1688, and were both rewarded for their services in that connection. This preferment, and the subsequent history of the two men materially reflect upon the question as to whether the real motive which prompted the move was regard for the public weal and in the interest of religion, as was alleged, or was in fact, a design to overthrow the Proprietary and entrench themselves in power. It has been well said in this connection, that "in times of revolution, men will rise to power, in whose mouths the alleged causes of revolution are but the watch-words to denote a party, or the calls to lure it on ; and whose hearts have never joined the service of the lip. But, as naturally as the muddy particles which float upon it denote the perturbed stream, does the elevation of such men indicate the over-excitement of the moment, and diminish the force of its allegations against those at whom the revolution is aimed".—(McMahon, p. 238.) Cheseldine was made Speaker of the Protestant Convention, which assembled immediately after the close of the revolution, and also of the first Assembly convened under the Royal Government, in 1692 ; he was also appointed Commissary General of the Province, from which office he was dismissed, in 1697, "*for carelessness and negligence in office*".—(Cl. Pro., H. D., Part 2d, p. 539.) What applied to him in office, seems to have developed in the case of his only son, Kenelm Cheseldine, into "carelessness and negligence" in morals.—(See 1st H. & McH. Maryland Reports, p. 103 ; 4th Ibid, p. 314 ; 2 Bland, p. 76.) After the revolution, Coade was made a Colonel of the militia, and also Receiver of Customs for the Potomac District, and, at the same time, was "asserting that religion was a trick, reviling the Apostles, denying the divinity of the Christian religion, and alleging that all morals worth having were contained in Cicero's offices". For this grossly blasphemous conduct, he was dismissed from office, and was presented by the grand jury of Saint Mary's County, for "*atheism* and *blasphemy*".—See Liber H. D. Part 2d, pp. 393-397.

T

Speaker of the Lower House of Assembly in 1658, the Council of Maryland met, in 1659.[1] "Bushwood" occupies a picturesque position on the commanding elevation overlooking the Wicomico. The house, a capacious brick building with two large wings and four-sided roof, capped with balustrade observatory, is strikingly imposing, and presents a charming specimen of colonial architecture. It at one time contained a great deal of handsomely-chiseled wood interior decorations, much after the design of those at "Sotterly", and said to have been the work of the same artistic hand, but this has, in recent years, been largely removed. On this, then very large estate, and near what is now known as "Bushwood Wharf", was located the once promising port and town of "Wicomico".[2]

On what part of "Saint Clement's Manor" the manor house stood has not been definitely ascertained, but it is believed to have been that part of it called "Brambly". Certain it is, that his son, Justinian, who was left in charge of the manor when Dr. Gerrard took up his residence in Virginia, and to whom he afterwards devised the greater part of it, lived there. In his will, dated 1685, he speaks of it as "my now dwelling house and plantation on said manor called Brambly,[3] and as early as 1664, Dr. Gerrard himself referred to it as "Gerrard's Brambly",[4] which, in connection with the further fact that Brambly appears to have been the name of the Gerrard homestead in England,[5] gives both color and strength to the theory that the beautiful and splendid estate of that name, on Saint

---

[1] Archives (Cl. Pro. 1690) p. 206; Ibid, 1659, p. 383; will, Luke Gardiner; will, John Coade; 4th H. & McH. Maryland Reports, p. 179; 1st Ibid, p. 153.

[2] Act, 1688, C. 6.   [3] Will Record, Annapolis.

[4] 1st H. & McH. Maryland Reports, p. 112.

[5] Tombstone of Thomas T. Greenfield, at Trent Hall.

Clement's Manor, was also the seat of Dr. Gerrard, the first proprietor and lord of the manor.

Of the style or character of the manor house at Saint Clement's, nothing is known, but it is highly probable that it was built of brick, as Dr. Gerrard employed a brick-maker on the manor, in 1643,[1] and which, it may be added, is the earliest reference the records furnish of brick making in Maryland. Saint Clement's Manor is also historical by reason of the fact that it was the spot on which the notorious rebellion of Governor Josiah Fendall was enacted. The details of this tragedy are given in Chapter III, "The First Capital", but it should here be noted, that the Legislature, through which this nefarious scheme was to be carried out, met for the purpose at the residence of Mr. Gerrard, on Saint Clement's Manor. The second day of the session, it adjourned to a house owned by Mr. Robert Slye, at Wicomico, before mentioned, and it was there that independence was formally proclaimed, and that Fendall issued his famous proclamation as Governor of the little Republic of Maryland.[2]

As the active friend and ally of Fendall, in this conspiracy, Mr. Gerrard was tried convicted, and sentenced to banishment, and confiscation of Saint Clement's Manor, and his other property in Maryland. The sentence, however, was commuted, and the order of confiscation dismissed, but he was politically disfranchised and prohibited forever from again holding public office.[3] After this, Mr. Gerrard moved across the Potomac into Virginia (leaving Saint Clement's in charge of his son, Justinian Gerrard), where he, in 1670, with John Lee, Henry Corbin, and Isaac Allerton, erected a "banquetting

---

1 Archives (Cl. Pro, 1643) p. 213.
2 Ibid, Ass. and Cl. Pro. 1659.
3 Ibid, Cl. Pro. 1660, p. 402.

house" at the corner of their respective lands.¹ In his will, dated 1672, he requested to be buried in Maryland by the side of his wife, Susanna, who was probably buried on Saint Clement's Manor. Mr. Gerrard was himself a Roman Catholic, but his wife, as well as a large number of the freeholders and tenants on Saint Clement's, were Protestants,² and a Protestant church was erected there, on Saint Paul's Creek, as early as 1642.³

After the death of Mr. Gerrard, information reached the Proprietary that Saint Clement's contained a much larger area of land than was set forth in the patent. A re-survey of the manor was ordered, by which it was ascertained to contain 11,400 acres, being 5,400 acres more than Mr. Gerrard had been paying the "annual quit-rent" upon.

A *scieri facias* was issued against Mr. Justinian Gerrard, his son and heir-at-law, and in 1678, the Provincial Court decided that the patent had been "unduly and illegally obtained", and ordered it to be canceled. A new patent was, however, issued to Mr. Justinian Gerrard for the manor, with

---

1 Meade's Virginia, 2, p. 146.   2 Day Star, p. 58.
3 Who Were the Early Settlers of Maryland.

Dr. Thomas Gerrard married, 1st, Susannah Snow, sister of Justinian and Abel Snow, and 2d, Rose Tucker, widow of John Tucker, of Virginia, who died in 1671. She left children by her first marriage— Sarah, who married ——— Blackiston, and Rose, who married William Fitzhugh of Virginia.--(Virginia Historical Society, Vol. 1, No. 3, January, 1894, p. 269.) Dr. Gerrard died in December, 1673, leaving by his first marriage, sons Justinian, Thomas, and John, and daughters Susannah, who married, 1st, Robert Slye, and 2d, John Coade ; Elizabeth, who married Nehemiah Blackiston, and Mary, and a grandson, Gerrard Peyton.—(See his will, Will Record, Annapolis.) His sons Justinian and Thomas both died without issue. John, his third son, left issue, Susannah, who died unmarried, and John, whose widow Jane, married Richard Llewellin, father of John Llewellin, of Brambly.—(Paper in possession of the Author, submitted to Thomas Stone, before 1750. for legal opinion as to heirs-at-law of Dr. Gerrard.)

SAINT MARY'S COUNTY

a "quit-rent" based on the correct acreage. Saint Clement's Manor was, in 1710, purchased by Charles Carroll, and the last official notice we have of it as a manor, is to be found in the celebrated case of Carroll and Llewellin, in 1750, over that part of it embraced within the limits of the estate called Brambly.[1]

Near Saint Clement's Manor, but not a part of it, was "Bushwood Lodge", noted as the early homestead of the Key family in Maryland,[2] and was at one time distinguished for the high character of its improvement. The mansion house, erected, it is said, about 1730, by Philip Key—the progenitor of the family in Maryland, a lawyer of first rank, and a member of the Privy Council—enjoys the reputation of having been one of the handsomest houses at that time in the Province. The parlor walls, tradition says, were made of alternate panels of carved wood and mirror. It was destroyed by fire early in the present century, the house now there being the second to occupy the place of the original.[3]

For an acconnt of "Newtown Manor", or "Little Bretton", as officially named, see Chapter IX, "Some of Maryland's Early Churches".

"Tudor Hall", the Key homestead, is situated near Leonard-Town. It was originally the home of the Barnes family, and on it may still be seen, the ancient tombstones,

---

[1] 1st H. & McH. Maryland Reports, p. 110.

[2] See will of Philip Key, 1764, Will Record, Saint Mary's County.

[3] The fact should not go unnoticed, that at "Bushwood Lodge" were born and reared, among others, Edmond Key, Attorney General of Maryland and a member of the committee which drafted the famous instructions for the Stamp Act Congress; Thomas Key, the father of Judge Edmond Key; and Francis Key, the father of Philip Barton Key, the distinguished jurist and statesman, and Ann Ross Key, wife of Chief Justice Roger Brooke Taney; and Francis Scott Key, author of the "Star Spangled Banner"—that national anthem whose "martial and inspiring strains" that have long since encircled the earth.

covering the graves of Major Abraham and Colonel Richard Barnes, two of early Maryland's most distinguished sons. The house, a handsome brick building, occupies a prominent and strikingly-pleasing position, overlooking Bretton's Bay, and is conspicuous for the graceful design and dignified simplicity of its architecture and finish.

Near it is a grove of stately oaks—sentinels of the primeval forest—one of which, a majestic white oak, is said to measure twenty-nine feet in circumference.

"Porto Bello" was the Hebb homestead. It is on the Saint Mary's River, nearly opposite Saint Mary's City. The house stands on a graceful eminence near the river, and commands an extensive and rarely beautiful view of both land and water. It is a large frame building, with brick foundations and gables, hipped roof, and semi-dormer windows, and presents an interesting specimen of colonial architecture. The interior finish, while not elaborate, is unique and handsome, and over the parlor mantel, built in the brick wall, is a large mirror, said to have been placed there when the house was erected.

Local history and family tradition say, that William Hebb, his friend, Lawrence Washington, and his neighbor, Edwin Coade—midshipmen in the British Navy—on their return, after the war between England and Spain, named their estates after persons and places connected therewith, Hebb calling his "Porto Bello", in honor of the celebrated battle of that name, in which he was engaged; Coade naming his "Carthegena", after the noted Spanish town of that name; and Washington giving his the name of "Mount Vernon", in compliment to Admiral Vernon, under whom they all served.

Among the other ancient estates in Saint Mary's, may be mentioned, "Evelynton Manor", in the "Baronie of Saint

Marie's", at Piney Point, granted to Hon. George Evelyn, in 1638; "Forrest Lodge", in Saint George's, granted to Patrick Forrest, in 1665; "Dryden", adjoining West Saint Mary's Manor, granted to Kenelm Cheseldine, in 1676; "Hunting Creek", adjoining "Park Hall", granted to Hon. Thomas Hatton, in 1654; "Snow Hill", near Saint Mary's City, granted to Abel Snow, in 1637; and the manors of "West Saint Mary's", opposite Saint Mary's City, containing 1370 acres; "Beaver Dam", between Indian Bridge and Leonard-Town, containing 7,680 acres; and "Chaptico", on the northwest side of Chaptico Bay and Run, containing 6,110 acres. These manors belonged to Lord Baltimore, and were retained by the Baltimore family, almost in their entirety, until the American Revolution.

Appendix.

※ ※ ※

AS shedding light upon the escapade referred to in note on pages 36 and 37—that of breaking open the old Vault, at Saint Mary's—the following letter, accidentally discovered, and never before published, is of historic interest and value. The letter, dated August 1st, 1799, was written by one of the participants, Dr. Alexander McWilliams, to his mother. The author was then a student of medicine under Dr. Barton Tabbs, who resided at Tabbs' Purchase, afterwards known as White Plains, near Saint Mary's City, and who was the son of Rev. Moses Tabbs, for many years Rector at William and Mary Parish. Dr. McWilliams afterwards served as surgeon in the navy, and subsequently located in Washington City. This letter, still in excellent preservation, is now in the possession of his nephew, Mr. James McWilliams, of Saint Mary's County. That part of it relating to family matters is, of course, here omitted :

August 1st, 1799.

DEAR RELATIONS :—

* * * * * * * * *

The oldest people now living, have for many years past spoken of a vault that was at Saint Mary's Church, in which was one of the first American governors and his lady, who were in leaden coffins and embalmed for the purpose of being sent and interred in England, but being disappointed in passage there, it was determined a vault should be erected and they enclosed therein, the door locked, and the key thrown into the river. This was the account which was handed us from the oldest people now living, who had been informed by their fathers, and they got it from their fathers, etc., but none of them remembered their names. Into this curious affair, Doctor Tabbs and Mr. James Biscoe were determined to search but never did. I hearing it mentioned proposed to Mr. George Campbell to accompany me there and open it, which request he willingly agreed to. Our intention was communicated to Mr. James Biscoe, Basil Biscoe and Doctor Tabbs who were all pleased with it and agreed to join us. Agreeable to appointment the 27th instant, all except Doctor Tabbs were there by 9 o'clock and nearly twenty others, although we were private as we could be or thought necessary. We first began to dig down as low as the door, but the ground being hard prevented us. The attempt was then made on top which was below the surface of the earth. However, after near four hours of excessive hard labor, we opened a small hole, and heard the bits of bricks rattle down on the coffins. I peeped in and saw two along side of each other. The hole being made larger, Mr. Campbell with a rope was let down and I followed him and to our astonishment we saw the coffins were of wood, the planks of which were easily separated, which we did, and behold it contained most elegant leaden coffins, the smaller of which was by a rope, with difficulty got out and conveyed to a shed close by where awaited the spectators anxious to behold the contents. We removed the lid and to our surprise saw within it another coffin of wood. The lid of this being knocked off, we saw the winding sheet perfect and sound as was every other piece of garment. When the face of the corpse was uncovered it was ghastly indeed, it was the woman. Her face was perfect, as was the rest of the body but was black as the blackest negro. Her eyes were sunk deep in her head, every other part retained its perfect shape. The loss of three or four of her upper fore teeth was supplied with a piece of wood between. Her hair was short, platted and trimmed on the top of her head. Her dress was a white muslin gown, with an apron which was loose in the body, and drawn at the bosom nearly as is now the fashion only not so low, with short sleeves and high gloves but much destroyed by time. Her stockings were cotton and coarse, much darned at the feet, the clocks of which were large and figured with half diamonds worked. Her gown was short before and gave us a view of all her ankle. Her cap was with long ears and pinned under the chin. A piece of muslin two inches broad which extended across the top of her head as low as her breast, the end was squared and trimmed with half inch lace as was the cap. The body was opened and the entrails removed and filled with gums and spice, and the coffin filled with the same. She was a small woman, and appeared delicate. In the coffin of the man was only the bones which were long and large. His head was sawed through the brain removed, and filled with embalmment, but he was not so well done as the other, or had been there much longer as he was much more gone. The winding sheet of the body was marked in such letters as these

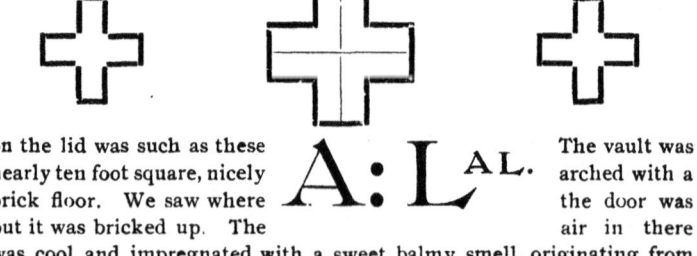

on the lid was such as these nearly ten foot square, nicely brick floor. We saw where but it was bricked up. The

The vault was arched with a the door was air in there

was cool and impregnated with a sweet balmy smell, originating from

APPENDIX

the coffins, but I thought proper to sprinkle it with rum. The length of time that these bodies have been here must have been two hundred years or more as we have not the smallest account who they were more than what I have mentioned. Since writing the above I have heard a man say who is sixty years of age, that it was one Copely. He got his information from his father who was eighty years of age when he died, and his was handed him by his great grand father who built the vault and came in as a servant to this Copely. This seems to be the best account, and most probable. After spending the day in hard labor we replaced them as before, and returned home, all acknowledging themselves perfectly satisfied and abundantly rewarded for their trouble. Numbers since regret their not knowing it as they might have been there. Others wish it again opened, and some are displeased at its being opened at all.

* * * * * * * * *

ALEXANDER Mc. WILLIAMS.

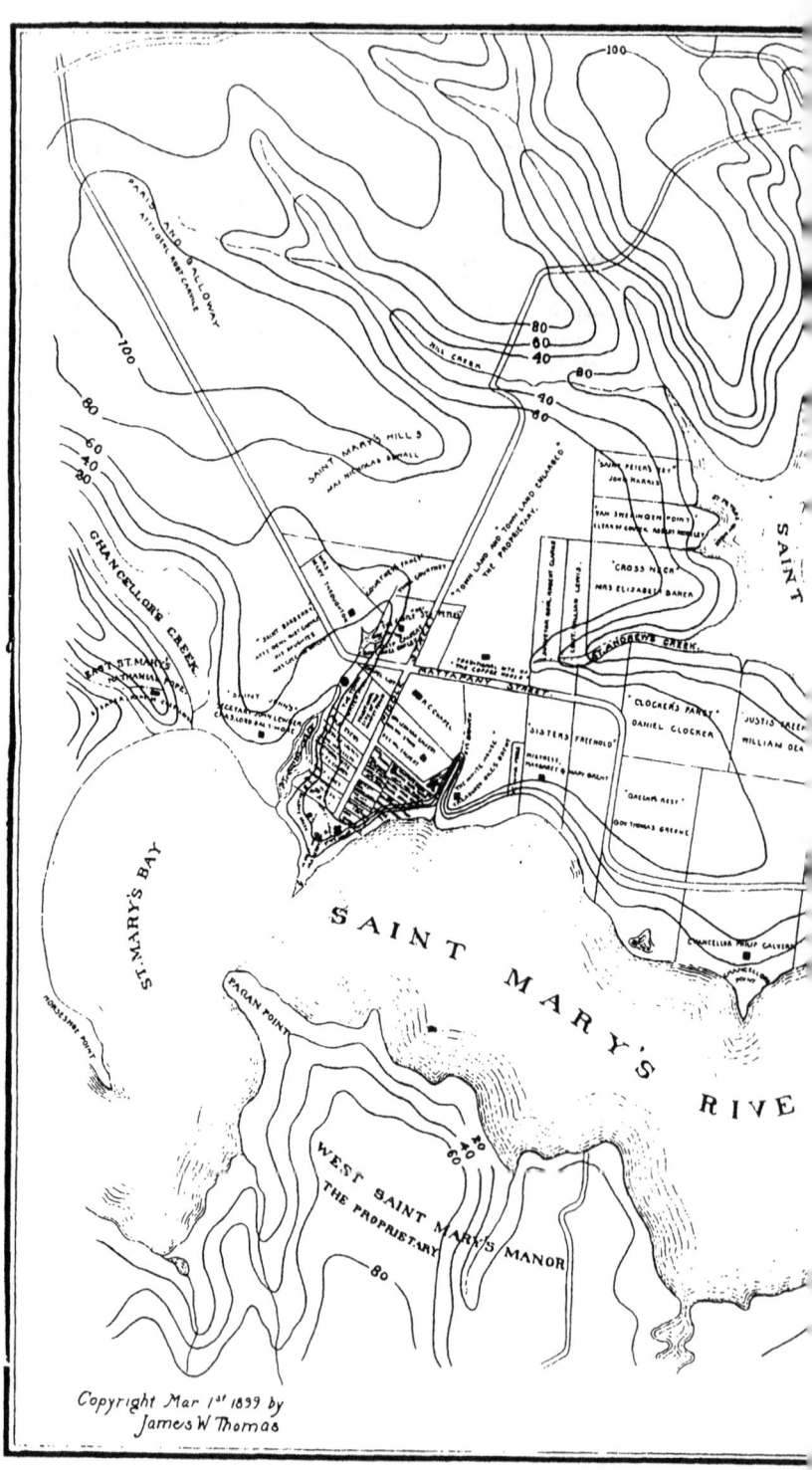

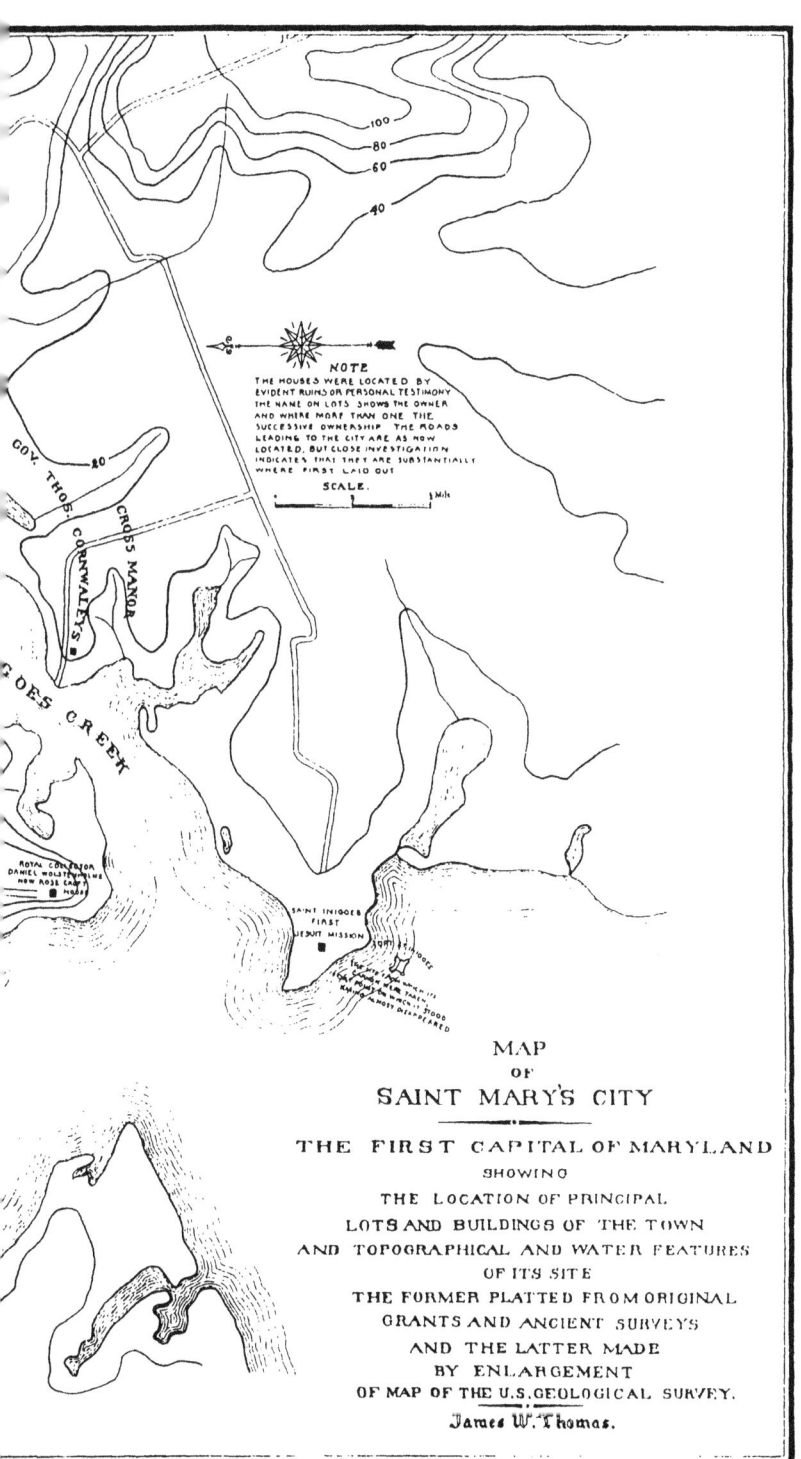

Errata.

On page 32, line 20, read sixty-two for fifty feet deep.
" " 53, last line, read Rosecroft for Rosecraft.
" " 58, last line, read Claiborne for Clayborne.
" " 148, reference 1, read Act, 1715, C. 48, for Act, 1715, C. 14.
" " 237, line 2 note, read were for was.
" " 241, line 2, read voluntatis, for voluntatics.
" " 241, line 1, reference 4, read paintings for painting.
" " 254, line 15, read erected for enacted.
" " 276, 278, 280, read Sothoron for Sotheron.
" " 285, last line note, read Camalier for Comalier,

Index.

Abbington Creek 264, 295
Abbington, John, gent,
  Curious warrant to . . note-102
Acknowledgments, see Deeds.
Addison, Col. Thomas . note-297
Addison, Judge 145
Admiralty, Court of 141
Aldermen of St. Mary's City, 25, 71
Allerton, Col. Isaac 315
All Faith Parish, History of, 216-220
All Saints' Church 212-213
Alms House 263-264
Anacosta .... note 20
Appeals, Court of 150-152
Appeals, right of 150-153
Ark and Dove 9, 10
Assize Courts 141, 142
Assembly, General 55, 56
Attorneys, regulations as to,
  and fees of 148
Augusta Carolina 353, 354

Bachelor's Hope 310, 311
Bailiff, Court 121
Baltimore, Lords, ...
  Instructions of 15, 23
  Report of note-24
  Makes religious toleration a
    cardinal rule .... note 57
  Home of Charles 48, 290
  Marriage of note-291
  Wills of ..... note, 98, 99
Barber, Dr. Luke, grant to, note, 308
Baron and Leet, Court .. 127 136
Barnes, Major Abraham, and
  Col. Richard ... 278, 279, 318
Bashford Manor ... 309-311
Battle Creek 307
Battle of the Severn ... note-64
Battle Town 307
Beaver Dam Manor 319
Blackiston's Island, identified
  as St. Clement's 13, 14

Blackiston, Col. Nehemiah, 13, 69, 70
Blackistone, James T. . note, 285
Blackistone, Gov. Nathaniel . 277
Bladen, Hon. William . . note-289
Bluff Point, estate 213, 313
Bordley, Judge 145
Borough, English, local mode
  of inheritance ..... note 107
Bowes, Timothy 279, 281
Bowles, Hon. James .. note, 297
Bozman, ... 12, 116, 256
Brambly, estate ... 314, 315, 317
Brent, Dep. Gov. Giles ... 50
Brent, Mistress Margaret . . 29, 50
Bretton, Hon. Wm., 232, note-234
Brice, Judge 145
Brome, Dr. John Mackall, note-51
Brome's Island 307
Brooke, Hon. Baker, married
  daughter of Gov. Calvert, note-63
  Lord of De-la Brooke Manor, 303
Brooke, Judge 145
Brooke, Gov. Robert ....
  President of Council ... 63
  Commander of County .. 254
  Deposed 255
  Religion of note-302
  Home of 307
Brooke Place Manor 307
Bud's Creek 257
Bushwood, estate ... 313, 314

Calvert, Lady Jane . 290, note-311
Calvert, Gov. Leonard ....
  Makes treaty with Indians, 16
  Laid out first town 17
  His home 29
  His Manors 288
  Aids in laying foundation of
    Government 36, 37
  Enforces religious toleration
    .... note, 58, 59

INDEX

First Chief Justice and Chancellor 115
Driven to Virginia 61
Expedition against Claiborne 249
His death 61
Life and character of . . . 62
Family of note-62
His monument 76, 77
His son and daughter, . note-63
Calvert Hon. Philip . . . . .
Appointed Governor . . . 65
Home of 52
Chancellor 52
Marriage of note-291
Calvert County . . . 254, 257, 307
Calverton Manor and town, 111, 307
Cannons from Fort St. Inigoes, 237
Canon 4,Title 2, not in force,note-197
Capital, Maryland's first . . .
Location of 21
Erected into a City 25
Map of . . . . Appendix
Character of improvements, 26
Houses, Public Buildings, 27-53
Polical History of 55, 80
An Historic Battle-field . 56, 60
Removal of 71, 74
Historical importance of . 78, 80
Carberry, Rev. Joseph 237
Carroll, Archbishop 295
Carroll, Charles of Carrollton note-295
Carroll, Gov. John Lee . note-302
Carthagena 318
Carvile, Attorney Genl. Robt. 47
Castle, Governor's 45
Causin, J. M. S. 286
Caution Money 86
Cedar Point, estate 295
Certificates 89, 90
Chancellor 115, 139
Chancellor's Point . . . . .
Place of first landing . . 18
View of 18
Chancery, High Court of . 139-141
Chapel, the first 41, 42
Used conjointly by Protestants and Roman Catholics, 42, 43
Later history of 43, 44
Its yard the place of burial, 45
Chapel of St. Clement's Manor 212
Chapels of Ease, 212, 218, note-221
Chaptico Manor 319
Chaptico town 212, 265
Charter, first municipal . . . 25

Charlotte Hall 274-276
Cherry Field Point 282
Cheseldine Kenelm . 49, note-313
Chesley's Hill, estate . . note-306
Churches, Early 203-238
Church Endowments, the
  earliest 208-213
Church Establishment . . .
Acts relating to 165-174
Character of 174
Maryland and English Establishment contrasted . 174-186
Clergy under 186 188
Their tenure . 180, 181, 185, 186
Induction of . 179, 180, 185, 189, 195, 196
English Ecclesiastical Law
  not in force under . . 174, 175
Tax under 189, 190
Swept away by revolution . 191
New conditions after . . 192-195
Law applicable to, note-171-174, 195-202
Church, Newtown . . . 231-234
Church, Poplar Hill . . . 205-208
Church, Sacred Heart 238
Church, St. Aloysius 238
Church, St. Inigoe's . . . 234-236
Church, St. John's 238
Church, St. Joseph's 238
Church Tax, controversy over, 189-190
Church, Trinity 39, 40
Church Wardens . . . 172, 178
Clergymen, Protestant . . .
First in the Province . . 163, 164
How benefice procured by . 179, 180, 185, 186
Tenure of . . 181, 185, 189, 196, note-197
Character of 186-188
Names of, 209, 210, 215, 219 220, 223 225
Clerks of Courts . . . 120, 121
Clocker's Fancy, place . . . 52
Coade, John 69, note-313
Cohongoronta, early name of
  Upper Potomac note-19
Commissary General . . . 137-139
Coin, Early Maryland 67
Conveyancing, methods of, 103-105
Colors for Counties . . . note-258
Cool Springs 276-278
Copley, Thomas 87, 235

INDEX 331

Copley, Sir Lionel, first Royal Governor 70
Death and burial of . . 36, 37, 70
Copley Vault . . . . . 37, note 70
Confiscation, Acts of 97 99, 101-102
Cornfield Harbor, estate . . . 289
Cornwaleys, Capt. Thomas. 40, 61 note-289
Council of Safety 278-281
Council Chamber 31
Court Houses, ordered built . . 122
At Leonard Town . . . 260-262
Courtes, Col. William . . . 70, 145
Courts, see several titles of Admiralty, Assize, Baron and Leet, Chancery, County, Oyer and Terminer, Prerogative and Provincial, King in Council
County Court . . . .
Organization of 118, 119
Judges of 121
Their compensation 121
Oath 124
Quorum 121
Terms of 121, 122
Administrative duties of, 122, 123
Rules of note-122
Jurisdiction of . . . 124, 126
Appeals from 127
Appeals to 117, 118
County Committee 281
Cremona, estate 304
Crier, Court 121
Cromwell's Commissioners. 63, 64, 242, 243
Cross Manor 289, 290
Cross Neck, place 52
Cuckold's (St. Cuthbert's) Creek 296, 301

Dalrymple confounds St. Clement's with Heron Island . . 12
Darnall, Col. Henry, Eleanor Brooke, Mary, John, Robert 294, note 295
Darnall, Justice 145
Deeds, acknowledgment and enrollment of . . . 104, note 105
Deep Creek 288
Deep Falls, estate 308, 309
De la Brooke Manor . . . 202, 204
Descent, rule of 106, 107
Digges, Col. William . . . .
Secretary of the Province . 30

In command at St. Mary's at time of its evacuation, 1689, 68
His manor the site of Fort Warburton, afterwards Fort Washington note-291
Districts, Commissioners for laying out 258
Dorsey, Clement 286
Dryden, estate 319
Ducking Stool 122
Dunmore's Fleet 282

Early County Offices, note-283-285
East St Mary's, place 49
Escheats 93
Egerton, Charles . . . note-289
Enrollment of Conveyances . 104
Entailments 107-108
Evelynton Manor 318

Fealty 93
Fendall, Gov. Josias, rebellion of 65, 66, 315
Fenwick's Manor 300, 301
Flag, the Maryland, design of, 248
Early uses of 249
Fines 94
Fleet, Capt. Henry 16
Forrest Hall, estate 308
Forrest Lodge, estate 308
Fort St. Inigoe's . . . 27, 236, 237
Fort St. Mary's 27, 28
Fort Warburton . . . note-291
Fort Washington . . . note-291

Garrison, Mattapany . . . 69, 291
General Court 153
Gerrard, Dr. Thomas . 13, 312, 317
Gerrard, Justinian . . . 316, 317
Gerrard's Creek 312
Gibbet Hill 270
Glebes . . . 176, 208, 212, 223
Goldsborough, Justice . . . 145
Graveyards, early, 45, 207, 208, 233, 238, note-301, note-304, note-306, 309
Green's Rest, place 51
Ground Rents 97

Hall, Justice 145
Hamburg 266, 308
Hands, Justice 145
Harford, Henry, last Proprietary 98, note-99
Harvey Hundred and Town, 258, 264

332 INDEX

Haywood, Justice 145
Henry, Justice 145
Hepburn, Justice 145
Heron Island 12, 14
Hooper, Justice 145
Hundreds, civil divisions . 257, 258
Hunting Creek 316

Indentures 105
Indians . . . .
  Characteristics and habits, 10, 11
  Religion 17
  Names 19, 20
  Manors 111, 112
  Money note-111
  Attempted colonization of . 111
Indian Town, estate 308
Induction, its uses and abuses
            179-186, 195, 196
Ingle, Richard 61
Inheritance, modes of . . note-107

Jail, first one erected . . . 26, 32
Jail, Leonardtown 263
Jellie's Tavern 38, 39
Jenifer, Daniel, home of . . . 31
Jenifer, Justice 145
Jesuit Fathers, note-87-90, note-235, note-237
Jordan, Jeremiah 279-281
Judges, appointment and compensation . 121, 137-138, 141-144
  Character of 154-162
  Oath note-124
Judicial System . . . . . .
  Gradual development of, 115-118
  Various courts under, 116-118, 127, 136, 139 141, 143, 150
  Characteristics of . . . 154-162
Jury, selection and compensation of 123, 145, 146
  Right to trial by . . . 123
  Of Manorial Courts, 128 note-134
Justices of the Peace . . . .
  Jurisdiction and powers, 117, 118
Jutland, estate 289

Key, Hon. Philip, 283, 285, note-317
Key, Hon. Edmund . . . 282, 317
Key's Creek 25, 27
King and Queen Parish . 210-216
King in Council, appeals to . 151

Land Office, establishment of, 91
  Records of note-99

Land Tenure, character of . 81-84
  How and by whom land could be obtained 84-90
  In what quantity 85-87
  Methods of transferring, 103-106
  Descent of 106-107
  System aristocratic in tendency 111-114
Law Chambers 31
Law of Province 115-116
Leonard-Town, history and
  map of 260-264
Levy, first County 258-259
Lewger, Secretary John . . .
  His home 47
  Conflict with Jesuits . . note-87
Little Bretton Manor . . . 233-234
Livery of Seisen 103-104
Longworth Point, estate . . . 313
Lowe, Susannah Maria . note-201
Lowentown 264
Luckland, estate 308

Mail route, the first . . . 268, 269
Manors, privileges and powers incident to 83, 108, 111
Manorial Courts 127-136
Map of Leonard-Town . . . 262
Map of St. Mary's City . Appendix
Marriages, early records of,
                note-225-232
Market Square 41
Maryland, area of note-64
Maryland, loss of territory . 64
Maryland Reports, early . 151, 152
Mattapany, estate 290, 292
Mayor and Aldermen of St.
  Mary's City note-71
Mattapany Street 27, 41, 52
Middle Street 27, 29-31
Mills, early . . . note-41, 269, 270
  Act for establishment of . . 27
Money, various kinds in use,
            95, note-111, 244
Morecroft, John 25
Mortmain, statutes of, enforced
                87-88
Mulberry tree, historic old 35-38, 76

Newtown Manor and Church,
            231, note-234
Nicholson, Gov. Francis, 71, 73, 276
Notley Hall, estate 311
Nuthead, Richard, first printer
  of Province 67-68

INDEX 333

Oyer and Terminer, Court of . 131
Palatine, Maryland a 81
   Nature of note-81-83
Parishes, Province divided into, 203
   Names of 203
Patents, land, how obtained, 89-91
Peake, Indian money . . note-111
Persons, names of, notes-71, 100,
   128, 136, 225, 232, 275, 278-281
Piepoudrea, Court of . . . note-41
Pillory 122
Pine Hill River, located . 255, 256
Piney Neck, estate . . . note-289
Plains, the, estate 306, 307
Plater, Hon. George . . . 296-298
Plater, Gov. George . 297, note-300
Point Patience, estate 307
Point Lookout 9
Poplar Hill Church . . . 205 208
Poplar Hill, estate note-295
Porto Bello, estate 318
Ports, public 266
Potomac River . . notes-9, 10, 19
Prerogative Court . . . 136-141
Preston, Richard 64, 137
Primogeniture 106, 107
Prince Frederick 307
Printing press 60, 67, 68
Protestant Revolution . . note-313
Provincial Court 143-162
Public roads 266-268

Queen Tree, place 265
Quia-emptoris, statute of, dispensed with note-83
Quigley, Capt. William, builder of first State House 32-35
Quit rents 94-99

Relief 94
Religious denominations, relative early growth of . . . 81, 82
Religious toleration, practical existence of note-57
Rent Rolls 99, 100
Resolutions, Stamp Act . . . 282
Resurrection Manor 296
Roads, early public 266-568
Roanoke, Indian money . note-111
Rock Creek Parish . . . 224-232
Roman Catholic places of worship 41-43, 231-238
Rosecroft, place 53
Rousby, Col. Christopher . . 292

Rousby Hall, place 293
Rousby, Col. John . . . 193
Royal Government 70

Seal, the Great, unique . . . 239
   The first lost 239
   Great Seal of 1648 240
   Captured, but restored . . 242
   Lesser Seals at Arms . . 243-244
   Stamped on money . . . 244
   Great Seal retained after Revolution 245
   New Seal adopted 245
   Second new Seal 247
   Third Seal, after one of 1648 247
   The one now in use 248
   Great Seal of United States, 245
   Illustrations . 241, 242, 243, 249
   Under Royal Government . 243
Sacred Heart Church 238
School, early system 273
Sheppard's Old Fields . . 260
Sheriffs, their appointment and duties 119 130
Sotterly 296-298
Spring, Governor's 47
State House, Maryland's first described 32-34
   Picture of 34
   Grant of 75
   Destruction of 76
Stocks 122
Susquehannah, estate . . 292-294
St. Aloysius' Church 238
St. Andrew's Parish . . . 220-224
St. Clement's Island . . . .
   Historic spot 9-11
   Rescued from oblivion . . 11-14
St. Clement's Manor . . . 311-317
   Courts of 128-136
St. Elizabeth Manor 288
St. Gabriel Manor 288
St. Inigoes Church 234-236
   Fort 236
   Mission note-237
St. John's Church 238
St. Jerome's Town 264
St. Joseph's Church 238
   Manor 295
   Town 264
St. Katherine's Island . . 13-14
St. Leonard's Creek 307
St. Margaret's Island 13
St. Mary's City, see Capital

INDEX

St. Mary's County
   Attractions of 251-253
   Character of houses . . . 287
   Civil divisions of 257, 258
   County seat of 259-263
   Delegates to conventions, 278-281
   Early officers of note-283
   After Revolution . . . 284-285
   Features of 251-253
   Governors of 286
   Historical interest of . . 251-253
   Limits of 254, 257
   Old estates of 288-319
   Other towns of . . . 264-265
   Ports of 266
   Representatives of in Congress, etc. 285-286
   Seat of learning in . . . 274-276
   Traditions of . . . note-270
   Will records of 271-273
St. Mary's Parish 205
St. Mary's River 21-22
St. Michael's manner 288
Snow Hill Manor 319
Stars and Stripes, history of, note-249-250
Stone, Gov Wm., note-59, note-62, 63, 64

Tabbs, Rev. Moses, 267, appendix
Taney, Chief Justice Roger B. 63
Tavern rates, established by law, note-39
Taxation . 28, 41, 166, 169, 189, 190
Tench, Justice 145
Tenure 92
Thomas, Capt. John Allen, 280, 281, 284
Thomas, Maj. William, Sr., 215, 279, 284, 311
Thomas, Maj. William, Jr., 63, 276, 281, 283, 285, 304
Thomas, Gov. James, note-283, 286
Toleration, Religious, practical existence of 57-60
Tomaquoakin (Tomakokin) Creek 312
Trent Hall, estate 304
Trinity Church 39
   Manor 288
Truman, Maj. Thomas . . 304, 305
Tubman, Maj. Henry, 275, 280, 284, 285
Tudor Hall 312
Turner, Edward . . note-128, 310

Urquhart, Rev. John . . . 220-221

Vault, Copley, 36, 37, 70, appendix
Vestry, law applicable to, 166-168, 174-179, 190-194, 196, 197
Vestrymen, names of, 205, 215, 217, note-224

Waldron's Old Fields, site of
   St. Andrew's Church . . . 221
Wardens, Church 172
Warrants, land 90
Warehouses, public 206
West St. Mary's Manor . . . 319
White, Father Andrew . . 9, 13, 18
Whipping post 122
Wicomico Town 264, 315
Wills, records of 138, 271
Walstenholme, Daniel . . 52, 53

Yaocomico, Indian town . . 16
   Site of First Capital . . . 17, 18

Zachiah Swamp 211, 267

www.ingramcontent.com/pod-product-compliance
Lightning Source LLC
Chambersburg PA
CBHW050615300426
44112CB00012B/1508